Life on the LUXURY

by Colin Scott

Remembering the Brown Bombers

First published in Great Britain in 2021
by Bryngold Books Ltd.,
100 Brynau Wood, Cimla,
Neath, South Wales SA11 3YQ.

www.bryngoldbooks.com

Typesetting, layout,
editing and design
by Bryngold Books

ISBN 978-1-905900-56-5

Printed in Wales.

www.bryngoldbooks.com

Contents

About the author

Colin Scott has been interested in transport for as long as he can remember, with buses and trains being his main focus right up to the present time. This is his third book and one that marks the culmination of a long held passion for all that made the N&C luxury coach company a transport legend.

Brought up in Bridgend, almost half way between the N&C's two main destinations of Swansea and Cardiff, much of Colin's teenage time was spent observing events at the town's busy bus station, which introduced him to the Brown Bombers.

Later, the service became his daily method of travel to and from work. Over time this, together with excursion organising and depot visits, led to the forging of friendships with many of the company's staff. All of this has played a part in the publication of ***Life on the Luxury*** which is a tribute to everyone involved with the N&C throughout its 40 year existence.

Combining nostalgic memories and down-to-earth tales of life on the N&C shared by many of its fellow devotees with facts, figures and photographs all help to ensure that though the company may be long gone, it will never be forgotten, something of which Colin is justifiably proud.

Life on the Luxury follows Colin's two previous books, the first, titled Diesels, Dragons & Daffs was a railway-based pictorial reflection of the changing scene captured with his camera again during the final years of British Rail.

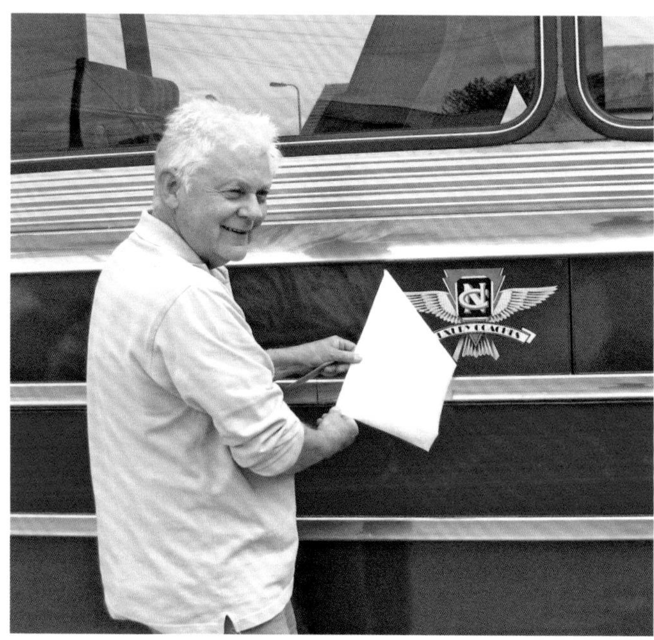

Colin Scott puts the final touch to a tribute vehicle created by the Brown Bombers group.

The second was his much acclaimed history of the Western Welsh Omnibus Company Ltd, titled Red, Cream and a touch of Gray, which sold out and was reprinted with the benefit of extra, fascinating material.

Colin spent much of his working life in local government across South Wales as a draughtsman, graphic designer and surveyor. Early retirement brought with it the opportunity to persue his transport interests further including an involvement in a preserved N&C vehicle and also an exhibition-carrying tribute coach.

Twists and turns

The story of the legendary Neath & Cardiff Luxury Coach Company contains as many twists and turns as the roads it operated on and reflects times far different to those in which its modern counterparts operate.

The N&C became well known for its pioneering Swansea to Cardiff express services. Its reputation grew from the way in which its proud management and staff linked arms to provide a fast and efficient service for the travelling public. It was highly regarded within the passenger transport industry, among its regular customers, and became the envy of its competitors.

Looking back, it's difficult to comprehend that N&C only lasted for 40 years, and that by the end of 1970 its vehicles and their distinct livery had all but vanished from the roads of South Wales.

Gerald Truran, N&C's Chief Engineer from 1965, wrote a technical account of the company's history and the specifications of its vehicles in his book Forty Years of Brown Bombers in 1971. Later, in 1998, I was instrumental in encouraging him to publish a revised second edition.

Now, half a century since its demise, this book aims to ensure the legend lives on. The N&C is still much talked about and tributes abound to those who made it all happen. Company histories rarely recall the staff, both depot and road crew, who were the human ingredient — the lifeblood — of any successful company. The publication of this book, 90 years since the first coach rolled out of the N&C depot on the company's maiden journey and 50 years since its demise, was born of my desire to record the human and social side of the remarkable 'Brown Bombers' before the memories fade.

Research unearthed countless fascinating tales and experiences that are still held close to the hearts of so many of the N&C's former management, staff and its passengers alike, making my task a privilege and a pleasure.

Life on the Luxury it certainly was, and not only for the travelling public. Many an employee described working for the company as the best job they ever had. They considered it a joy to go to work, even when schedules were tight and traffic heavy. There was a rigorous discipline, instilled by the military background of its management. With that came a caring and benevolent, family-based philosophy that rubbed off on the rank and file, and in turn even reached out to its passengers. Both sides remained fiercely loyal and happy, for most of the time, despite the daily challenges that life in the fast lane brought.

I hope this book will evoke a plethora of memories for many people who to this day still hold an affection for a unique company which overcame the odds and became an unforgettable transport legend.

Colin Scott, 2021.

Foreword

by Professor Stuart Cole, CBE. Emeritus Professor of Transport (Economics and Policy) University of South Wales — and a supporter of bus travel in South Wales for over 60 years.

Life on the Luxury is about a time when passenger transport between two of Wales biggest cities, Cardiff and Swansea, was far different from that of today, with exciting developments for travellers.

The passing of the Transport Act in 1930 changed many things. Most importantly, as this book shows, it gave birth to an express coach legend – the N&C Luxury Coach Company Limited. The company's history is uniquely told here using a fresh approach to social commentary – through the everyday life of its passengers, owners, managers and road staff (many of whom Colin knew) using previously unpublished illustrations, timetables and publicity.

This was a highly successful company whose demise Colin Scott saw as a sad affair brought about by another Transport Act. This established the National Bus Company which had a determination to centralise its brand and the operations of the coach and bus businesses it took over.

The events that unfolded day by day between those two Acts have been transformed into this book. Colin has painstakingly turned what he witnessed into a fascinating journey back in time reflecting the world of the N&C.

The book's style rather than concentrate on the engineering aspects has cleverly focused on a more nostalgic theme with many personal anecdotes from speeding drivers stopped by constabulary, bad weather and no lighting during the Second World War. These colourful memories print an indelible image of an express service envied by other operators and remembered by many, including myself as a young bus and coach traveller.

The timetables required an average speed of 30 mph much of it along that perilously designed road the A48 with its middle two-way lane. No wonder the road death figure was double the present number despite there being only 10 per cent of the car numbers. Though not due to the 'Luxury.'

Often bus operators think they run buses. Not so of course; their real function is carrying passengers and that's what the following pages are about on good days and bad.

Colin Scott's recollections deny the old quotation 'if you can remember the 1960s you weren't there'. The characters in this book do remember those days and have given their evidence to its author.

Bus companies have invariably been part of big groups (BET Federation, Tillings, Red & White) who allowed their subsidiaries to have a character of their own. Famous brands – South Wales Transport, United Welsh, Thomas Bros, Associated Motorways and of course N&C – disappearance was sadly unnecessary. This book keeps their (and especially N&C's) memory alive.

Bus and coach enthusiasts will all find something to interest them in 'Life on the Luxury.'

Chapter 1

One man's vision

During the first week of April 1930, various events hit the headlines around the world. Scientists in America predicted that man would land on the moon by 2050; the film The Blue Angel starring Marlene Dietrich premiered in Berlin, while in Los Angeles, The Broadway Melody won Outstanding Picture in the second Academy Awards ceremony.

Each of these events brought with them their own particular brand of excitement. Closer to home, in the industrial South Wales heartland, a memorable event of an entirely different kind was unfolding as a coach carefully, almost without being noticed, nosed its way out of a garage, tucked away in a narrow, terraced cul-de-sac on the fringe of the bustling market town of Neath.

At the wheel was driver Eddie Bailey, proudly attired in the smart uniform that was to become one of the hallmarks of the newly-born N&C Luxury Coach Company. To Eddie, it may have been just another job. He may not have realised as he headed out of that dusty Burrows Road garage for the open road and Cardiff, behind the wheel of the gleaming 20-seat Morris Viceroy vehicle, that he was at the launch of what was to become an exciting 40-year adventure in British passenger transport history.

Driver Bailey's run that day marked the start of a transport adventure that was to last for 40 years. It was one that saw the creation of a legend in the region it served through thick and thin, and one that is still recalled fondly to this day.

As the miles ticked by on the Viceroy's debut run to Cardiff that day, still more than two decades away from becoming the Welsh capital, daily life was far from easy for the majority of the country's population.

Britain was in the grip of the great depression that plagued the country throughout the 1920s and peaked with the Wall Street crash of 1929. Millions of workers lost their jobs as a result of a massive downturn in the economy. Some areas of the

United Kingdom were hit more than others. The worst affected were those dependent on heavy industries such as coal, iron and steel and South Wales was without doubt one of these that suffered most.

Those who found themselves out of work received no wages, and the unemployment benefit of the time was barely enough to pay the rent, let alone support a family. People could no longer afford to buy essentials, which contributed to more businesses declaring themselves bankrupt and in turn creating more unemployment.

It was a vicious circle that had all too quickly become a way of life. In the worst hit areas, hope all but vanished. Thousands of former hardworking men were left with little to do and could often be seen gathered in groups on street corners.

There remained however, pockets of prosperity among the poverty. While there was a housing shortage and slum housing everywhere across the valleys, in the Uplands and Sketty areas of Swansea, and the Cyncoed and Roath districts of Cardiff, hundreds of private houses were being built for a prosperous middle class.

The Vale of Glamorgan was agriculturally rich and buoyant from its home-grown livestock and produce. Major petrochemical plants were being planned and developed across south west Wales.

So while some may have given in to the horrors of such a devastating economic downturn others had a different approach. Among these was a man with a clear vision of the route he felt would take him on the road to better times.

This far sighted businessman with a solid military background, who had served with distinction in the First World War, was none other than Colonel R Godfrey Llewellyn. At the time Colonel Llewellyn gave his

LOOK OUT

FOR

THE N.C. LUXURY COACHES

The Express Motor Coach Service from Neath, Briton Ferry & Port Talbot to Cardiff.

COMMENCING APRIL 2ND

Surprisingly low return fares enable you to visit Cardiff at a fraction of previous cost.

REGULAR SERVICE THROUGHOUT DAY

First Bus leaves Alfred Street 8-40 a.m. Last Bus leaves Cardiff after Theatre.

Intermediate Buses Frequent.

--- Full Time Tables ---
--- Obtainable From Coaches ---

A newspaper advertisement announcing the new N.C. service from April 1930.

address as Waunceirch House on the outskirts of Neath. It was a grand house which stood in verdant grounds and would probably have enjoyed the support of a number of servants.

Not too far away in neighbouring Swansea, Colonel Llewellyn's family had for some years been steadily building up the C K Andrews Ltd motor vehicle distribution business. In its early days C K Andrews was described as a coach company. That may suggest that they were involved with constructing horse drawn coaches before motor vehicles.

By 1930 C K Andrews was in possession of two Morris Viceroy chassis. Both were turned into 20 seat vehicles using the company's skills and material.

When these vehicles emerged from the workshop they proudly displayed the fleet name of N C Luxury coaches, an operator with which Llewellyn had a significant involvement in setting up and eventually running. The '&' between those letters had yet to be born.

With an obvious optimism for the future, Colonel Llewellyn would probably have been well aware of the passage through Parliament of the Road Traffic Bill which eventually became law in 1930.

It is probable too, that he saw this as paving the way for the establishment of a profit making enterprise. In readiness, on 28 October, 1929 the Andrews company applied for licences in respect of motor coach services between Swansea, Neath and London, and also between Neath and Cardiff.

The Licensing Committee met on 7 January, 1930 with Colonel Llewellyn himself acting for the firm. Not surprisingly, there were objections from existing operators including South Wales Transport and Western Welsh. These objections, despite the Colonel's passionate defence of his applications, appeared to have hit home. The result — only four licences were granted. These were for the Neath to Cardiff service only.

At that time the C K Andrews company held the licences and supplied the vehicles to operate the service. Writing in 1971, the Colonel, by now Sir Godfrey Llewellyn, recalled that the Andrews name was used in applying for the licences because they didn't want to form a new company entailing extra expense, until they knew they could get them. It was agreed however, that should the licences be granted, a seperate company would be formed to operate it.

On April 1, 1930, a day before the service eventually began, a special journey carried civic representatives of the boroughs of Neath and Port Talbot — the only towns to licence the service — to Cardiff and back. As Sir Godfrey explained in later years: "The very first trip we took was to show councillors that we meant business and what a good service it was going to be."

The peculiarities of the licensing system meant that arrangements had to be made for the service to terminate on private land that was within the boundary of the Borough of Cardiff.

"We arranged to run into the yard of coach operator E R Forse at Cardiff because we

Neath and Cardiff Luxury Coaches (Ltd.).

A private company, registered on April 4, Capital, £1.000 in £1 shares. Objects: To carry on the business of char-a-banc, omnibus, coach, lorry, cab, car or taxi-cab proprietors, &c. The subscribers (each with one share) are: R. G. Llewellyn, Waunceirach House, Neath, company director: W.G. Hayes 12, Glanmor-crescent, Swansea, company secretary. R. G. Llewellyn is the first director. Qualification: 50 ordinary shares. Remuneration: As fixed by the company. Registered office: 21, Uplands-crescent, Swansea.

A public notice of the company registration which appeared in various publications early in 1930.

NEATH & PORT TALBOT ENTERPRISE

The proprietors of the new 'Bus Service between Neath, Port Talbot and Cardiff are indeed, to be commended on their enterprise in filling a much needed want.

A trial trip was made on these luxurious coaches last Monday week, when the Neath and Port Talbot Councillors accepted Col. Llewelyn's invitation to personally test the efficiency of the 'buses.

The coaches are the new Morris Commercial "Viceroy" type, seating 20 passengers, and proved to be the final word in comfort, satisfaction being expressed by every member of the company.

It is intended to run a most complete time table. The last 'bus leaves Cardiff for home at 10.45, which will be much appreciated by shoppers and theatre-goers to Cardiff, who have previously been unable to take advantage of Cardiff's attractions because of the too-early train home.

The remarkably cheap fare of 3s. 9d. return will prove a special inducement.

Time tables and full particulars may be had of the proprietors of the Garage, or from the conductors.

A newspaper review of the new service and inaugural run which was published in April 1930.

couldn't get licences to pick up or set down in Cardiff itself," continued Sir Godfrey.

"The entrance to E R Forse's yard, which was afterwards enlarged, was very narrow and on leaving with the councillors we hit one of the pillars of the gate and knocked it down, which was not a very good start."

The first public service ran the following day with an unassuming departure from Neath at precisely 8.40am. Driver Eddie Bailey's pride at being at the wheel of the first Morris Viceroy to take to the road must have been immense. It never left him during the long years that followed and was still evident when he shared some of the memories that contribute greatly to this salute to the N&C in 1987.

"We started on 2 April, although it was suggested that we might start the day before, 1 April," explained Sir Godfrey, "but being slightly superstitious, I refused to open up on 1 April, and that's why we started on 2 April."

The restriction within the Borough of Cardiff was strict, as the N&C company was not

The N&C's pioneering workforce gather for the camera at Neath in 1938. In the centre of the picture are Captain J J Newbury and Colonel R G Llewellyn. On the extreme right is the engineer, F H Beddoes.

licensed to set down and pick up passengers within its boundary. The terminus could not be on public land, which is why an agreement was made with E R Forse for doing so at their Kingsway garage.

Passengers could only travel out of Cardiff if they held a return ticket. This rule was strictly enforced by the Cardiff police who escorted each vehicle to and from the Borough boundary at Culverhouse Cross.

The agreement to use Forse's garage was nevertheless challenged by the police and in October a summons saw Driver John Baskerville and N&C fined for permitting the plying for hire at Forse's. Despite the defence that the contract was made on private property, Baskerville was fined 10 shillings, and the company £2 plus costs.

Neath & Cardiff Luxury Coaches Limited was finally incorporated on April 4, 1930, with Colonel Llewellyn, as Managing Director.

The Colonel, who served in the London Home Guard, lived in Tredilion Park, near Abergavenny at the time, and was described by some as an eccentric. He had been awarded the OBE in 1942, and was always very particular about the correct use of his military title whenever mail was being addressed to him.

It mattered not about a precise geographical address — it was quite sufficient to address him as: 'Col. R G Llewellyn, Bart., CBE, MC, TD, DL, JP, Abergavenny.' but every abbreviation mattered. If mail arrived for him which didn't bear the precise order of the distinguishing letters after his name, it would be returned to sender, marked 'not known at this address'.

In the beginning, the company was managed by J H Williams with the assistance of Harry Paulson. Both these men had been associated with bus operators Willmore Services of Neath. Harry Paulson had invested in the new N&C company, and often took his turn behind the wheel. He was still driving for them in the early 1950s, but very slowly — just 25mph on times! He was remembered as a great colleague, but a problem to the conductors who were on the receiving end of so many complaints about his lack of speed.

The road rules begin to change

The Road Traffic Act of 1930 abolished the 20mph speed limit and set a variety of limits for different classes of vehicle. None was set for vehicles carrying less than seven people. New requirements were introduced for all licences and a special system was created for public service vehicles, including a 30mph speed limit for buses and coaches.

PSV regulations became centralised under a system of regional traffic commissioners. There were tighter rules regarding the construction of vehicles and the conduct of drivers, conductors and passengers. There was also a limitation on the number of hours a driver could continuously drive.

The Act aimed to protect incumbent operators from any predatory behaviour from others who fancied a slice of the action over their more profitable routes. Cross-subsidy of routes was encouraged to protect rural services, and to help avoid fare increases.

The outcome meant operators had to apply to the commissioners both to introduce or amend existing services, and if they wished to increase fares. The authority hitherto vested upon local councils to licence and regulate services was now no longer theirs.

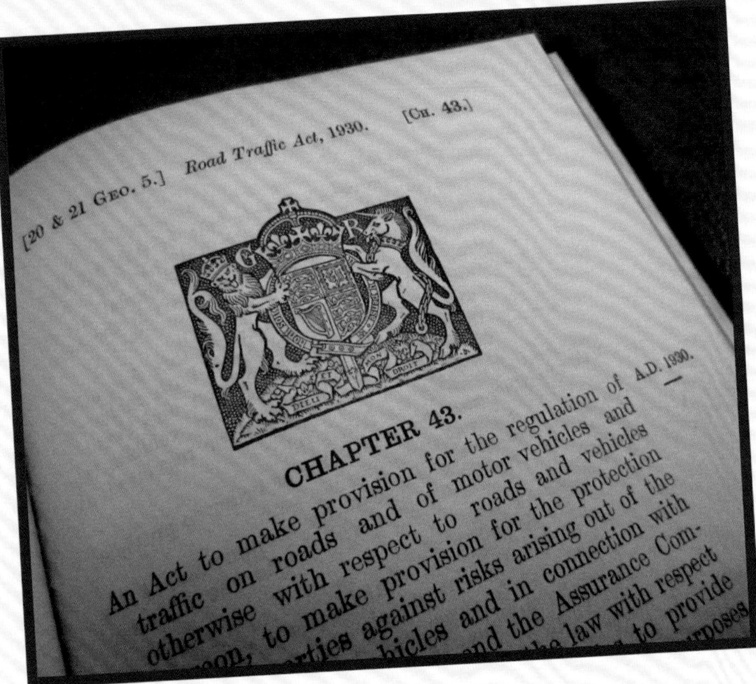

Originally the N&C livery was pale yellow with white around the windows and a brown side flash. This is probably why they were originally given the nickname of Flying Bananas. However when N&C changed its livery to mainly brown in 1932, they quickly became known as the Brown Bombers.

That said, the N&C vehicles were often referred to by passengers as simply 'The Luxury.' The question would often be: "Are we catching the Luxury?" There was never any misunderstanding as to what particular company was being referred to. The N&C stood out.

After the Second World War, bright red was added to the brown. Occasionally other liveries were trialled, but for various reasons, these were generally short lived.

While decisions were being made about the best livery in those early days, out on the road there were more serious issues facing the rapidly growing company. Not least among these was the conundrum of where to set down in Cardiff. The borough council and its police never seemed to run out of obstacles to put in the way of common sense on the issue.

"When we did get permission to run into Cardiff," recalled Sir Godfrey, many years later, "We were allowed to go to Fitzhamon Embankment. This was when the new Traffic Commissioners came in and reviewed the situation which had not previously allowed us to go into Cardiff officially.

"Other companies were running into Westgate Street, so we applied to terminate there, which wasn't objected to by Cardiff Council, but instead by its police. Eventually the matter had to be decided by a special independent court."

Sir Godfrey's frustration was evident when he recalled those difficult times: "One objection was that too many buses were already running into Westgate Street and that there was also a car park outside a block of flats running along the street which prevented buses from stopping on that length of the road."

An artist's impression of how the first Morris Viceroy vehicles may have looked in their early livery.

The hearing resulted in good news for N&C. The Cardiff police were overruled and after much effort the company was finally allowed to run right into Westgate Street.

"We started on a Sunday morning," recalled Sir Godfrey, "and I and Captain Newbury went up in a car to see the reception in Westgate Street.

"We found that the police had aggravated the position by lengthening the car park considerably, thereby endeavouring to make us stop opposite the Fire Station which was one of the objections they had put up.

"Eventually we proved that we could stop without stopping in front of the fire station. The police were waiting for us there and took the name of the driver and conductor and also all the passengers. This went on for a day or two. The police had threatened us previously if we ran into Westgate Street. We contacted the Traffic Commissioners who told us to comply with the licences as issued.

"Subsequently, the police carried on with this procedure, but only took the name of the driver and conductor. This then led to what we called the 'Royal Escort'. The mobile police met us at the borough boundary, escorted us into Westgate Street, where they took the name of the driver and conductor, and then escorted them out again when the time came. This went on for a long time and must have cost the police quite a lot of time and fuel.

"After a considerable time, this was supplanted by an officer sitting in a window opposite, taking notes and photographs, including flashlights, until finally, after a very long time, methods to worry us ceased.

"One amusing incident happened when this somewhat sad performance — which we considered persecution — was going on. In order to try and make us stop in front of the fire station, instead of going up the street clear of it, they cut the lower branches of a line of trees in that part of the street, leaving them in heaps so that when the bus came in it would have to stop, so they thought, behind the heap, thereby stopping in front of the fire station doors.

"I think Eddie Bailey was the driver at that time and he had his head screwed on. When he saw his dilemma, instead of stopping, as no doubt the opposition had intended, behind the heap, he propelled the heap in front of the bus, up in front of him until he was clear of the exit from the fire

Timings that bred success

N.C. LUXURY COACHES LTD.

Neath, Briton Ferry, Port Talbot – Cardiff.

3/9 Return. 3/- Single.

TRAVEL BY ROAD

TIME TABLE.

Depart.	Week Days.							Sundays.			
Neath Alfred St............	8-40	12-0	2-0	3-30	5-15	7-45	9-15	1-45	2-45	5-30	8-0
Lodge, Briton Ferry...	8-47	12-7	2-7	3-37	5-22	7-52	9-22	1-52	2-52	5-37	8-7
Villiers St, B. Ferry.....	8-50	12-10	2-10	3-40	5-25	7-55	9-25	1-55	1-55	5-40	8-10
Baglan Church...........	8-53	12-13	2-15	3-43	5-28	7-58	9-28	1-58	2-58	5-43	8-13
Cardiff, ARR...............	10-10	1-30	3-30	5-0	6-45	9-15	10-45	3-30	4-30	7-0	9-30

Week Days.		Sundays.	
Dept. Cardiff	Arr. Neath	Dept. Cardiff	Arr. Neath
10-20 a.m.	11.40 a.m.	3-50 p.m.	5-15 p.m.
1-45 p.m.	3.15 p.m.	6-0 "	7-30 "
3-30 "	5-0 "	7-30 "	9.15 "
5-15 "	6-45 "	9-45 "	11-15 "
7-15 "	8-45 "		
9-45 "	11-15 "		
11-0 "	12-30 a.m.		

This timetable illustrates how bare and random the service was when it began. Services were continually developed until N&C became a force to be reckoned with by its competitors.

station, but at the moment the front of his bus got close to the heap in the first place, there was a great ringing of bells, the fire station doors were thrown open and out came the fire engine, no doubt hoping that the bus would be in the way.

"By now though, the bus had gone further up the street! The result was that the fire engine went up to the Angel Hotel, turned, came back and went back into the station."

Not everyone shared this hatred of the N&C however. The letter to the editor of the Neath Guardian on 27 March 1931, reproduced alongside paid a glowing tribute to the company's service.

In 1932 Captain J J Newbury, MBE became the General Manager, a post he occupied until 1964. He had been an Army colleague of Colonel Llewellyn. Whilst demonstrating hand grenades to the local Home Guard he blew his own hand off, and as a result wore a brown leather glove to disguise his loss. The captain was assisted by yet another military figure, Colonel J Lloyd, TD, DL.

Colonel Llewellyn, Captain Newbury and J H Williams had all served their country, and the operation of the N&C company was greatly influenced by this military background. They could never have been described as pen pushers, and much preferred being out in the field instead of sitting behind a desk in the James Street, Neath garage where the company had soon relocated.

The yard there was overlooked at one end by the offices. When the colonel, accompanied by one or both of the others, gathered for a meeting, instead of using one of the offices, they would parade, military style, up and down the yard, side by side, with hands clasped behind their backs. They were always in step and made an almost choreographed shuffle to turn at each end in an exact imitation of a military parade. Then, as soon as their meetings were over, they would quickly drive off, the colonel being chauffeur driven.

Returning to the early years, hot on the heels of Eddie Bailey came A J H (Mick) Williams, who joined the company on the day after that first service and stayed for its entire lifetime. Eventually he became chief inspector and recalled that in the first year the fare from Neath to Cardiff was three shillings and nine pence (3s 9d) return; it was 3s 6d from Port Talbot and 2s from Bridgend.

"Those early coaches were one-man operated and the hours were long," Mick recalled. "We worked every day, including turns on Sundays. Wages were £2 10s a week and if you worked an additional shift to Cardiff you got an extra five shillings."

Praises and pride in print

Sir,

Colonel R G Llewellyn's pride in the Neath to Cardiff Luxury Coach Service is well justified, and Neath can't very well let him down. To travel to Cardiff this way is equal to the amenities of a private car, less its risk, expense, or worry. When I express my appreciation of the pleasure, comfort, smoothness and speed of the journey; the astonishing cheapness (cheap train excursion rates); its conveniences (the handy stopping places, freedom to use the return half any time, day or week), and particularly the skill and marked unfailing courtesy of the drivers, I also voice the feelings of thousands of other residents of Neath and district. We might well pause to reflect on the sort of privileges the public would receive in the journey by road to Cardiff had it been left to some big combines we know to originate such a service. Happily for Neath, Neath & Cardiff Luxury Coaches leads the way, and their present position should be unassailable so long as their efficient and attractive standard is maintained.

Yours, etc.

Adam Jewell, Windsor Road, Neath.

Fred 'Jock' Cross was another stalwart whose career with N&C began in those pioneering early days. Such was his determination to find work in the dark days of the Great Depression that he walked from Scotland to Newport, where he met Colonel Llewellyn,

> **" I got engaged on the N&C! I was from Cardiff and his family lived in Port Talbot, so we met half way. Those really were the days. "**
>
> ***Anita Hanney***

who offered him a job and also accommodation. For this kindness, Jock always remained loyal and served with the company until the end. He shunned the offer of promotion to inspector, as he preferred life on the road. His skills were many and his dedication, like so many others, was beyond reproach. He had a 99 per cent accident free record, blotted only by one minor incident in which he unfortunately injured his hands.

It wasn't only Cardiff Council that hassled the N&C company over its legitimate operations. In a meeting of Port Talbot Council's General Purposes Committee in May 1953, the scheduled timetable for bus services between Port Talbot and Cardiff was considered. Councillor Percy Gaen said that the Western Welsh company's schedule for the 37 miles to Cardiff was 1 hour 51 minutes, whereas the N&C Company's scheduled time for the same journey was just one hour 30 minutes. He felt that such a schedule was hardly conducive to safe driving, and must lead to N&C coaches exceeding the speed limit.

On behalf of the company, Mr R Lloyd pointed out that the N&C Company was an express service, with fewer stopping places than the Western Welsh services. This was bound to lead to a quicker run to Cardiff. Some N&C drivers who had formerly driven for Western Welsh had stated that they had been obliged to drive faster to keep to the N&C schedules, but at some places in Port Talbot the average speed was only 9mph and at no point was it higher than 20mph.

The committee was to receive further reports later, but it was hardly any of their business; any scheduling decisions were that of the Traffic Commissioners.

In any event, Councillor Gaen's information was wrong: the published timetables in 1953 gave journey times for Western Welsh services at 1 hour 31 minutes, and N&C's at 1 hour 15 minutes. Port Talbot Council would have spent their time more wisely had they considered a way of easing the traffic congestion that always seemed to disrupt bus services through the town.

A proud line-up of many of the vehicles that comprised the N&C fleet, together with their drivers at the Fairfield, Neath, during the mid-1930s.

Chapter 2

Route to success

The advent of the 1930 Road Traffic Act, with its aim of protecting operators from predatory behaviour on profitable routes, sent many rushing to start new services. It brought a neutrality to vehicle and service licensing by replacing decision making local councils with independent regional traffic commissioners.

Originally, a further licence to extend the embryonic N&C service to Swansea had been sought, but the South Wales Transport and Western Welsh companies had also both applied for licences for a Swansea to Cardiff (via Neath) service. Not unexpectedly perhaps, N&C had objected to these bids.

The decision of who should be granted a licence for this route was deferred until the newly-appointed traffic commissioners were in place, in order that the matter could be decided without prejudice. Eventually in November 1931 the licence was granted — with conditions — to a jubilant N&C company. The refusal of the applications by both Swansea-based South Wales Transport Company and Cardiff-based Western Welsh remains a puzzle. Both were large operators with substantial back-up. The move however handed the newly established minnow, the N&C Luxury Coach Company, a boost without compare and one which would set it on its way as a major player on the route and give it the foundation on which it would operate successfully for the 40 years that followed.

There was however one stipulation in the granting of this licence and that was that at no point would N&C be allowed to operate double deck vehicles on the service.

Early on, N&C bought the licences of Morriston-based operator Bromham in order to gain its tours licences. The company also bought the business of A J David Limited, Haulage, which was operated from James Street, Neath, but sold this before the outbreak of the Second World War, something which Colonel Llewellyn later suggested was a great mistake.

N&C's simple original fare structure began as an experiment, but it became such a success that it remained unaltered for the following 25 years. This success exceeded all expectations but brought the company close to bankruptcy because the demand was so great that the vehicles were unable to withstand the tremendous daily hammering, which led to vehicle shortages and incurred almost prohibitive maintenance costs.

"I think it would be good to mention how close this enterprise came to ending when the original coaches wouldn't stand up to the job," revealed Sir Godfrey writing in 1971. "I remember at one time a passenger in the early days asking an inspector how the company could possibly afford to run at such a low fare to which he replied: Never mind, you exploit us while the going's good and use us as much as possible. Actually, as I have pointed out, it was the low fare which nearly broke us, but for quite a different reason, it was simply the overwhelming response which made the rolling stock incapable of coping."

Most operators had believed that if more revenue was required, the remedy was to increase fares. N&C believed that this was wrong thinking. They believed that what was required was a fare that would attract the most customers, thereby generating more sustainable revenue.

It was thanks to the foresight and energy of Colonel Llewellyn as Managing Director and his General Manager Captain J J Newbury, together with his assistant Colonel Lloyd and Chief Engineer H Beddoes, that the N&C company overcame these difficulties with better, sturdier vehicles and, within a very short time, grew strong and flourished.

The N&C Company occupied rooms at Neath's Great Western Chambers at the town end of Bridge Street, but contrary to popular belief, this was never intended as their Registered Office. This, along with Captain Newbury's office, until the move to Briton Ferry, was always at James Street. Great Western Chambers was purely a Booking and Tours office, and none of the day to day running of the company took place there.

The Second World War brought about changes as fuel rationing led to a significant reduction in services. While the Government terminated express services generally, N&C was treated leniently because of its relatively short route mileage. However, all relief and duplicate journeys were suspended. Three of the company's coaches were requisitioned by the Army, and others were sold as surplus or loaned to other operators. The fleet was halved from 24 to 12, a badly timed move as the service frequency had just increased to hourly.

By 1942, the company was employing women as conductors. The blackout and heavy air raids,

One of a pair of Gloster Gardner vehicles that entered service in 1934, WN6536 is pictured at Bridgend bus station in 1950. These vehicles had complicated gearboxes, but were fast coaches and survived until 1953. *Alan B Cross*

The unusual Duple body styling of the Maudslay Magnas is clearly illustrated as ENY68 and ENY66 pick up at Bridgend bus station in 1950 during a busy period evidenced by much duplication of services. *Alan B Cross*

particularly in Swansea, brought about a number of hair-raising escapes and accidents – including one involving two N&C vehicles near Bridgend. All in all, it was a time of great uncertainty for the company, whose continuing expansion could by no means have been assured.

Enid Dewitt travelled weekly to Bridgend during the Second World War and remembered those times clearly. She recalled that only the tiniest of lights could be shown by vehicles, but even so, N&C's timekeeping was always spot on. Despite the enforced cutbacks and fuel rationing, speed and comfort did not suffer it seems:

"All was peaceful on those journeys until we got to Stormy Down, where there was an RAF camp," recalled Enid. "The peace and tranquillity of the journey was often shattered when around 40 squaddies from the camp who were intent on a night out in Bridgend piled on, but of course there was never any trouble. They were happy times."

"The N&C vehicles were just that little bit different. They were clean, luxurious and punctual. The staff were marvellous."

Joan Lloyd was another who used the N&C service during the war, for her shopping trips to Bridgend. She particularly remembered the superb timekeeping of the company's coaches: "In 1945, despite hostilities having ended, rationing was still rife, she said.

"We had heard that a shop in Bridgend had received a delivery of shoes, so we caught the 7am coach and queued for hours."

Joan couldn't have realised that a journey home from the theatre in Cardiff aboard an N&C coach with some friends would lead to romance and the journey of a lifetime.

"I counted the people ahead in the queue," she recalled. "I quickly realised we'd be standing for the journey home. Once aboard however, two men in a nearby seat offered to squeeze up and I sat with them, three in a seat. I ended up exchanging contact details with one of them, and the following day he rang me at work and we chatted. That resulted in us going out for a date, again by N&C coach, and we ended up getting married just after the war in 1946."

When peace returned, the company struggled to resume a full service with its worn out fleet. Due to the heavy bomb damage at Swansea, the terminus moved from Alexandra Road to New Street, and later to Clarence Street. Materials continued to be in short supply for many years, and in an attempt to speed up vehicle production, the N&C company established its own coachbuilding business in secluded former Government premises at Longford, Neath.

Captain Newbury managed this business, and the first coach bodied by the company was proudly rolled out of the factory in 1948. It was a 33-seat vehicle mounted on an AEC Regal III chassis. A further 16 coaches by Longford were introduced between 1948 and 1952. There were liveries of metallic copper and sand, and desert sand and tan. It then became customary for N&C's new coaches to wear a variety of colours. Vehicles built at the company's works all had a stylish, individual touch which resulted in no two coaches being identical.

Apart from supplying N&C's own needs, the Longford Manufacturing and Coachbuilding Company's variety of coach, bus and lorry bodies were supplied to many other operators until 1952/3. By that time, bodies had once again become available from the established suppliers, and so a decision was taken that the business would be closed.

There is no doubt that this relatively short lived business diversion would have provided some exciting opportunities for the N&C Company. History is unclear as to whether the venture was a profitable one though.

In general, the 1950s saw a period of eye-catching, flamboyant designs of coach bodywork. This was in stark contrast to what had been available during the war years. Many would contend that this must have helped attract an increasing number of passengers eager to exploit their newly-restored freedom. For most, it would be many years before the explosion in family car ownership would impact significantly on the passenger transport industry. N&C was no exception.

In the heady years that followed, there would often be three or four N&C crews awaiting the call for relief work. They would

The Longford Manufacturing and Coachbuilding company's works at Neath Abbey, with production in full swing in 1948. In the distance one of the N&C's AEC Regal IIIs is in the course of receiving its body.

stand by in the United Welsh canteen at the old Swansea bus station. To comply with N&C's licence conditions, there were strict operating rules that had to be observed when operating duplicate journeys, particularly with regard to picking up and setting down points. The waiting crew would decide the best way to run the reliefs as efficiently as possible, not only to support the scheduled service, but to be back home at a decent hour.

These relief services were originally known as 'Bolters', then later as 'Flyers'. It made sense to direct passengers onto these coaches depending on their destination. One coach for example, would run non-stop to Cardiff via the Bridgend by-pass, while another would run up to Pyle or Bridgend only. It was always the unofficial aim of the Cardiff 'Bolter' to catch up the service vehicle that may have been an hour ahead leaving Swansea. That meant the relief driver went hell for leather, and before the opening of Briton Ferry bridge, would run via Jersey Marine, avoid the circuit around the centre of Neath, and miss out Bridgend altogether.

The only pinch point was, of course, the notorious bottleneck in the centre of Port Talbot where, if the level crossing gates were closed, between five and 10 minutes extra was added to the running time. It was always the aim to reach Cardiff in an hour

Used as a demonstrator by Longford Coachworks, KNY 198 was a Gardner-engined Tilling Stevens front entrance 33 seat coach. It joined the N&C fleet in late May 1950 and is seen at Alfred Street, Neath. *Alan B Cross*

and a half, which would allow an earlier service to be duplicated back to Pyle or Neath to end the day.

Trevor Burley joined the company straight from school in 1948 as a junior clerk in the James Street garage. His mentor and boss was Inspector Dai John, for whom he had enormous respect.

"I was 16, had my own office and loved the place and the people," recalled Trevor. "In those heady days of mass departures, whenever they had a choice, passengers would pick what they regarded as the nicest of the standing coaches.

"If the best one was on the relief for Cardiff only, people were reluctant to board the old banger waiting behind. The passengers who were bound for the intermediate stops tried to get away with sitting still and not moving. It would be very annoying if this was only discovered en-route and the 'Bolter' had to make an unscheduled stop.

"One driver had a wonderful way of ensuring he only carried the passengers he wanted. Eddie Williams would stagger up to the coach looking completely dishevelled and would literally frighten his unwanted passengers off the vehicle. He had the uncanny ability to hunch his back, drop his jaw and adjust his sleeves so one arm looked longer than the other. His colleagues would lift him, dribbling, into the cab, whereupon his bulging eyes would duel with each other to focus forward. Needless to say, as soon as the conductor asked the startled passengers to change coaches, they were gone!

"When working the Bolters," continued Trevor, "the fastest part of the journey was between Bridgend and Cardiff. We could overtake on the Golden Mile and our passengers were always pointing and laughing at those in the slower coach. One of the drivers would play a brilliant trick when this happened, he would duck down, out of sight, his view of the road being from under the steering wheel. For the passengers on the overtaking vehicle, it was quietly explained by the conductor that the N&C was experimenting with driverless coaches. What a character!"

The early post-war years were a time of great progress for N&C. The company was enjoying a runaway success with its express services, but had created problems among competitors and police, and when it was announced that changes to the Traffic Act were to come about, Col. Llewellyn decided to sell his interest to the British Electric Traction (BET) Group.

Accordingly, the company found itself under the BET umbrella in 1953. It was controlled by a board of directors under the chairmanship of W T James, OBE. Col. Llewellyn remained Managing Director and J J Newbury the General Manager. The decision to sell was a good one. Appreciative of their newly acquired asset, BET provided major investment in new and rebodied vehicles. It was a massive vote of confidence that enabled the company to continue to provide its sterling service for the 15 glorious years that followed. And glorious years they certainly were.

Under this new regime, in June 1954, Trevor Burley was given the job of bringing one of the first Guy Arabs on its delivery run from Park Royal in London. To get there he took one of six Longford-bodied AEC Regals that had been selected for rebodying. There was a convoy of three AECs up, and three Guys back, duly repeated so that all six vehicles

Longford bodywork on show at Bridgend bus station in 1950. On the left is JTX339, a new Daimler CVD6DD in the desert sand and tan livery, and on the right, HNY913, a two-year old AEC Regal Mk III. *Alan B Cross*

N&C operated 12 Guy Arab LUF coaches with Park Royal bodywork, delivered in two batches of six in 1954 and 1955. One of the latter delivery, LCY781, is seen near Victoria Station, Swansea in the early 1960s. *The Bus Archive*

were exchanged. The drivers were well over their normal hours behind the wheel, so at Gloucester they parked up and went to the cinema to get some rest!

As the new Guy Arabs entered the fleet, N&C was granted a half hourly service frequency in a bid to cut down the amount of duplicate services that had been needed at the time. The restriction on picking up at Cowbridge and Pyle was also lifted at this time, allowing for both locations to appear on the coaches.

Other service improvements included the introduction of Cheap Day Return tickets and use of the newly-opened Central bus station in Cardiff where they received what could be described as the prime spot for departures.

By the mid-1950s, a further six Guy Arabs had arrived, and the six retained AEC Regal IIIs had received striking new bodies from Park Royal, built to the newly permitted 8ft width. Many will recall these fabulous coaches which provided the backbone of the company's services during the late 1950s and early 1960s. To the bystander, they were unmistakable, as they were the first coaches to be fitted with radial tyres and they made a humming or swishing sound as they passed by. They undoubtedly set the scene for the N&C's glorious heyday.

The AEC Reliance underfloor-engined chassis was introduced to N&C in 1956, and thereafter was the preferred make of vehicle, supplied with a variety of bodies over the ensuing years.

The company continued to grow from strength to strength and by July 1960 its fleet stood at an all time maximum of 35 coaches. In 1967, under the helm of chief engineer Gerald Truran, N&C entered its final glorious era with the fleet becoming entirely of AEC manufactured vehicles.

The two Morris Viceroy luxury coaches which began the express service between Neath and Cardiff on 2 April 1930, proved to be the pioneers of what became one of the most popular and useful links in public transport in South Wales.

Three decades later, N&C was still on top of its game, and moving with the times.
In 1962 they had 35 coaches with an average age of five years. During that same year those hard working vehicles carried 1,330,924 passengers.

N&C LUXURY COACHES LTD

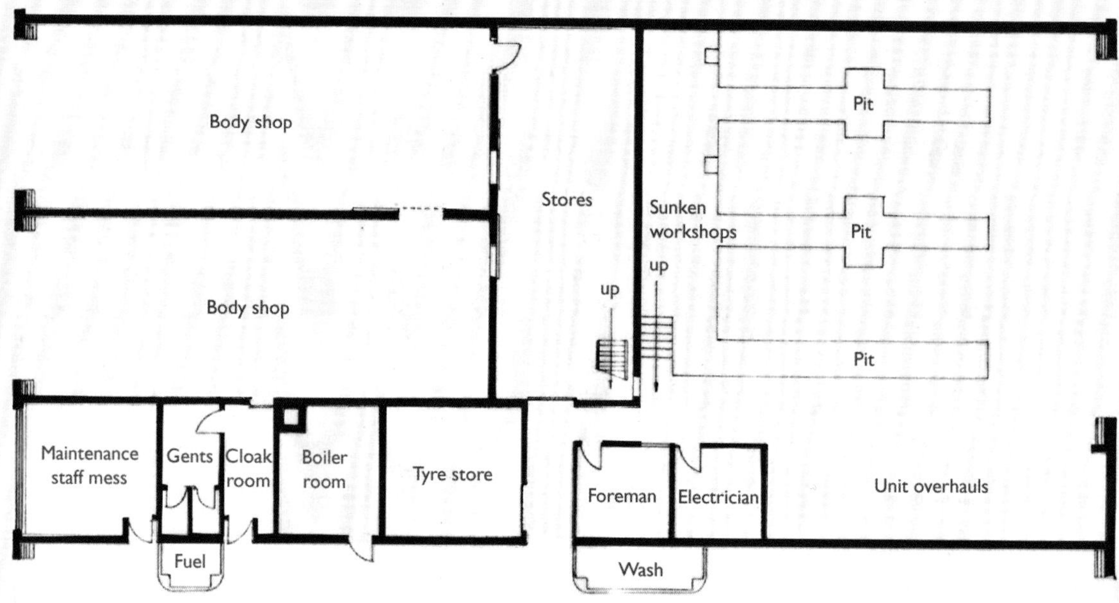

Stabling garage

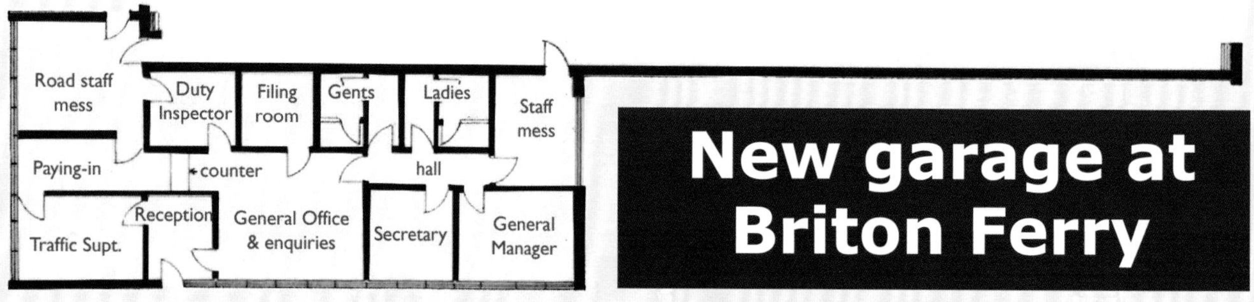

New garage at Briton Ferry

For many who had worked in the damp and difficult conditions of N&C's James Street, Neath operating centre, the prospect of working in a modern purpose built building must have been an exciting prospect. This architect's drawing of the new Briton Ferry garage and offices shows just how improved everything was to be. The map to the right indicates the convenient location of the new set-up, alongside Briton Ferry roundabout and the eastern end of Neath River Bridge which in the early 1950s was the UK's biggest civil engineering project. Above right is a view of the new engineering bay complete with sunken inspection pits. When N&C left the premises they were used for many years by Calor Gas while it later became the home of Swansea Motor Vehicle Auctions.

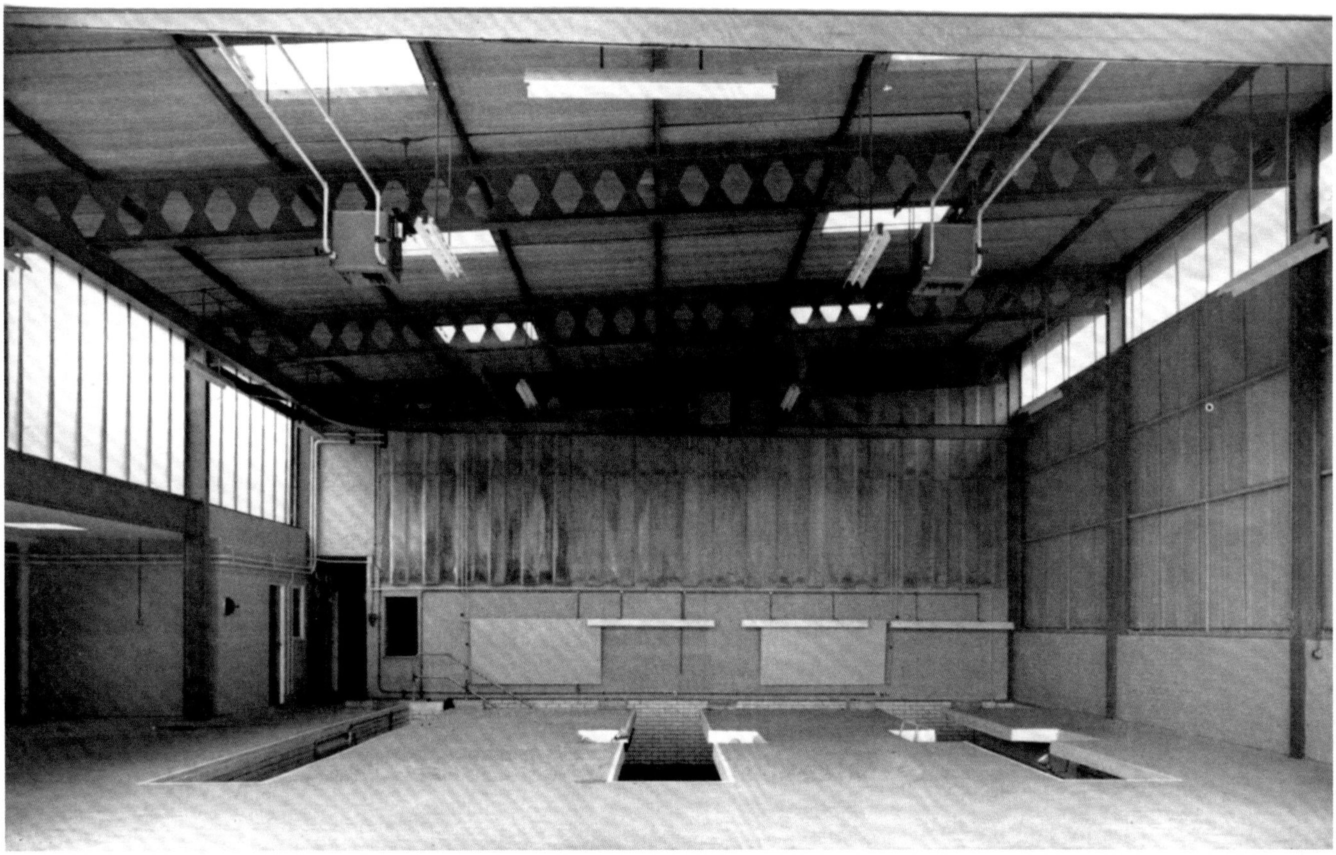

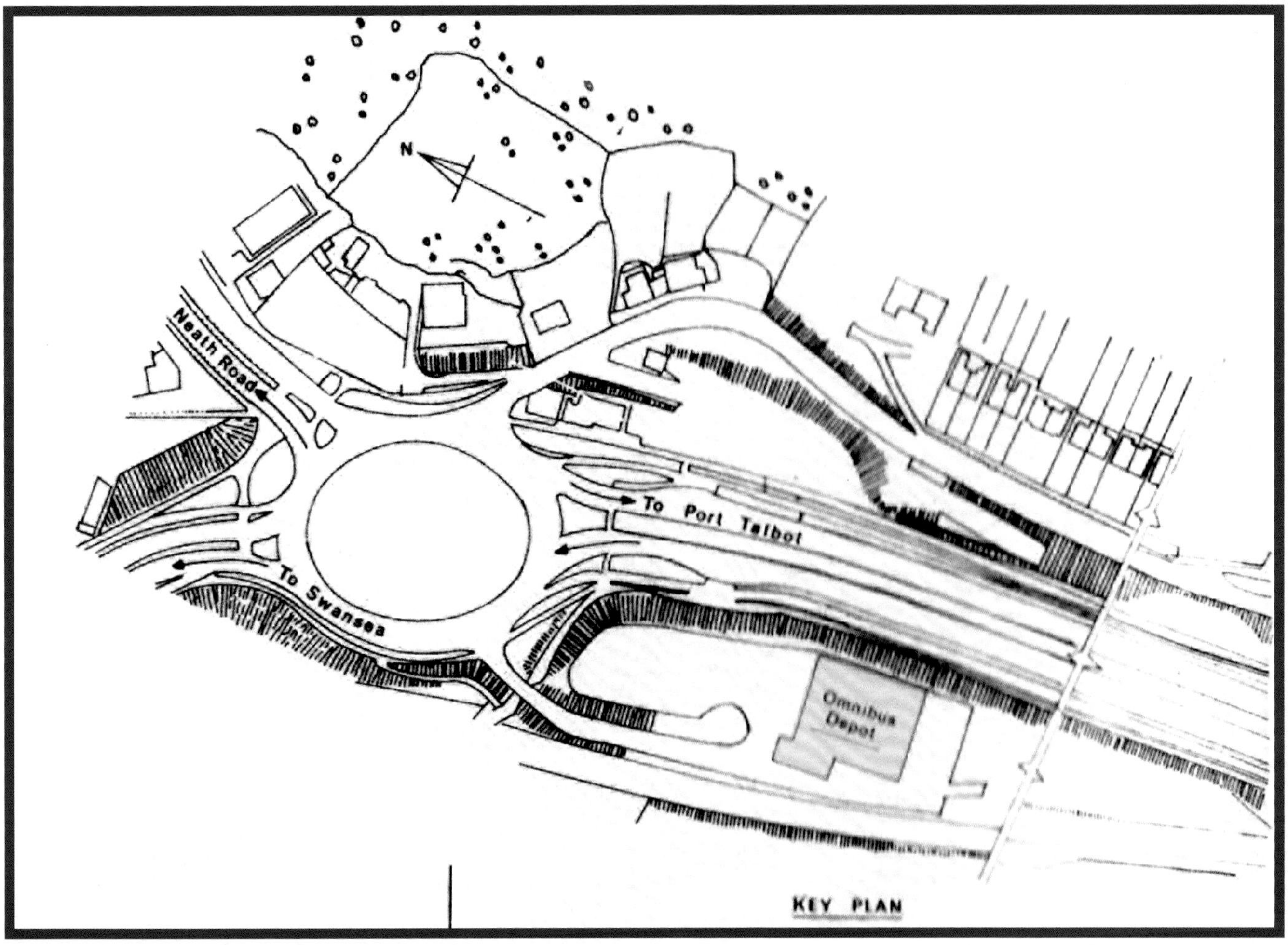

KEY PLAN

The long and winding road

The original point-to-point mileages for Swansea to Cardiff via Neath were as follows:

Swansea - Cardiff Read down			**Cardiff - Swansea Read up**	
----	----	Swansea (Clarence Street)	48.4	4.2
4.2	4.2	Morriston (The Cross)	44.2	1.1
1.1	5.3	Llansamlet (Star Inn)	43.1	2.6
2.6	7.9	Skewen (Station Road)	40.5	2.0
2.2	10.1	Neath (Victoria Gardens / Parade)	38.5	1.9
1.9	12.0	Briton Ferry (Lodge)	36.6	0.8
0.8	12.8	Briton Ferry (Roundabout)	35.8	1.3
1.3	14.1	Baglan (Post Office)	34.5	1.9
1.7	15.8	Port Talbot (Bethany Square)	32.6	0.3
0.3	16.1	Port Talbot (Old Empire)	32.3	0.6
0.6	16.7	Port Talbot (Taibach)	31.7	1.3
1.3	18.0	Port Talbot (Tollgate Island)	30.4	1.0
1.0	19.0	Margam (Post Office)	29.4	3.3
3.3	22.3	Pyle Cross	26.1	1.8
1.8	24.1	Stormy Down	24.3	2.0
2.0	26.1	Bridgend (Laleston)	22.3	2.3
2.1	28.2	Bridgend (Bus Station)	20.0	1.1
1.1	29.3	Bridgend (Police Headquarters)	18.9	5.9
5.9	35.2	Cowbridge (Town Hall)	13.0	8.4
8.4	43.6	Cardiff (Culverhouse Cross)	4.6	2.7
2.7	46.3	Cardiff (Victoria Park)	1.9	1.9
2.9	48.3	Cardiff (Central Bus Station)	----	----

Tilling Stevens K6MA7, HTX545 new in 1948, was fitted with a Gardner 6LW engine. It was livelier than the 5LWs in the subsequent trio which entered service in 1950. All had Longford 33-seat bodies.

Driver Fred 'Jock' Cross at the wheel of AEC Reliance PTX 830F in the yard at Briton Ferry when new in 1968.
Gerald Truran

N&C's new purpose-built depot was opened in Briton Ferry on Tuesday 26 November, 1963. The move from Neath to Briton Ferry was an enforced one as a result of Neath's new town redevelopment proposals which involved complete redevelopment of the James Street area. The company had encountered a few difficulties in its search for alternative premises, which began back in 1958, but the former Vernon tinplate works adjacent to the new Briton Ferry roundabout became available, and so the brownfield site was chosen for a modern garage with ancillary plant, together with the company's offices, all in compact modern conditions. The design of the garage allowed for a roof height of 15ft which catered for the possible future operation of double deck vehicles. Situated on a two acre site, it was unusual in that it consisted of two bays, one a drive-through garage with its own fuel point and stabling area; while the other consisted of workshops and stores. In between were rooms for staff and toilets. The total floor area was nearly 13,000 square feet and altogether 14 maximum-length coaches could be housed within. There was a separate paint shop, body shop and servicing area. Alongside the garage were offices and mess rooms, and room for a further 16 coaches outside. It was ideally placed for N&C's operations, being situated just where the route split, and this allowed dead mileage to be kept to a minimum. The premises were freehold, the land being bought outright for £6,500. The cost of erecting the buildings was £57,759.

Colonel Llewellyn received a baronetcy in 1959 and became first Baronet of Baglan under his new title of Sir Godfrey Llewellyn. Retired for 10 years, he made a special visit to celebrate the official opening of the new depot. He had been managing director since the company became a subsidiary of British Electric Traction in 1953. Also present was former company secretary, Captain J J Newbury, who was now general manager, along with secretary, H E Exton; accountant, R J Franklin; engineer, J G Winn; Chief Clerk, S J Raisen and traffic superintendent, R J Gallanders.

The formal opening ceremony was novel with the chairman of the South Wales Traffic Commissioners, Ronald J Jackson, complete with his PSV driver's badge, driving into the depot with one of the latest coaches to break the tape. The human touch which had always

official opening of a new

OMNIBUS DEPOT AND OFFICES

by Ronald R. Jackson Esq

CHAIRMAN OF THE TRAFFIC COMMISSIONERS,
SOUTH WALES TRAFFIC AREA

ON TUESDAY 26th NOVEMBER 1963

NEATH AND CARDIFF LUXURY COACHES LTD.

REGISTERED OFFICE: BRITON FERRY, GLAMORGAN *TELEPHONE:* BRITON FERRY 3393/4

DIRECTORS

W. M. DRAVERS, Chairman
Col. Sir GODFREY LLEWELLYN, BART., C.B., C.B.E., M.C., T.D., D.L., J.P., Managing Director
T. V. WOODS, C.B.E. **Sir JOHN GUTCH,** K.C.M.G., O.B.E. **F. K. POINTON**

COMPANY OFFICERS

J. J. NEWBURY M.B.E. General Manager
H. E. EXTON *SECRETARY* · **R. J. FRANKLIN** *ACCOUNTANT* · **J. G. WINN** *ENGINEER*
S. J. RAISEN *CHIEF CLERK* · **R. J. GALLANDERS** *TRAFFIC SUPERINTENDENT*

3

signified the company's relations with its road and garage staff was evident when a silent tribute was called for by chairman W M Dravers, to salute one of N&C's older employees, garage electrician David Davies, who had collapsed there from a fatal illness the previous Saturday. Better known to his workmates as 'Dai Dai', he had passed away after being taken to hospital.

Three-quarters of the road and garage staff had been invited to the opening — everyone who could be spared from the road. There was no difference between 'top' and other tables, and the generosity of the company impressed all who attended.

This happy atmosphere was noted in a speech by chairman W M Dravers. He began by saying that one of the principal reasons for building the new premises was to improve working conditions for the staff who for many years had worked under great difficulties in unattractive conditions. "Despite these difficulties," said Mr Dravers. "They had always turned out vehicles second to none in cleanliness and mechanical efficiency. They deserved the greatest credit for that," he added.

Sir Godfrey gave a witty speech in which he recalled the company's characters - all of whom had proved their loyalty over the years. Mr Ronald Jackson recalled the company's beginnings with the Morris Viceroy coaches in the 1930s: "They were a most attractive sight," he said, "with their colouring earning them the nickname of The Flying Bananas."

Many will remember the impressive sight of the fleet parked in line along the landscaped sunken front yard of the modern Briton Ferry depot. All available coaches were enticingly faced outwards towards the A48, while it was customary to park coaches arriving at the depot facing into the grass bank to await inspection.

N&C had become the envy of many other operators, admired from afar, yet resented by local companies who were overcome with jealousy, having been incapable of providing any meaningful competition.

In March 1964, just a few months after the new depot opened, General Manager J J Newbury retired. He had worked for the company for 34 years, and yet was still to reach his 60th birthday. A presentation was made by Jock Cross at the Cambrian Hotel, Windsor Road, Neath. Mr Newbury thanked those present and recalled that a number of them had been with the company since they were boys. 'Jock', who had made the presentation, had done much, particularly during the war years, for the benefit of his fellow workmen who were in the armed forces, but such work was too readily forgotten with the influx of new staff.

> **"Those N&C coaches had a double seat in front, and it gave you a bird's eye view of the road. I loved it when we managed to occupy it!"**
>
> ***Allison Thomas***

Mr Newbury also expressed the hope that the staff would continue to work together, as teamwork was essential for success. This was very important, as every new car on the road meant the loss of at least one fare-paying passenger. "Only last week," continued Mr Newbury, "the firm carried 2,000 less passengers than in the same week the previous year. Fare increases had never been the answer as it becomes a vicious circle. As fares increase, passengers decrease and a resistance is set up. This called for understanding both by management and staff." Mr Newbury added that he planned to spend more time aboard his yacht 'Quo Vadis', and for that he said he would need the continued help of his old colleagues to ensure that he kept to his proper routes!

N&C LUXURY COACHES
Swansea Cardiff Express Services

A full yard at Briton Ferry depot, probably on a Sunday morning around 1963-64. In contrast just five years later when the main image was captured by Brian Maguire 36-footers had become the norm.

The mid-1960s saw a change at the top. Chief engineer F H Beddoes retired in 1963 and was replaced by J G Winn. Then in 1964, general manager J J Newbury retired to be succeeded by Dennis N Flower. W T James was replaced as chairman of the board by W M Dravers. Meanwhile, Winn's stay was short-lived, and he left the company in 1965, to be succeeded by Gerald Truran who came from Devon General, but had served his apprenticeship with Western Welsh and in a very short time clearly made his mark at Briton Ferry.

It came as no surprise that Sir Godfrey was not interested in retirement just yet. However, in 1967, he was horrified to learn that the BET Group was becoming worried about its future, due to the gathering political pressure to sell to the state-owned Transport Holding Company (THC) under plans for a national bus company. A few months later, his worst fears were realised, and BET sold its interests – before its hands were forced. Tragically, this meant the beginning of the end for the proud and passionate N&C.

The company found itself under new management in March 1968, although THC remained temporarily under BET control until the formation of the National Bus Company had been completed. The inevitable further change of directors in mid-1968 led directly to the retirement of Sir Godfrey, who broke his association with the N&C Company after more than 38 years. During 1969, shortly after delivery of the final two 'proper' N&C coaches, control of the engineering department passed to South Wales Transport. Then came the major revision to express services that saw the Western Welsh 301 service combine with N&C to form a 20-minute frequency between Briton Ferry and Cardiff. The N&C no longer ran an express service, and had been delivered into the hands of South Wales Transport and Western Welsh, who couldn't wait to destroy all the good work. That's just what they did, and with shockingly indecent haste. Killed, as the staff claimed, by nationalisation and mourned by all.

PUBLIC SERVICE VEHICLE
GG
7773
CONDUCTOR

GG
37024

General manager Dennis Flower left the company at the end of 1969, and South Wales Transport didn't replace him. In March 1970, the Bell Automaticket machines were replaced by overhauled Setrights converted for decimal currency. Then in July, the final two vehicles arrived bearing the N&C name – but minus the word 'Express'. They had been ordered by SWT in line with their purchasing policy. Plaxtons, to be fair, fitted them with various coach-type embellishments to numb the fact that they were built on bus frames, but the pair were never going to be popular — politics ensured that!

The final nail in the coffin came with the closure of Briton Ferry garage in January 1971, after just over eight year's operation. At this date, once Western Welsh had taken their share of N&C vehicles, the remainder, together with most of the Briton Ferry based staff, were transferred to the former United Welsh bus company's Swansea depot in the city's Clarence Terrace.

Despite the N&C's painful demise, it can be said to have enjoyed a most romantic career. It was a small company that successfully challenged the competition provided by the powerful Great Western Railway and two major bus companies, Western Welsh and South Wales Transport, until political pressure forced its hand. N&C was highly regarded by its proud staff and loyal customers alike, and was a truly awe-inspiring example of what private enterprise can achieve.

Chapter 3

Life on the road

The origin of the A48 trunk road which stretches between Gloucester and Carmarthen dates back to Roman times, and between Cardiff and Neath some sections of the N&C's route closely followed this direct, but often undulating historic route.

However, there were sections that didn't follow the original road, and in the N&C's early days these were often narrow and winding. In the 1930s, much of the traffic on the A48 was still horsedrawn. Despite all of this, with so little traffic about generally, the journey from Neath to Cardiff took only about an hour and a half.

From 1932, N&C's full route between Swansea and Cardiff via Morriston and Neath stretched to 48 miles. When the new Neath River Bridge at Briton Ferry opened in October 1955, alternate services by-passed Morriston and Neath, and ran direct to Cardiff via the A483 Fabian Way dual carriageway, reducing the run to 42 miles.

During the 40 years that N&C plied the A48, many thousands of journeys were made between Swansea and Cardiff. Initially, the timetable was irregular and consisted of more afternoon journeys than those in the morning. There were more services by 1932, but still not of a regular pattern, probably due to the limited number of vehicles available, rather than lack of passengers.

In 1937, there were 15 journeys each way on weekdays and six on Sundays, but during the Second World War this was reduced to eight and two respectively. It wasn't until 1946 that a regular time-interval timetable was compiled and operated. From this point services left Swansea on the half-hour from 6.30am to 9.30pm, and from Cardiff on the hour between 7am and 11pm. Oddly, as there was only one overnight coach out-stationed at Cardiff, there was no 8am westbound departure for Swansea.

By 1952, around half of the fleet had been upgraded with sturdy new AEC Regals, and in 1954, with major investment now coming

from the BET Group, the service doubled to half hourly. A year later, alternate journeys crossed the new Neath River Bridge at Briton Ferry and saved 15 minutes on the time taken via Neath. This pattern of services remained largely unaltered for the next 15 glorious years, with 33 weekday journeys each way, and 13 on Sundays.

To most of the travelling public in immediate post-war Britain, a bus or coach was something that took them on their daily journey to school, work, shopping, or to the cinema, theatre or pub in the evening.

The vast majority of passengers didn't give a thought about the vehicle or crew that carried them, as long as the service was on time and the fare was reasonable.

The N&C was different. It aimed high on all counts and as a result was genuinely revered by its customers, who recognised instantly that the service they were being offered was first rate in every respect. They were carried in absolute style and comfort, were looked after by the road staff, and of course, the service was nearly always punctual.

All of this meant that there was often some lively running needed to keep to schedule, but generally speaking, traffic was light and vehicles were smaller, so there was more room on the road, and overtaking was permitted at many places then, that were later frowned upon as being too dangerous.

N&C took delivery of its first underfloor engined coaches, three Longford–bodied AEC Regal Mk IVs, between May 1951 and May 1952. Each had minor differences in styling but they were all well liked, despite their heavy handling. The third of these vehicles, LTX111 is seen at Victoria Gardens, Neath, in the late 1950s.

With the number of motor vehicles on the road increasing annually, various improvements were made to the A48. Notable among these were several three-lane stretches between Waterton and Culverhouse Cross, laid down during the war years. It seems bizarre in the 21st Century to accept that oncoming traffic was meant to share this centre, or overtaking lane, but that's exactly what happened.

It was often jokingly suggested this centre lane on the A48 was created specifically for the N&C! Later, in the 1960s, when a dual carriageway by-passing Cowbridge and the A48(M) by-passing Port Talbot were built, N&C was quick to seize the opportunity of providing additional non-stop 'flyer' journeys and took advantage of reduced end-to-end timings. A great many services continued to be duplicated at busy times. As the decade drew to its close, it would have been reasonable to assume that the N&C would continue to go from strength to strength for many more years.

A group of N&C drivers and conductors in front of AEC Regal Mk IV, LTG226 at Swansea, early 1950s.

Trevor Burley recalled times in the late 1940s and early 1950s when construction of the Abbey Works at Port Talbot was underway. The decommissioned RAF base at Stormy Down was used for accommodating many construction workers, and the N&C carried them to and from the massive construction site. This meant transporting a huge number of people at peak morning and evening times, something that required many relief coaches. The workers enjoyed the speedy ride and always cheered the fastest drivers – but also booed the slowest!

It was rare for an N&C employee to be unhappy in his work. The management, engineers and staff were loyal and diligent workers who strove to retain the valued custom of an equally loyal travelling public.

During the summer of 1935 there had been a prolonged and vitriolic strike by busmen in South Wales, but once again the N&C company had stood alone throughout by maintaining its service to the public.
This was not without its problems as there was a lot of ill-feeling displayed towards N&C staff by the striking busmen. They often found themselves on the receiving end when tempers boiled over. Strikers at Neath had been endeavouring in vain to induce the N&C crews to join them, as theirs was the only service running through the town.
Services were regularly escorted by police

Telegrams : "NELUXCO"
Telephone : NEATH 2227/8

NEATH AND CARDIFF LUXURY COA

TIME TABLE—27th JUNE, 1960

EXPRESS SERVICE

SERVICE NO. 7—SWANSEA, MORRISTON, LLANSAMLET, SKEWEN, NEATH ABBEY, NEATH, STORMY DOWN, BRIDGEND COWBRIDGE, CA

SERVICE NO. 10—SWANSEA, PORT TENNANT, BRITON FERRY (RIVER BRIDGE), BAGLAN, PO COWBRIDGE, CARDIFF.

WEEKDAY SERVICES

	Ser. No. 7	Ser. No. 7	Ser. No. 7	Ser. No. 7	Ser. No. 10	Ser. No. 7	Ser. No. 10	Ser. No. 7	Ser. No. 10	Ser. No. 7	Ser. No. 10	Ser. No. 7	Ser. No. 10	Ser. No. 7	Ser. No. 10	Ser. No. 7	Ser. No. 10	Ser. No. 7
		†																
	a.m.	a.m.	a.m.	a.m.	a.m.	a.m.	a.m.	a.m.	a.m.	a.m.	a.m.	a.m.	p.m.	p.m.	p.m.	p.m.	p.m.	p.m.
	Starts from Neath	Via Morriston & Neath	Via Morriston and Neath	Starts from Morriston	Via Port Tennant and B' Ferry Bridge	Via Morriston & Neath	Via Port Tennant and B' Ferry Bridge	Via Morriston & Neath	Via Port Tennant and B' Ferry Bridge	Via Morriston & Neath	Via Port Tennant and B' Ferry Bridge	Via Morriston & Neath	Via Port Tennant and B' Ferry Bridge	Via Morriston & Neath	Via Port Tennant and B' Ferry Bridge	Via Morriston & Neath	Via Port Tennant and B' Ferry Bridge	Via Morriston & Neath
SWANSEA (Clarence St.) dep.		**6 45**	**7 15**		**8 00**	**8 15**	**9 00**	**9 15**	**10 00**	**10 15**	**11 00**	**11 15**	**12 00**	**12 15**	**1 00**	**1 15**	**2 00**	**2 15**
Swansea (Dyfatty St.)		6 47	7 17			8 17		9 17		10 17		11 17		12 17		1 17		2 17
Swansea (Harbour Road)					8 02		9 02		10 02		11 02		12 02		1 02		2 02	
Port Tennant (Union Inn)					8 07		9 07		10 07		11 07		12 07		1 07		2 07	
Port Tennant (Vale of Neath Inn)					8 10		9 10		10 10		11 10		12 10		1 10		2 10	
Crumlyn Burrows					8 13		9 13		10 13		11 13		12 13		1 13		2 13	
Jersey Marine (Road Junction)					8 14		9 14		10 14		11 14		12 14		1 14		2 14	
Morriston (Cross Roads)		6 55	7 25	7 55		8 25		9 25		10 25		11 25		12 25		1 25		2 25
Llansamlet (Star Inn)		6 59	7 29	7 59		8 29		9 29		10 29		11 29		12 29		1 29		2 29
Skewen (Station Road)		7 07	7 37	8 07		8 37		9 37		10 37		11 37		12 37		1 37		2 37
Neath Abbey		7 09	7 39	8 09		8 39		9 39		10 39		11 39		12 39		1 39		2 39
NEATH (Victoria Gdns.)	**6 45**	**7 15**	**7 45**	**8 15**		**8 45**		**9 45**		**10 45**		**11 45**		**12 45**		**1 45**		**2 45**
Briton Ferry (Lodge Cinema)	6 50	7 20	7 50	8 20		8 50		9 50		10 50		11 50		12 50		1 50		2 50
Briton Ferry (Post Office)	6 52	7 22	7 52	8 22		8 52		9 57		10 52		11 52		12 52		1 52		2 52
Briton Ferry (River Bridge)					8 20		9 20		10 20		11 20		12 20		1 20		2 20	
Baglan (Swan St.)	6 53	7 23	7 53	8 23	8 21	8 53	9 21	9 53	10 21	10 53	11 21	11 53	12 21	12 53	1 21	1 53	2 21	2 53
Baglan (Post Office)	6 54	7 24	7 54	8 24	8 24	8 54	9 24	9 54	10 24	10 54	11 24	11 54	12 24	12 54	1 24	1 54	2 24	2 54
Baglan (The Elms)	6 56	7 26	7 56	8 26	8 26	8 56	9 26	9 56	10 26	10 56	11 26	11 56	12 26	12 56	1 26	1 56	2 26	2 56
PORT TALBOT (Gram. Sch.)	**7 00**	**7 30**	**8 00**	**8 30**	**8 30**	**9 00**	**9 30**	**10 00**	**10 30**	**11 00**	**11 30**	**12 00**	**12 30**	**1 00**	**1 30**	**2 00**	**2 30**	**3 00**
Port Talbot (Old Empire)	7 01	7 31	8 01	8 31	8 31	9 01	9 31	10 01	10 31	11 01	11 31	12 01	12 31	1 01	1 31	2 01	2 31	3 01
Port Talbot (Taibach)	7 03	7 33	8 03	8 33	8 33	9 03	9 33	10 03	10 33	11 03	11 33	12 03	12 33	1 03	1 33	2 03	2 33	3 03
Margam (Co-operative)	7 05	7 35	8 05	8 35	8 35	9 05	9 35	10 05	10 35	11 05	11 35	12 05	12 35	1 05	1 35	2 05	2 35	3 05
Margam (Landore Avenue)	7 06	7 36	8 06	8 36	8 36	9 06	9 36	10 06	10 36	11 06	11 36	12 06	12 36	1 06	1 36	2 06	2 36	3 06
Margam (Post Office)	7 09	7 39	8 09	8 39	8 39	9 09	9 39	10 09	10 39	11 09	11 39	12 09	12 39	1 09	1 39	2 09	2 39	3 09
PYLE (Cross Roads)	**7 15**	**7 45**	**8 15**	**8 45**	**8 45**	**9 15**	**9 45**	**10 15**	**10 45**	**11 15**	**11 45**	**12 15**	**12 45**	**1 15**	**1 45**	**2 15**	**2 45**	**3 15**
Stormy Down (Cross Roads)	7 17	7 47	8 17	8 47	8 47	9 17	9 47	10 17	10 47	11 17	11 47	12 17	12 47	1 17	1 47	2 17	2 47	3 17
Laleston (Mackworth Arms)	7 26	7 56	8 26	8 56	8 56	9 26	9 56	10 26	10 56	11 26	11 56	12 26	12 56	1 26	1 56	2 26	2 56	3 26
Bryntirion (Hostel)	7 27	7 57	8 27	8 57	8 57	9 27	9 57	10 27	10 57	11 27	11 57	12 27	12 57	1 27	1 57	2 27	2 57	3 27
Bryntirion (Phillips Avenue)	7 28	7 58	8 28	8 58	8 58	9 28	9 58	10 28	10 58	11 28	11 58	12 28	12 58	1 28	1 58	2 28	2 58	3 28
BRIDGEND (Bus Station)	**7 30**	**8 00**	**8 30**	**9 00**	**9 00**	**9 30**	**10 00**	**10 30**	**11 00**	**11 30**	**12 00**	**12 30**	**1 00**	**1 30**	**2 00**	**2 30**	**3 00**	**3 30**
Bridgend (Waterton Cross)	7 33	8 03	8 33	9 03	9 03	9 33	10 03	10 33	11 03	11 33	12 03	12 33	1 03	1 33	2 03	2 33	3 03	3 33
COWBRIDGE (Town Hall)	**7 45**	**8 15**	**8 45**	**9 15**	**9 15**	**9 45**	**10 15**	**10 45**	**11 15**	**11 45**	**12 15**	**12 45**	**1 15**	**1 45**	**2 15**	**2 45**	**3 15**	**3 45**
Ely (Culverhouse Cross) arr.	8 00	8 30	9 00	9 30	9 30	10 00	10 30	11 00	11 30	12 00	12 30	1 00	1 30	2 00	2 30	3 00	3 30	4 00
Cardiff (Victoria Park)	8 10	8 40	9 10	9 40	9 40	10 10	10 40	11 10	11 40	12 10	12 40	1 10	1 40	2 10	2 40	3 10	3 40	4 10
Cardiff (Canton Cinema)	8 12	8 42	9 12	9 42	9 42	10 12	10 42	11 12	11 42	12 12	12 42	1 12	1 42	2 12	2 42	3 12	3 42	4 12
Cardiff (Neville St.)	8 13	8 43	9 13	9 43	9 43	10 13	10 43	11 13	11 43	12 13	12 43	1 13	1 43	2 13	2 43	3 13	3 43	4 13
CARDIFF (Central Bus Stn.)	**8 15**	**8 45**	**9 15**	**9 45**	**9 45**	**10 15**	**10 45**	**11 15**	**11 45**	**12 15**	**12 45**	**1 15**	**1 45**	**2 15**	**2 45**	**3 15**	**3 45**	**4 15**

	Ser. No. 10	Ser. No. 7	Ser. No. 10	Ser. No. 7	Ser. No. 10	Ser. No. 7	Ser. No. 10	Ser. No. 7	Ser. No. 10	Ser. No. 7	Ser. No. 10	Ser. No. 7	Ser. No. 10	Ser. No. 7	Ser. No. 10	Ser. No. 7	Ser. No. 10	Ser. No/ 7
	a.m.	a.m.	a.m.	a.m.	a.m.	a.m.	a.m.	a.m.	a.m.	a.m.	a.m.	p.m.	p.m.	p.m.	p.m.	p.m.	p.m.	p.m.
CARDIFF (Central Bus Stn.) dep.	**7 00**	**7 00**	**7 30**	**8 00**	**8 30**	**9 00**	**9 30**	**10 00**	**10 30**	**11 00**	**11 30**	**12 00**	**12 30**	**1 00**	**1 30**	**2 00**	**2 30**	**3 00**
Cardiff (Neville St.)	7 02	7 02	7 32	8 02	8 32	9 02	9 32	10 02	10 32	11 02	11 32	12 02	12 32	1 02	1 32	2 02	2 32	3 02
Cardiff (Canton Cinema)	7 03	7 03	7 33	8 03	8 33	9 03	9 33	10 03	10 33	11 03	11 33	12 03	12 33	1 03	1 33	2 03	2 33	3 03
Cardiff (Victoria Park)	7 07	7 07	7 37	9 07	8 37	9 07	9 37	10 07	10 37	11 07	11 37	12 07	12 37	1 07	1 37	2 07	2 37	3 07
Ely (Culverhouse Cross)	7 15	7 15	7 45	8 15	8 45	9 15	9 45	10 15	10 45	11 15	11 45	12 15	12 45	1 15	1 45	2 15	2 45	3 15
COWBRIDGE (Town Hall)	**7 30**	**7 30**	**8 00**	**8 30**	**9 00**	**9 30**	**10 00**	**10 30**	**11 00**	**11 30**	**12 00**	**12 30**	**1 00**	**1 30**	**2 00**	**2 30**	**3 00**	**3 30**
Bridgend (Waterton Cross)	7 43	7 43	8 13	8 43	9 13	9 43	10 13	10 43	11 13	11 43	12 13	12 43	1 13	1 43	2 13	2 43	3 13	3 43
BRIDGEND (Bus Station)	**7 45**	**7 45**	**8 15**	**8 45**	**9 15**	**9 45**	**10 15**	**10 45**	**11 15**	**11 45**	**12 15**	**12 45**	**1 15**	**1 45**	**2 15**	**2 45**	**3 15**	**3 45**
Bryntirion (Phillips Avenue)	7 47	7 47	8 17	8 47	9 17	9 47	10 17	10 47	11 17	11 47	12 17	12 47	1 17	1 47	2 17	2 47	3 17	3 47
Bryntirion (Hostel)	7 48	7 48	8 18	8 48	9 18	9 48	10 18	10 48	11 18	11 48	12 18	12 48	1 18	1 48	2 18	2 48	3 18	3 48
Laleston (Mackworth Arms)	7 49	7 49	8 19	8 49	9 19	9 49	10 19	10 49	11 19	11 49	12 19	12 49	1 19	1 49	2 19	2 49	3 19	3 49
Stormy Down (Cross Roads)	7 58	7 58	8 28	8 58	9 28	9 58	10 28	10 58	11 28	11 58	12 28	12 58	1 28	1 58	2 28	2 58	3 28	3 58
PYLE (Cross Roads)	**8 00**	**8 00**	**8 30**	**9 00**	**9 30**	**10 00**	**10 30**	**11 00**	**11 30**	**12 00**	**12 30**	**1 00**	**1 30**	**2 00**	**2 30**	**3 00**	**3 30**	**4 00**
Margam (Post Office)	8 06	8 06	8 36	9 06	9 36	10 06	10 36	11 06	11 36	12 06	12 36	1 06	1 36	2 06	2 36	3 06	3 36	4 06
Margam (Landore Avenue)	8 09	8 09	8 39	9 09	9 39	10 09	10 39	11 09	11 39	12 09	12 39	1 09	1 39	2 09	2 39	3 09	3 39	4 09
Margam (Co-operative)	8 10	8 10	8 40	9 10	9 40	10 10	10 40	11 10	11 40	12 10	12 40	1 10	1 40	2 10	2 40	3 10	3 40	4 10
Port Talbot (Taibach)	8 12	8 12	8 42	9 12	9 42	10 12	10 42	11 12	11 42	12 12	12 42	1 12	1 42	2 12	2 42	3 12	3 42	4 12
Port Talbot (Old Empire)	8 14	8 14	8 44	9 14	9 44	10 14	10 44	11 14	11 44	12 14	12 44	1 14	1 44	2 14	2 44	3 14	3 44	4 14
PORT TALBOT (Gram. Sch.)	**8 15**	**8 15**	**8 45**	**9 15**	**9 45**	**10 15**	**10 45**	**11 15**	**11 45**	**12 15**	**12 45**	**1 15**	**1 45**	**2 15**	**2 45**	**3 15**	**3 45**	**4 15**
Baglan (The Elms)	8 18	8 18	8 49	9 18	9 49	10 18	10 49	11 18	11 49	12 18	12 49	1 18	1 49	2 18	2 49	3 18	3 49	4 18
Baglan (Post Office)	8 20	8 20	8 51	9 20	9 51	10 20	10 51	11 20	11 51	12 20	12 51	1 20	1 51	2 20	2 51	3 20	3 51	4 20
Baglan (Swan St.)	8 23	8 23	8 54	9 23	9 54	10 23	10 54	11 23	11 54	12 23	12 54	1 23	1 54	2 23	2 54	3 23	3 54	4 23
Briton Ferry (River Bridge)	8 25		8 55		9 55		10 55		11 55		12 55		1 55		2 55		3 55	
	Via Briton Ferry Bridge & Port Tennant		Via Briton Ferry Bridge & Port Tennant		Via Briton Ferry Bridge & Port Tennant		Via Briton Ferry Bridge and Port Tennant		Via Briton Ferry Bridge and Port Tennant		Via Briton Ferry Bridge & Port Tennant		Via Briton Ferry Bridge & Port Tennant		Via Briton Ferry Bridge and Port Tennant		Via Briton Ferry Bridge & Port Tennant	
Briton Ferry (Post Office) arr.		8 24		9 24		10 24		11 24		12 24		1 24		2 24		3 24		4 24
Briton Ferry (Lodge Cinema)		8 26		9 26		10 26		11 26		12 26		1 26		2 26		3 26		4 26
Neath (Windsor Road)		8 29		9 29		10 29		11 29		12 29		1 29		2 29		3 29		4 29
NEATH (Cattle Market)		**8 30**		**9 30**		**10 30**		**11 30**		**12 30**		**1 30**		**2 30**		**3 30**		**4 30**
Neath Abbey		8 36		9 36		10 36		11 36		12 36		1 36		2 36		3 36		4 36
Skewen (Station Road)		8 38		9 38		10 38		11 38		12 38		1 38		2 38		3 38		4 38
Llansamlet (Star Inn)		8 46		9 46		10 46		11 46		12 46		1 46		2 46		3 46		4 46
Morriston (Cross Roads)		8 50		9 50		10 50		11 50		12 50		1 50		2 50		3 50		4 50
		Via Neath & Morriston		Via Neath & Morriston		Via Neath & Morriston		Via Neath & Morriston		Via Neath & Morriston		Via Neath & Morriston		Via Neath & Morriston		Via Neath & Morriston		Via Neath & Morriston
Jersey Marine (Road Junction)	8 31		9 01		10 01		11 01		12 01		1 01		2 01		3 01		4 01	
Crumlyn Burrows	8 32		9 02		10 02		11 02		12 02		1 02		2 02		3 02		4 02	
Port Tennant (Vale of Neath Inn)	8 35		9 05		10 05		11 05		12 05		1 05		2 05		3 05		4 05	
Port Tennant (Union Inn)	8 38		9 08		10 08		11 08		12 08		1 08		2 08		3 08		4 08	
Swansea (Harbour Road)	8 43		9 13		10 13		11 13		12 13		1 13		2 13		3 13		4 13	
Swansea (Palace Theatre)		8 58		9 58		10 58		11 58		12 58		1 58		2 58		3 58		4 58
SWANSEA (Clarence St.)	**8 45**	**9 00**	**9 15**	**1000**	**1015**	**1100**	**11 15**	**12 00**	**12 15**	**1 00**	**1 15**	**2 00**	**2 15**	**3 00**	**3 15**	**4 00**	**4 15**	**5 00**

NOTE:—† Starts from Swansea MONDAYS ONLY—TUESDAYS TO SATURDAYS (inclusive) STARTS FROM N

NOTE:—SERVICE No. 7 (VIA NEATH). No passenger may be accepted at SWANSEA, MORRISTON, LLANSAMLET, SKEWEN, NEATH ABBEY or NEATH for an (*i.e.* SWANSEA direction) after leaving Baglan Swan Street.

SERVICE No. 10 (VIA BRITON FERRY RIVER BRIDGE). No passenger may be accepted at SWANSEA or any intermediate point for any fare short of BRIT SWANSEA after leaving BRITON F

The Company will make every effort to maintain the services enumerated, but can accept no responsibility for loss or delay.

The Company reserves the right to alter, augment, reduce or withdraw all or any part of these services without further notice.

ES LIMITED Regd. Office: JAMES STREET, NEATH, GLAM.
Ref. No.: TGR.395/1—TGR.395/23

ON FERRY, BAGLAN, PORT TALBOT, PYLE,

LBOT, PYLE, STORMY DOWN, BRIDGEND,

EXPRESS SERVICE

er. o. 7	Ser. No. 10	Ser. No. 7	Ser. No. 10	Ser. No. 7	Ser. No. 10	Ser. No. 7	Ser. No. 10	Ser. No. 7	Ser. No. 10	Ser. No. 7	Ser. No. 10	Ser. No. 7 S.O.	Ser. No. 7
m.	p.m.	p.m.	p.m.	p.m.	p.m.	p.m.	p.m.	p.m.	p.m.	p.m.	p.m.	p.m.	p.m.
15	4 00	4 15	5 00	5 15	6 00	6 15	7 00	7 15	8 00	8 15	9 00	9 15	9 45
17		4 17		5 17		6 17		7 17		8 17		9 17	9 47
Morriston & Neath	4 02	Via Morriston & Neath	5 02	Via Morriston & Neath	6 02	Via Morriston & Neath	7 02	Via Morriston & Neath	8 02	Via Morriston & Neath	9 02	Via Morriston & Neath	Via Morriston & Neath
	4 07		5 07		6 07		7 07		8 07		9 07		
	4 10		5 10		6 10		7 10		8 10		9 10		
	4 13		5 13		6 13		7 13		8 13		9 13		
	4 14		5 14		6 14		7 14		8 14		9 14		
25	Via Port Tennant and B' Ferry Bridge	4 25	Via Port Tennant and B' Ferry Bridge	5 25	Via Port Tennant and B' Ferry Bridge	6 25	Via Port Tennant and B' Ferry Bridge	7 25	Via Port Tennant and B' Ferry Bridge	8 25	Via Port Tennant and B' Ferry Bridge	9 25	9 55
29		4 29		5 29		6 29		7 29		8 29		9 29	9 59
37		4 37		5 37		6 37		7 37		8 37		9 37	10 07
39		4 39		5 39		6 39		7 39		8 39		9 39	10 09
45		4 45		5 45		6 45		7 45		8 45		9 45	10 15
50		4 50		5 50		6 50		7 50		8 50		9 50	10 20
52		4 52		5 52		6 52		7 52		8 52		9 52	10 22
	4 20		5 20		6 20		7 20		8 20		9 20		
53	4 21	4 53	5 21	5 53	6 21	6 53	7 21	7 53	8 21	8 53	9 21	9 53	10 23
54	4 24	4 54	5 24	5 54	6 24	6 54	7 24	7 54	8 24	8 54	9 24	9 54	10 24
56	4 26	4 56	5 26	5 56	6 26	6 56	7 26	7 56	8 26	8 56	9 26	9 56	10 26
00	4 30	5 00	5 30	6 00	6 30	7 00	7 30	8 00	8 30	9 00	9 30	10 00	10 30
01	4 31	5 01	5 31	6 01	6 31	7 01	7 31	8 01	8 31	9 01	9 31	10 01	10 31
03	4 33	5 03	5 33	6 03	6 33	7 03	7 33	8 03	8 33	9 03	9 33	10 03	10 33
05	4 35	5 05	5 35	6 05	6 35	7 05	7 35	8 05	8 35	9 05	9 35	10 05	10 35
06	4 36	5 06	5 36	6 06	6 36	7 06	7 36	8 06	8 36	9 06	9 36	10 06	10 36
09	4 39	5 09	5 39	6 09	6 39	7 09	7 39	8 09	8 39	9 09	9 39	10 09	10 39
15	4 45	5 15	5 45	6 15	6 45	7 15	7 45	8 15	8 45	9 15	9 45	10 15	10 45
17	4 47	5 17	5 47	6 17	6 47	7 17	7 47	8 17	8 47	9 17	9 47	10 17	10 47
26	4 56	5 26	5 56	6 26	6 56	7 26	7 56	8 26	8 56	9 26	9 56	10 26	10 56
27	4 57	5 27	5 57	6 27	6 57	7 27	7 57	8 27	8 57	9 27	9 57	10 27	10 57
28	4 58	5 28	5 58	6 28	6 58	7 28	7 58	8 28	8 58	9 28	9 58	10 28	10 58
30	5 00	5 30	6 00	6 30	7 00	7 30	8 00	8 30	9 00	9 30	10 00	10 30	11 00
33	5 03	5 33	6 03	6 33	7 03	7 33	8 03	8 33	9 03	9 33	10 03	10 33	11 03
45	5 15	5 45	6 15	6 45	7 15	7 45	8 15	8 45	9 15	9 45	10 15	10 45	11 15
00	5 30	6 00	6 30	7 00	7 30	8 00	8 30	9 00	9 30	10 00	10 30	11 00	11 30
10	5 40	6 10	6 40	7 10	7 40	8 10	8 40	9 10	9 40	10 10	10 40	11 10	11 40
12	5 42	6 12	6 42	7 12	7 42	8 12	8 42	9 12	9 42	10 12	10 42	11 12	11 42
13	5 43	6 13	6 43	7 13	7 43	8 13	8 43	9 13	9 43	10 13	10 43	11 13	11 43
15	5 45	6 15	6 45	7 15	7 45	8 15	8 45	9 15	9 45	10 15	10 45	11 15	11 45

r. o. 7	Ser. No. 10	Ser. No. 7	Ser. No. 10	Ser. No. 7	.Ser No. 10	Ser. No. 7	Ser. No. 10	Ser. No. 7	Ser. No. 10	Ser. No. 7	Ser. No. 7 N.O.	Ser. No. 10	Ser. No. 7 N.O.
n.	p.m.	p.m.	p.m.	p.m.	p.m.	p.m.	p.m.	p.m.	p.m.	p.m.	p.m.	p.m.	p.m.
00	4 30	5 00	5 30	6 00	6 30	7 00	7 30	8 00	8 30	9 00	9 30	10 00	10 30
02	4 32	5 02	5 32	6 02	6 32	7 02	7 32	8 02	8 32	9 02	9 32	10 02	10 32
03	4 33	5 03	5 33	6 03	6 33	7 03	7 33	8 03	8 33	9 03	9 33	10 03	10 33
07	4 37	5 07	5 37	6 07	6 37	7 07	7 37	8 07	8 37	9 07	9 37	10 07	10 37
15	4 45	5 15	5 45	6 15	6 45	7 15	7 45	8 15	8 45	9 15	9 45	10 15	10 45
30	5 00	5 30	6 00	6 30	7 00	7 30	8 00	8 30	9 00	9 30	10 00	10 30	11 00
43	5 13	5 43	6 13	6 43	7 13	7 43	8 13	8 43	9 13	9 43	10 13	10 43	11 13
45	5 15	5 45	6 15	6 45	7 15	7 45	8 15	8 45	9 15	9 45	10 15	10 45	11 15
47	5 17	5 47	6 17	6 47	7 17	7 47	8 17	8 47	9 17	9 47	10 17	10 47	11 17
48	5 18	5 48	6 18	6 48	7 18	7 48	8 18	8 48	9 18	9 48	10 18	10 48	11 18
49	5 19	5 49	6 19	6 49	7 19	7 49	8 19	8 49	9 19	9 49	10 19	10 49	11 19
58	5 28	5 58	6 28	6 58	7 28	7 58	8 28	8 58	9 28	9 58	10 28	10 58	11 28
00	5 30	6 00	6 30	7 00	7 30	8 00	8 30	9 00	9 30	10 00	10 30	11 00	11 30
06	5 36	6 06	6 36	7 06	7 36	8 06	8 36	9 06	9 36	10 06	10 36	11 06	11 36
09	5 39	6 09	6 39	7 09	7 39	8 09	8 39	9 09	9 39	10 09	10 39	11 09	11 39
10	5 40	6 10	6 40	7 10	7 40	8 10	8 40	9 10	9 40	10 10	10 40	11 10	11 40
12	5 42	6 12	6 42	7 12	7 42	8 12	8 42	9 12	9 42	10 12	10 42	11 12	11 42
14	5 44	6 14	6 44	7 14	7 44	8 14	8 44	9 14	9 44	10 14	10 44	11 14	11 44
15	5 45	6 15	6 45	7 15	7 45	8 15	8 45	9 15	9 45	10 15	10 45	11 15	11 45
18	5 49	6 18	6 49	7 18	7 49	8 18	8 49	9 18	9 49	10 18	10 49	11 18	11 49
20	5 51	6 20	6 51	7 20	7 51	8 20	8 51	9 20	9 51	10 20	10 51	11 20	11 51
23	5 54	6 23	6 54	7 23	7 54	8 23	8 54	9 23	9 54	10 23	10 53	11 24	11 53
	5 55		6 55		7 55		8 55		9 55			11 25	
24	Via Briton Ferry Bridge & Port Tennant	6 24	Via Briton Ferry Bridge and Port Tennant	7 24	Via Briton Ferry Bridge & Port Tennant	8 24	Via Briton Ferry Bridge & Port Tennant	9 24	Via Briton Ferry Bridge & Port Tennant	10 24	10 54	Via Briton Ferry Bridge and Port Tennant	11 54
26		6 26		7 26		8 26		9 26		10 26	10 56		11 56
29		6 29		7 29		8 29		9 29		10 29	10 59		11 59
30		6 30		7 30		8 30		9 30		10 30	11 00		12 00
36		6 36		7 36		8 36		9 36		10 36	To Neath Only		To Neath Only
38		6 38		7 38		8 38		9 38		10 38			
46		6 46		7 46		8 46		9 46		10 46			
50		6 50		7 50		8 50		9 50		10 50			
Neath & Morriston	6 01	Via Neath & Morriston	7 01	Via Neath & Morriston	8 01	Via Neath & Morriston	9 01	Via Neath & Morriston	10 01	Via Neath & Morriston		11 31	
	6 02		7 02		8 02		9 02		10 02			11 32	
	6 05		7 05		8 05		9 05		10 05			11 35	
	6 08		7 08		8 08		9 08		10 08			11 38	
	6 13		7 13		8 13		9 13		10 13			11 43	
58		6 58		7 58		8 58		9 58		10 58			
00	6 15	7 00	7 15	8 00	8 15	9 00	9 15	10 00	10 15	11 00		11 45	

S.O.—Saturdays Only **N.O.**—Neath Only

hort of BAGLAN (SWAN STREET) and no passenger may be accepted in a westerly direction

RRY (RIVER BRIDGE). No passenger may be accepted when travelling in the direction of
RIVER BRIDGE).

J. J. NEWBURY, M.B.E., General Manager.

TOUR
PRIVATE
RELIEF COACH
BRIDGEND ONLY
NEATH ONLY
CARDIFF VIA BRITON FERRY BRIDGE
SWANSEA VIA BRITON FERRY BRIDGE
CARDIFF VIA NEATH
SWANSEA VIA NEATH
CARDIFF NON-STOP
SWANSEA NON-STOP

throughout the affected area between Neath and Swansea.

One of a number of incidents that occurred at this time came on Thursday, 29 August. A coach was passing through Melyncrythan, Neath, when a stone was hurled at its windows, and one of the panes was cracked, although not broken. A police constable who was following the coach saw the stone being thrown and gave chase to a man, who disappeared along a canal bank.

> **"Living in Taibach, we were on the N&C route. The coaches were always on time and their seats were covered in luxurious upholstery so we used to call N&C the Nice and Comfy!"**
>
> ***Joan Berry***

On the night of 3 September, a coach left Alfred Street at 9.50pm, driven by William Evans. There were 25 passengers aboard, and it was escorted by a police car with two constables inside. At Alford Lane a crowd of around 30 men had gathered and there was a crash of glass and also a noise like a gunshot. The coach immediately pulled up and the two police officers accompanying the vehicle went in pursuit of the men believed to have been responsible, who had run away.

An examination of the vehicle showed that the glass on the nearside window of the driver's cab had been smashed and stones were found inside the cab. A pane of glass in front of the passenger seats was also broken. Driver Evans had suffered a minor cut to the side of his mouth. Conductor Charles Chinnock reported that several of the passengers were frightened and hysterical, while children lay on the seats and refused to sit properly. General Manager J J Newbury had seen the 9.50pm coach off and was following in his own car. He immediately came across the incident and took charge of the coach as far as Port Talbot. Garage foreman George Matthews was on duty at James Street and examined the coach when it returned to the depot. He noticed a small hole in the first nearside window and inside, under the nearside seat, he found a lead pellet with two small fragments of glass sticking to it.

Five men later appeared on remand at Neath Court, accused of causing malicious damage and of unlawful assembly. Three were bus drivers and two were conductors, all living locally. Ironically, one of the defendants was a friend of Driver Evans, who was surprised to learn of his involvement in the incident. He received a full apology in court.

The magistrates accepted there was no case to answer on the charge of malicious damage, as the five individuals could not all have committed the two offences listed. However, regarding the charge of unlawful assembly the case was referred for trial. Later, at Cardiff Crown Court, a jury returned a not guilty verdict as there was a lack of evidence and witnesses to the incident.

Despite the usual loyalty of its staff, there were occasional disputes within the N&C camp itself. Among these were two in particular which unfortunately led to the staff taking direct action.

The company had been operating for over 30 years before a dispute brought about strike action within N&C for the first time. This was over the introduction of the first 36ft long coaches whose large seats hindered conductors who couldn't pass any standing passengers when taking fares and returning to the front to operate the door. The number of permitted standees was consequently reduced and the following year's intake of coaches had narrower seats, more grab rails and a driver operated door lever which gave the appearance of a second handbrake.

A lesser dispute arose concerning the Burlingham Seagull coaches, which had heavy, one-piece boot doors.

One of the Longford-bodied Maudslay Magnas, CTG293 at an embryonic Cardifff Central bus station, awaiting a journey back to Swansea, in the early 1950s.

NEATH AND CARDIFF LUXURY COACHES
LIMITED

THE PUBLIC ARE ADVISED THAT PART OF THE N. & C. SERVICE IS NOW OPERATING VIA

BRITON FERRY RIVER BRIDGE

AND THE FOLLOWING

CHEAP DAY FARES

ARE IN OPERATION:–

After 9.30 a.m.

From	To	s.	d.
BRIDGEND ...	CARDIFF	2	10
PYLE	"	3	6
PORT TALBOT	"	4	0
BRITON FERRY	"	4	6
NEATH	"	4	9
SKEWEN	"	5	0
LLANSAMLET	"	5	6
MORRISTON ...	"	5	9
SWANSEA	"	5	9
BRIDGEND ..	SWANSEA	3	3
PYLE	"	2	9

After 11 a.m.

Cheap Half-Day Return

CARDIFF 5/- SWANSEA

EXPRESS SERVICE

every half-hour

between

CARDIFF and SWANSEA

And in the Reverse Direction.

Copies of Time Tables can be obtained from the Conductor or from the Company's Offices, Great Western Chambers, NEATH. Telephone 2227-8.

Many conductors had refused to use them, but Gwilym Williams didn't agree with this practice and struggled one day to load a pram into the coach boot at Bridgend, before going aboard to take fares.

Climbing Crack Hill, near Bridgend, his driver slammed into second gear to pass a lorry, and as he did so, the boot door opened and out rolled the pram, gathering speed as it careered back down the hill almost causing a multi-vehicle pile-up. Gwilym admitted later he was sorry he hadn't listened to his colleagues' advice.

The second strike came as the company's existence drew to an unhappy close in 1970. By this time, the Cardiff-based crews had been taken into the employ of Western Welsh, but the men were aggrieved that their seniority had been compromised. Tempers flared one day over the use of a Western Welsh vehicle for an N&C private hire. The dispute escalated into three days of strike action, and was never totally resolved. A costly ban on private hire lingered and caused considerable loss of revenue.

How different things might have been today if those blinkered politicians of the late 1960s had not engineered the actions that brought about N&C's demise. What may have come next? London had appeared on the destination blinds of the Guys, maybe in optimism for the future, and with the completion of the M4, it would not have been beyond the realms of possibility that a service to the English capital would have been operated by N&C. Like today's National Express network, N&C's 'Flyers' would certainly have used the motorway between Briton Ferry and Coryton interchange at Cardiff and served the university and civic offices at Cathays.

Reclamation of Cardiff Bay could well have seen a link from Cardiff West and Culverhouse Cross terminating in the city centre. If N&C had continued to operate, it would certainly have flourished, and today we would be seeing a mainly high-specification, double-deck fleet, operating around the clock both on the A48 and the M4 – but inevitably without conductors. Smart ticketing, stand alone ticket machines at bus stations and, ultimately, full cash-free travel would have streamlined the entire operation.

Whether N&C would have expanded west is another question to which the answer will always remain a mystery. It is however, something that would have been more than likely. Llanelli was often talked about. It may have worked on a Saturday, but would have been unlikely to have attracted any regular clientele without by-passing Swansea on weekdays.

A Flyer from Pontardawe and Clydach, non-stop to Cardiff, is more likely to have been a winner, hugely time-saving and unhindered by competition, providing new commuter and shopping opportunities.

An express service with a 15-minute frequency may even have had a minor effect in terms of reducing the number of cars on the M4. All towns between Newport and Carmarthen — still N&C — and even further afield to Bristol and Bath, or Swindon and Oxford may have been contenders. Instead, we have the prospect of spending billions of pounds on relief roads, if ever the go-ahead on such cash swallowing schemes is given.

Tight timings and tea breaks

Most people who use buses expect them to be punctual and reach their destination on time. They would also expect the vehicles to be comfortable, clean and mechanically sound.

Licensing regulations in the 21st Century dictate that buses should be no earlier than one minute and no later than five minutes at any stage of their journey.

In N&C's days the rules may not have been as stringent, but strict standards were set and had to be followed. Passengers gave little thought to the efforts of those who created timetables and duty rosters but it was no easy task.

Even working to the given roster could present problems. And it was all for a wage that most would consider meagre in the years that followed.

The rates of pay for drivers and conductors in 1967 appear poor when viewed now. A structured pay award agreed for a 48-hour, six-day week that year saw conductors start on £12-1s-0d rising after six months to £12-3s-0d and after 12 months to £12-5s-0d. Drivers on the other hand started on £12-8s-9d, rising after six months to £12-10s-9d and after a year to £12-12s-9d.

A selective look at some of the staff duties of the 1960s can be seen alongside. It is noticeable that, despite the tight timings, reasonable comfort breaks were provided at the end of each journey. That allowed, in the rare event of a delay to an inbound service, for the subsequent departure to be punctual, even if it meant a quicker cup of coffee for the crew. The coach door was usually left open for passengers to step aboard as they arrived — there was no waiting outside in the cold and never a queue to pay the driver before leaving.

Duties of the daily schedule

Using 1967 as a guide N&C's staff rosters amounted to 21 turns of duty for Briton Ferry staff, and seven for their Cardiff counterparts. They were repetitive in the number of journeys and routes covered. For example BF1 crew would sign on at Briton Ferry at 06:25, travel light to Neath then form the 06:45 to Cardiff, arriving 08:15. They would return to Swansea via Briton Ferry Bridge at 08:30. There they had a meal break before returning to Cardiff at 11:00, arriving 12:45. A teabreak of 15 minutes followed before they would leave at 13:00 to Briton Ferry, where they handed over to turn BF2. They had run 122.4 miles in service, with a 3.3 dead run to start the day. This was repeated daily until Saturday, then they rested on Sunday. Duty BF2 signed on at 14:10 and at 14:23 took over from BF1, running to Swansea via Neath. They had a 15-minute turnaround at Swansea before returning to Briton Ferry at 15:15. They repeated this short run to Swansea and back at 16:23 before having their meal break at Briton Ferry between 17:53 and 18:53. They then had a full run to Cardiff and back to Swansea via Briton Ferry Bridge, by 22:15 before a light run back to the depot to sign off at 22:40 totalling 128.7 route miles and 6.3 dead miles.

Duty BF1Monday – Saturday

Sign on 06:25		**R.M.**	**D.M.**
06:35	Light Briton Ferry to Neath	----	3.3
06:45 – 08:15	Neath to Cardiff	38.2	----
08:30 – 10:15	Cardiff to Swansea via Briton Ferry Bridge	42.4	----
Meal Break			
11:00 – 12:45	Swansea to Cardiff via Briton Ferry Bridge	41.8	----
13:00 – 14:23	Cardiff to Briton Ferry		
Hand over to Duty BF2			
Sign off 14:35		**122.4**	**3.3**

Duty BF2 Monday – Saturday

Sign on 14:10			
Take over from Duty BF1			
14:23 – 15:00	Briton Ferry – Swansea via Neath	12.6	----
15:15 – 15:53	Swansea – Briton Ferry via Neath	12.8	----
Hand over to Duty BF14			
Take over from Duty CF29			
16:23 – 17:00	Briton Ferry – Swansea via Neath	12.6	----
17:15 – 17:53	Swansea – Briton Ferry via Neath	12.8	----
Hand over to Duty CF26			
Meal Break			
Take over from Duty CF30			
18:53 – 20:15	Briton Ferry – Cardiff	35.5	----
20:30 – 22:15	Cardiff to Swansea via Briton Ferry Bridge	42.4	----
22:15	Light to Briton Ferry depot	----	6.3

Sign off 22:40		**128.7**	**6.3**

Duty BF13 Monday – Saturday

Sign on 06:20

Stand by at Depot to cover staff failures, etc. In the event of any staff failure, this duty covered the duty concerned including any overtime allocated. Staff reporting late for duty worked Duty 13 until normal time of finishing unless told otherwise by the Duty Inspector.

Sign off 13:20

Duty BF14 Monday – Saturday

Sign on 15:40		**R.M.**	**D.M**
Take over from Duty BF2			
15:53 – 17:15	Briton Ferry – Cardiff	35.5	----
17:30 – 19:15	Cardiff – Swansea via Briton Ferry Bridge	42.4	----
Meal Break			
20:00 – 21:45	Swansea – Cardiff via Briton Ferry Bridge	41.8	----
22:00 – 23:45	Cardiff to Swansea via Briton Ferry Bridge	42.4	----
23:45	Light to Briton Ferry depot	----	6.3
Sign off 00:05		161.1	6.3

Duty BF15 Monday – Friday

Sign on 07:10			
07:10 – 12:20	Spare as required and relief duty to Cardiff	35.5	----
12:30 – 14:15	Cardiff – Swansea via Briton Ferry Bridge	42.4	----
Meal Break			
15:00 – 15:23	Swansea to Briton Ferry via Briton Ferry Bridge	6.3	----
Hand over to Duty BF10			
Sign off 15:25		84.2	----
Saturday			
Sign on 09:10			
Take over from Duty CF27			
09:23 – 10:00	Briton Ferry – Swansea via Neath	6.6	----
10:15 – 12:15	Swansea to Cardiff via Neath	48.3	----
12:30 – 14:15	Cardiff – Swansea via Briton Ferry Bridge	42.4	----
Meal Break			
15:00 – 15:23	Swansea to Briton Ferry via Briton Ferry Bridge	6.3	----
Hand over to Duty BF10			
Sign off 15:25		103.6	----

Duty CF28 Monday – Thursday and Saturday

Rest Day Cover

Monday Work Duty 26
Tuesday Work Duty 30
Wednesday REST DAY
Thursday Work Duty 29
Friday

		R.M.	D.M.
Sign on 14:40 (Driver)			
14:40	Penarth Road		
Standby Central Bus Station then			
17:25 - 18:40	Non-stop Cardiff to Swansea (R10)	42.4	----
Light to Briton Ferry Depot		----	6.3
19:02 Passenger to Cardiff then standby Central bus station			
Sign on 17:00 (Conductor to Pre-book)			
17:25 Cardiff to Swansea			
(Non-stop Journey)			
then work with Duty 32 Driver			
17:30 - 18:10	Cardiff to Bridgend (Non-stop)	20.0	----
Light to Penarth Road. Standby as required until		----	20.1
Sign off 21:00			
Driver		42.4	6.3
Conductor		20.0	20.1
Saturday	**Work Duty 32**		
Sunday			
Sign on 13:00 Penarth Road			
13:05	Light to Central Bus Station	----	0.3
13:15 - 15:15	Cardiff to Swansea (R7)	48.4	----
BREAK			
15:40 - 17:40	Swansea to Cardiff (R7)	48.3	----
MEAL BREAK			
18:15 - 20:00	Cardiff to Swansea (R10)	42.4	----
BREAK			
20:55 - 22:40	Swansea to Cardiff (R10)	41.8	----
Light to Penarth Road		----	0.3
Sign off 22:50 (Conductor)		180.9	0.6
22:55 (Driver)		128	

One of the three 1958 Weymann Fanfare-bodied AEC Reliances, RCY803, waits at Station Road, Port Talbot, in the late 1960s. The days of bumper-to-bumper traffic queues through the town had vanished with the opening of the A48(M).
Damian Owen/Port Talbot Historical Society

Coaches entering Bridgend from the west had to negotiate turns at Dunraven Place to enter Market Street, then four more 90 degree turns to reach stand 18 in the town's bus station. The one piece boot door of the Burlinghams is clear to see.

Chapter 4

Tried and tested

Over N&C's 40 years of operation, a wide variety of vehicles were tried and tested. Some were better than others at coping with the demanding schedules, and the drivers and garage staff naturally had their favourites — and their bugbears.

The early 20-seater Morris Viceroys proved to be a disappointment as they were unable to withstand the heavy daily pounding they received. The company operated eight altogether, plus two larger Morris Dictators. By 1932, however, they changed direction when several larger Dennis Lancets entered the fleet and over the following years, these showed a great deal more promise.

This was just the beginning of a 10-year process of evaluating various marques of vehicle in what appears to have been an attempt to find a suitable vehicle that would stand up to the work required of it.

Long term employee Trevor Burley had mixed views on the vehicles he drove in those early days: "My opinions take into account the many developments in engineering, both mechanical and civil, that have been made in the 65 years since I last drove an N&C vehicle," said Trevor.

"In my time, the N&C was the king of the road, and the coaches were the best of their time. I was, and still am, proud of my association with the marvellous N&C family concern. My opinion of the coaches is purely a description of what they were like, and not meant as any kind of criticism.

"Between the Dennis Lancets, two Glosters came in 1934 and were an expensive experiment, as only 12 were ever made. In their day, they were unstoppable and would outstrip any police car! They were the fastest coaches in the fleet and were fitted, uniquely, with a fifth gear which could only be engaged when travelling over 40 mph in fourth gear. On the flat, they would build up to 80mph plus, but died at the sight of a hill. Then, to change down through the box the fifth gear had to be disengaged before the speed dropped below 40mph. If there was an unexpected need to brake suddenly the opportunity would be lost, the gear could not be disengaged, and the coach required the services of a mechanic.

"The other coaches in the fleet could not exceed 45mph," continued Trevor, "except when freewheeling downhill and with a prayer at the bottom!"

By the time he became a fully-fledged 'Bomber' driver, the Glosters were banished to James Street's top yard and only used as a last resort. "They didn't go out unless we were desperate," said Trevor, "and I only drove them about three or four times, on reliefs. They were, to say the least, exhilarating to this 21-year-old at the time."

Next, in the late 1930s, came two Maudslays which received N&C's own bodies. "These were known as the big Qs," recalled Trevor, "Their five cylinder Gardner engines

'Built as only Britain can build' – Morris Commercial Vehicles advertisement from the 1930s.

throbbed unevenly and sounded like a Second World War German bomber, guaranteeing a headache for the driver who sat alongside. They had four-speed crash gearboxes with no synchromesh between 1st and 2nd gears. With a following wind, they could reach 42 mph. Even so, we enjoyed what we had and they were happy times."

Two local operators were acquired by N&C around this time: firstly, in 1936, Jones of Danygraig, who had a petrol-engined Maudslay; then in 1938, Bromham of Morriston contributed two, petrol-engined Dennis Lancets.

Then, just before the Second World War the company bought four more Maudslay Magnas with odd looking Duple bodies.

"These became known as the small Qs and they were cramped and had blind spots for the driver," recalled Trevor.

"The driving position was directly in line with the windscreen pillars. In later years health

New in 1937, CTG293, was one of two Maudslay Magnas given rather ungainly coachwork by N&C itself, a decade before Longford Coachworks began vehicle building in 1947. *Alan B Cross*

BUILT AS ONLY BRITAIN CAN BUILD

R.P. 20-SEATER PASSENGER CHASSIS

. . A reliable low-cost 20-passenger chassis BUILT FOR THE LOAD. Complying with the Ministry of Transport Regulations, it embodies many important features, including :—

FOUR-WHEEL BRAKES . . TWIN REAR TYRES ENGINE DEVELOPS OVER 45 H.P. . . FULLY-FLOATING REAR AXLE . . LOW STURDY FRAME . . 13 ft. 6 in. WHEELBASE . . FOUR-SPEED GEARBOX . . CHROMIUM-PLATED RADIATOR DIPPING BEAM HEADLIGHTS . . THERMOSTATICALLY-CONTROLLED RADIATOR SHUTTERS . . GEARBOX-DRIVEN TYRE PUMP FULL EQUIPMENT

For full details see separate folder. Copy on request.

"Cambridge" Service Bus

R.P. CHASSIS

£282

ex Works

"VICEROY" 24/26-SEATER PASSENGER CHASSIS

. . Built in the heavy vehicle section of the largest commercial vehicle works in Europe, the Morris-Commercial "Viceroy" chassis presents a first-class engineering job embodying finest quality materials, yet marketed at an unusually low figure for a vehicle of this class.

For full details see separate folder. Copy on request.

"VICEROY" CHASSIS

£545

ex Works

and safety regulations would probably have banned them from being driven in the dark and wet. Their curved fronts were impressive, quite lovely for the era, but curved glass for windscreens had yet to be developed, so they featured no fewer than six panes of straight glass, set at different angles, producing multiple reflections from the interior lights. The driver's forward view was obstructed by the numerous frames to support these panes. There was only one windscreen wiper, immediately in front of the driver, and it was tiny because of the small screen. There were no heaters nor demisters in the cab, and no way of reaching the glass when it misted up in the rain, due to the heat from the engine. To add to the challenge, these coaches had a small wheelbase and narrow cross-ply tyres, so you quickly learned how to correct skids."

Many of the staff thought the Maudslays were coaches designed by a group of apprentices after a Saturday night out. They may have been ahead of their time, considering that 70 years ago the half-cab was still very much the norm. It is possible that the shortfalls of these odd coaches may well have fuelled the idea of N&C going forward to produce their own bodies at the Longford works.

In 1939, N&C's first AEC, full-fronted Regal, ENY 65, arrived – in a livery of French grey and red, as it had been intended for Valiant Direct Coaches of London. It was fitted with an experimental overdrive gearbox and was a very fast vehicle. Regrettably, its original Strachan body was destroyed in an accident when only a year old.

Further AEC Regals entered the fleet immediately after the Second World War, including two former Green Line examples which had seen service with the armed forces during hostilities.

A handful of Daimlers followed the AECs as the company entered its second decade. "These were powerful beasts, but known for their erratic behaviour," recalled Mike John. "They had a column-mounted pre-selector switch, and a very dangerous clutch pedal

The A48 was a quieter road back in the days when N&C's Guys were providing the mainstay of the service. This one is heading west out of Cowbridge. *Phil Trotter*

New in 1939, Duple-bodied Maudslay ENY 66 crosses Cardiff Bridge heading for Swansea soon after the Second World War. The driver's vision was impaired by the windscreen set-up of six flat panes of glass, each mounted at a different angle.

that would neutralise the gear box in the event of misuse, by shooting out about 15 inches, forcing your knee into the steering wheel. You could break your wrist and even your leg if you weren't careful. According to transport expert Lyndon Rees, nothing else could match them on the stiff climb up Primrose Hill, heading out of Cowbridge towards Cardiff.

Two Crossley double deckers were purchased in 1946 with a view to reducing the number

The sweeping lines of the stylish Longford body are evident on Daimler KNY197 at Swansea's Clarence Street terminus in 1950. Alan B Cross

In the late 1940s, to overcome post-war shortages of new vehicles, N&C obtained two former Green Line AEC Regals that had seen Army service before passing to operators in Merthyr and Bootle, Lancashire. The first to arrive, in November 1946, HB6138, is seen above alongside what later became Cardiff Central bus staion, while EM3855, below, which arrived in early 1947, heads a line of N&C vehicles laying over across the River Taff at Fitzhamon Embankment.

Awaiting its call for the evening peak service from Cardiff is Guy Arab LCY783, seen on the perimeter road at Central Square in 1962. *Glyn Bowen*

of duplicated journeys, but the application for their use was refused by the Traffic Commissioners. The vehicles, already wearing N&C colours, were sold without ever operating on service, although not before one became stuck under the Angel Street railway bridge in Neath, right outside the Great Western Chambers premises.

Much later, in October 1959, alterations to Port Tennant railway bridge led to the hiring of a Leyland Atlantean from James of Ammanford, which was tested with BET and N&C officials on board. Clearly, N&C were still keen to use double deckers to avoid duplication, but again, it came to nothing. It conjured up visions of Ribble-style, coach-seated Atlanteans plying the A48.

Six more AEC Regals, this time fitted with Longford bodies, entered the fleet in 1948. They were so successful that they were rebodied during the mid-1950s and survived until 1964. They retained their half-cab design, but were now 8ft wide and were attractive, hard working vehicles. N&C tried four Tilling-Stevens types between 1948 and 1950, again bodied by Longford. The first, HTX 545, had a large Gardner 6LW engine, and the other three were fitted with Gardner 5LWs. "They were comfortable, but underpowered and slow," recalled Trevor Burley.

At the start of the 1950s, something completely different entered the bus arena. This was the advent of the underfloor-engined chassis which significantly influenced future bus and coach design. N&C were quick to recognise the benefits of this arrangement. "The AEC Regal Mk IVs came in 1951/2 and had pre-selectors that

> **"They seemed to get up to 70mph and kept up the speed all the way. Motorists knew they were on a tight schedule and just got out of their way. It was always a thrilling ride!"**
> ***Colin Simper***

were difficult to master," remarked Trevor, "they were heavyweights, but were by far the easiest and nicest coaches to drive, the most superior vehicles in the fleet, despite being flat out at 43-45mph.

Next came the Guys, which comprised two batches of six, delivered in 1954 and 1955. "The Guys were troublesome and had their engine, gearbox and rear axle drive so far

The Park Royal bodywork on Guy Arab LCY781 gleams in the afternoon sun at Central Square, Cardiff, as she awaits her next rush hour relief working, 5 September, 1966. *Robert Thomas*

In April 1962 the first 36ft vehicles joined the fleet in the shape of two 51-seat Harrington Cavaliers. Newly refurbished 232BWN is seen here near Llandarcy in 1967. *Gerald Truran/Omnibus Society*

Ready to head west for Swansea from Cardiff bus station in August 1970, CTX986C still sports a sticker from a private hire trip to Longleat arranged by the author. *Mike Street*

A firm favourite among the road staff for its ease of handling and free running was Plaxton Panorama 1, LTX829E. *Gerald Truran/The Omnibus Society*

from the drivers' ears that with the passenger noise in the open saloon, it was difficult to time the gear changes.
With passengers sat alongside, it could be embarrassing when drivers had to struggle, listening to the revs to establish the correct gear. They were lightweight and fast, but the brakes weren't that clever," remarked Trevor.

"Once you were familiar with the gearbox, what at first seemed impossible suddenly became easy, and it was even possible to avoid use of the clutch once you were used to them."

Lyndon Rees thought highly of the Guys: "Once those old girls made it to the top of Tumble Hill, Swansea-bound, and wound themselves up in fifth gear, they went like the clappers! Some were a little hard on the suspension as the chassis had been intended for double-deckers."

Chief Engineer Gerald Truran made an interesting comparison between the Guys and the later AEC Reliances: "The Guys used to suffer from damaged fronts, because the brakes were not all that good. The brakes on Reliances were much better and drivers tended to forget to adjust stopping distances when they were driving the Guys. Their engines used to suffer from the effects of flood water, since they had a duct behind the radiator which carried the water straight to the engine, which did them no good."

Brian Metcalfe worked in the garage as an electrician, and did relief work in the summer if there was a shortage of drivers. He also had a soft spot for the Guys and Burlingham-bodied AECs, and recalled: "Time went quicker on these coaches.
You could chat to the front seat passengers en-route."

The idiosyncratic handling characteristics of some of the coaches were well known by the garage and road staff alike. For instance, Weymann Fanfare RCY804 was known as 'The Flyer' because the speed governor did not kick in at the usual speed of around 55mph and so it would fly up Crack, Primrose and Tumble Hills, even with a standing load. Stopping was more of a problem, however, and could explain why 804 had a plain lower front panel which differed from 803 and 805.

It has often been suggested that ordinary motorists using the A48 were, to say the least, aware of the Brown Bombers' propensity to exert their rights of passage, particularly with regard to dominance of the centre lane. Car drivers in particular, were usually minded to hold back and let them through. Dennis Flower gained a memorable first impression of the company when he was travelling down to Wales to take up his role as general manager in 1964. He was enjoying the journey, peacefully descending Crack Hill in his Ford Zodiac, when he was suddenly shaken by a brace of N&C Guys that appeared from nowhere, shot past him and disappeared into the distance on a concerted bombing mission. Confirming all he had been told in advance, he was shaken but not stirred – maybe he was even suitably impressed by the incident!

By this time, the Guy Arab coaches were approaching life expiry. A refurbishment scheme was initially planned for them, but Gerald Truran, the new chief engineer, favoured acquiring second-hand AEC Reliances. As a result the Guys had all been withdrawn by the start of 1967 and the N&C fleet was entirely of AEC manufacture.

Gerald enjoyed telling of how the N&C must have typically appeared to most car drivers of the time: "I sometimes followed the returning 'flyer' coach out of Cardiff on a Sunday evening, usually one of the Plaxtons, when it was returning light to Briton Ferry.

The two Plaxton Elites UNY831/2G, new in 1969, were stylish vehicles, but were unable to display N&C's familiar destination locations along the cove panels due to the large panoramic windows. Prior to entering service, UNY 831G poses for a photoshoot at Briton Ferry on March 15, 1969.

The driver of ill-fated TWN557 looks a little fed up of the slow-moving traffic along Station Road, Port Talbot, during the early 1960s.

My Morris Minor, would keep up at first, but once over Tumble Hill, that was the last I would see of it.

"The 'NCY' Burlinghams, and later the 36ft Reliances used to run out of fuel on the last trip down from Cardiff, unless the fuel tanks had been refilled at Penarth Road during the day," continued Gerald, "They had only 20-gallon tanks. We fitted 32-gallon tanks to the NCYs and larger 40-gallon tanks to the 36 footers, and that solved a lot of problems."

When the 36ft AEC era arrived, each annual intake of coaches looked the same, but they had idiosyncrasies. In each batch, there was a good one and a bad — or not so good — one. Out of the 231/232 pair 232BWN was the stronger for example; 567ECY was much more sluggish than her sister 568, and it was the same with CTX985/986C and LTX828/829E – the latter in each pair was the superior. LTX829E was everyone's favourite, it was like a GT version of the family car, and just as easy to drive. PTX830F, a 41-seater, was somewhere in between. With the second batch of Commanders, HTG602D — the only 36-footer — was understandably slower than 600/601 which were smaller, lighter coaches, but with the same engines.

"I once had to collect one of the 36ft Harringtons which had blown its head gaskets at Cardiff," recalled Gerald Truran, "We used our BMC lorry to take up some water, which we used to refill the coach's cooling system. Once this was done, I brought the coach out of Cardiff, followed by the truck. Once over Tumble and keeping an eye on the temperature gauge, I let it go and when I got to the Cowbridge bypass, I knocked it out of gear and let it run, in an effort to cool the system down, as I didn't want to waste time stopping to top up with water. On the downhill side, she went off the clock and drifted up the incline on the other side before I put it back into gear and continued back to the garage. When I got back, my driver in the truck said to me, "You weren't half moving down the bypass, weren't you?", and then went on to say "Didn't you see the police car following you?"

Needless to say, I hadn't seen the police car and I was fortunate that I wasn't stopped."

Byron Westlake worked as a fitter with Western Welsh at Bridgend when he was called upon one day to look at 567, which had pulled in having developed a fault: "The gear linkage had to be welded back together. The tubular rod often broke where it was clamped to the rear selector on top of the six-speed gearbox," he recalled.

The Duple Commanders worked day in, day out, and were true workhorses, albeit none too nippy. An entry on the vehicle defect sheet of 985 in 1969 read: "Overtaken on Crack Hill by a woman pushing a pram. Fit larger engine in coach."

Under the technical leadership of Gerald Truran, Plaxtons built the bodies of his beloved AEC Reliances from 1967. Two extremely stylish 51-seater, Panorama 1s arrived that year, followed by a 41-seater in 1968. The penultimate coaches that arrived in 1969 were a pair of Plaxton Panorama Elites on the usual AEC Reliance chassis.

With metrication now becoming standard, they were 11 metres long, as opposed to 36 feet, so they were an inch longer, but looked longer still with their sleek bodywork. N&C's electrician, Brian Metcalfe, had the pleasure of being the first person to work on them, as they turned up with faulty alternators.

The last vehicles to be delivered were two Plaxton Derwent bodied AECs that looked like standard buses, but featured coach interiors. The company was now under South Wales Transport management and as a result, their registrations reverted to Swansea Borough rather than Glamorgan County Council.

These coaches were disliked by everyone. Fitted with column-mounted selectors, drivers claimed that there was no power in them and the steering was heavy, maybe on account of the extra weight of the coach seats they carried.

A coach for all seasons

The author's view of some of the N&C coaches he regularly travelled on:

1956 | NCY 885 – 887

AEC Reliance/Burlingham Seagull

These three were the oldest in the fleet, but they had classic lines and were sleek and stylish.

It was a thrilling experience to ride in the front seats next to the driver. With the windscreen and nearside window curved around you, the forward view of the road was now unsurpassed.

1958 | RCY 803 – 805

AEC Reliance / Weymann Fanfare

The Fanfares lacked the flair of the Seagulls and the windscreen arrangement was severe, but they were nippy coaches, and I remember one hot summer's day being bathed in escaping steam from under the floor as we climbed out of Ely on the way home!

1959 | TWN 556 – 558

AEC Reliance / Park Royal

These three were known as 'the boxes' and gave sterling service day in, day out. Their embellished bus-style bodywork made them unpopular, but they gave some very fast performances. One, 557, was written off prematurely in 1968 after an accident.

1960 | WWN 189 – 191

AEC Reliance / Harrington Cavalier

The Cavaliers transformed N&C's image and were stylish coaches. They always looked ahead of their time.

These first three led a sheltered life for many years, being kept back for tours and private hire work. 190 was given the experimental fawn and red livery in 1965.

The arrival of a pair of Plaxton Panorama 1 bodied AEC Reliances in 1967 marked a turning point for N&C. From the entry of LTX 828E into the fleet, driven here by Peter Parker. Bodywork by Plaxton was specified for all vehicles for the remainder of the company's life. *Gerald Truran/ The Omnibus Society*

1962 | 231 / 232 BWN

AEC Reliance / Harrington Cavalier

The first of two pairs of 36ft long 51-seaters that formed the backbone of the service for the years that remained.

They sometimes struggled with a full load because of their extra weight, but were improved when fitted with an overdrive sixth gear.

1963 | 567 / 568 ECY

AEC Reliance / Harrington Cavalier

This final batch of Cavaliers differed internally to the earlier pair and had narrower seats with lower headrests, extra grab handles and driver-operated doors. I began my daily commutes aboard 567, but 568 was the better performer of the two.

1965 | CTX 985 / 986C

AEC Reliance / Duple Commander

These coaches turned heads like no other when they first took to the streets and they saw extensive use on service right from the start.

I travelled on these two more than any of the other types. 986 was a little livelier than her sister.

1966 | HTG 600 – 602D

AEC Reliance / Duple Commander II

600 and 601 were 41-seaters and saw a lot of private hire work. 602 went straight into service but had no guts at all. She was soon repainted brown. I must have been one of the few who liked the fawn and deep red livery that these carried from new.

1967 | RCY 803 – 805

LTX 828 / 829E

AEC Reliance / Plaxton Panorama 1

These two were extremely stylish coaches and looked stunning inside and out. They featured a great deal of chrome which complimented the livery, while inside there was a lot of dark formica and black window frames. 829 was the best coach in the fleet.

1968 | PTX 830F

AEC Reliance / Plaxton Panorama 1

This 41-seater led a gentle life on tours and charters, and was kept away from service for 90 per cent of the time. It was usually tucked away inside the garage. It took a very long time before I actually got to ride on her. She had generous leg room as the body was of intermediate length.

1969 | UNY 831 / 832G

AEC Reliance / Plaxton Elite

There should have been more of these, as they looked sleek and modern in every sense. They certainly turned heads when pressed into service, but their clutch-controlled doors caused a few problems! Their body styling meant they lacked the room to carry roof destinations transfers.

1970 | UCY 979 / 980J

AEC Reliance / Plaxton Derwent

These two vehicles were disliked because of their bus-style bodies that were heavy due to their coach seats, and sluggish with their semi-automatic boxes. Like the proverbial camel, this was a horse designed by a committee!

Second-hand acquisitions

1960 | RRC 237 / 238

AEC Reliance / Weymann Fanfare

Acquired from Trent Motor Traction

These plush 37-seaters were as good as new when they came to N&C, having been used by Trent only for six summer seasons. They entered N&C service in the cream and red livery of their previous owner. I thought they were better than N&C's own Fanfares.

1966 | 3279 - 3248 WB

AEC Reliance / Burlingham Seagull

Acquired from Sheffield United Tours

If the Trents were good, the 'Sheffields'were bad. They were almost life expired when N&C received them, they couldn't run all day because of their small fuel tanks and they lacked destination blinds.

However, they were comfortable and their larger, fixed windows gave better vision than N&C's own Seagulls.

Two types of second-hand coach arrived late in 1966 as replacements for the worn-out Guys. On the left is Weymann Fanfare RRC238, which together with RRC237 came from Trent Motor Traction. Both were in excellent condition. On the right is 3281WB, one of six (3279-84) Burlinghams that were acquired from Sheffield United Tours, but which required a fair amount of work. Both types were more modern than N&C's own Weymann Fanfares and Burlingham Seagulls. Their daily mileage was limited by the fact that they only had small fuel tanks.
Gerald Truran/The Omnibus Society

Chapter 5

Law and order

Because of their tightly-timed schedules, N&C drivers frequently caught the attention of the boys in blue. In the early years, if the scheduled express timings were to be maintained, drivers often found themselves breaking speed limits.

The 1930 Road Traffic Act had laid down a maximum speed of 30mph for all public service vehicles, and it was precisely that — 30mph — that was the average speed required to run the service!

Imagine the stress on the drivers as minutes ticked by in heavy traffic or waiting for a long, slow, mineral train to cross at the notorious level crossing in the centre of Port Talbot. They were minutes that were unrecoverable without constantly breaking the law! It is quite remarkable that the drivers were prepared to work day in, day out, under such pressures, just to gain the kudos of working for the N&C. A typical newspaper report of the period recorded that an N&C coach was paced by police at Margam Road, Margam, on Thursday 28 August 1933 and its driver, Fred 'Jock' Cross was booked for exceeding the speed limit. He was fined £1 and his licence endorsed. His speed was given as between 40 and 42mph.

A J H (Mick) Williams was fined £2 for exceeding the speed limit in a public service vehicle in September 1938. A second charge of driving the vehicle with a defective speedometer was dismissed. The company was summoned for permitting the public service vehicle in question to be used without an efficient speedometer, but the summons against them was also dismissed. Mr P Haslan (Cardiff) for the defence, entered a plea of not guilty to all charges.

Mobile Police Officer R Tudball gave evidence of following the coach in a police car along the road between Cowbridge and the Coach & Horses in Bridgend. He found at times that the vehicle's speed varied between 40 and 45 miles per hour.

Mick Williams denied on oath that his speed was that alleged by the police officer. He said that he had looked in his mirror several times, but saw no sign of a police car following him. His speedometer had gone out of order on that very journey, but he was certain his speed was never anywhere near 40 miles per hour.

Occasionally there were instances of unruly behaviour by passengers. A former Mayor of Port Talbot was convicted of having conducted himself in a disorderly manner on a bus and for failing, when requested, to declare his destination or pay his fare. Councillor Taliesin Mainwaring, J.P., miners' agent and former Mayor, was fined £2 for each offence at Bridgend Court on Thursday 11 May, 1944, and was ordered to pay £6.8.11d costs.

Councillor Mainwaring, who denied the charge, was accused of boarding the coach at Taibach, Port Talbot and when the conductress asked him for his fare he said, "At my time and convenience." She went to the other passengers, then returned to him later, and he said "I am still not ready."

The ramshackle buildings and yard at James Street, Neath, belied the slick operations that came from within. One of the unpopular Tilling Stevens coaches, HTX545, is seen parked up in late 1959.

When she told him she had other work to do, he pulled out a number of bus tickets, the majority on respect of other buses, but one was for a journey to Bridgend. She asked where he was going and he told her Cardiff, so she asked him if he would take another ticket from Bridgend, and he replied: "No, I might be dead before I get to Cardiff."

She reported the matter to the inspector, who threatened to put him off at Laleston, but in the event the coach pulled up at Bridgend police station where the conductress asked him again and he said "I am not quite ready yet."

A number of passengers gave evidence, one of them saying Councillor Mainwaring's conduct so incensed the passengers that there were cries of "Throw him off the bus."

Police Sergeant W J Jones said Councillor Mainwaring told him: "I was doing a lawful duty travelling between Port Talbot and Cardiff and I was insulted." When he mentioned the word 'insulted' there was a general cry and one person said 'Throw him off, go on without him,' and another said 'What a specimen of man to have as a councillor.' He was very aggressive."

Neath conductor Delfryn John found himself in a spot of bother at Bridgend on Saturday 24 September 1946, as he turned a blind eye to carrying excess passengers.

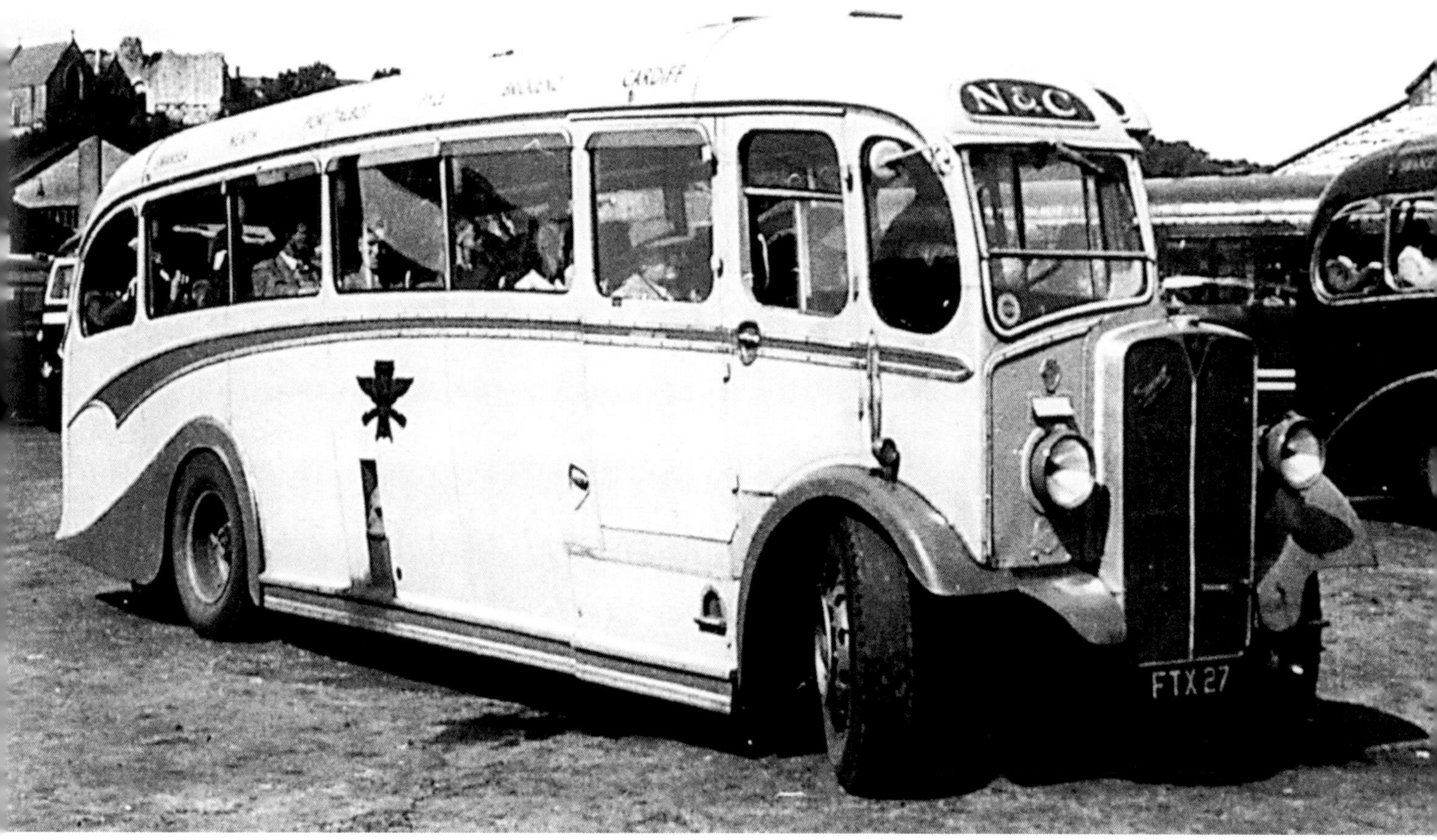

One of two AEC Regal Mk Is fitted with Duple 33-seat body, FTX27 entered service in 1946. It had received the desert sand and tan livery by 1950 when it is seen in Bridgend bus station with a healthy complement of passengers. *Alan B Cross*

Police evidence was given that his coach, heading for Cardiff, was stopped in Bridgend at 2.45pm, and it was pointed out to the conductor that all the seats were occupied, and there were 14 passengers standing. Defending, Mr O Glyn Davies pleaded that John, who had only just started on the job, had allowed his good nature to get the better of him during a peak period of traffic. John had found that once all the seats had been occupied, there were still a number of regular passengers waiting to board, and some were visiting hospitals in Cardiff.

Technically, the company itself was accused of permitting the offence. It was stated by Police Sergeant Mallinson that when he interviewed the company secretary, he was told: "You won't get any more trouble. We have issued definite instructions to all our conductors not to carry more than five standing passengers." Mr Davies remarked that with the difference that existed between rail and coach fares, many people preferred to travel by the latter means, and he was afraid that John had allowed his good-nature to get the better of his judgement. As far as the company was concerned, they were ignorant of what actually happened on the road, but they were now making every possible effort to keep the number of passengers down to the stipulated figure. Conductor John was fined 10 shillings and the company £5.

Driver Marsden Curtis found himself in a spot of bother at Port Talbot Police Court following an incident in June 1947, when Emrys Wheeler, a county planning officer from Baglan, Port Talbot, allegedly had to take avoiding action while driving his car along the town's Baglan Road at 30mph.

Wheeler claimed an N&C coach started to overtake him and was 75 per cent past him when it pulled in towards the left, forcing him to the kerb, and he had to pull up to avoid colliding with the side of the vehicle. He gave chase and subsequently ascertained the driver's name before lodging a complaint with the police about the manner in which the coach had been driven.

Charged with driving a bus without due care and attention, and without reasonable consideration for other road users, driver Curtis said that he was travelling at 25mph when he sounded his horn and intimated that he wished to overtake the car driven by Wheeler. There was no signal calling him on or any other indication, and he proceeded to overtake at his speed of 25mph.

Glyn Rees, of Cardiff, a passenger sitting in the front of the bus, said he had noticed that the driver of the small car did not wish to give way, and that, in his opinion as a regular driver of cars for the previous 12 years, the public service vehicle driver had conformed with the Highway Code in the manner that he overtook.

The magistrates decided to give Glyn the benefit of the doubt and dismissed both of the charges.

In one of the earliest N&C colour photographs, RCY804 and HTX407 are on the patch near the garage at James Street, Neath, around 1960. Briton Ferry Bridge first appeared on the destination blinds of the Fanfares. Before this the Burlingham Seagulls, like the Guys before them, listed Jersey Marine as the route indicator.
Anthony Warrener

Driver Thomas Moore, was fined £1 and had his licence endorsed for driving his coach at a speed of 41-43 mph along Baglan Road, Port Talbot at 7.50pm on Saturday 6 March, 1948. When Moore protested that the speedometer was not registering correctly, he was told that it was his responsibility to see that it did so. When he asked the magistrates how he was to go about seeing that it did register properly, the chairman informed him that the Bench could not tell him, but he would have to find out himself and that he could obtain the assistance of the police.

A further plea of not guilty was made by driver Oswald Feltham, following an incident involving a police mobile car and an N&C coach along Baglan Road, Port Talbot, on Saturday 24 July 1948.

Mobile Police Sergeant Cyril Lewis said he was driving the police car from Port Talbot to Neath when, nearing the Shell Mex filling station at Baglan, a luxury coach driven by the defendant and coming from the direction of Neath, emerged from behind a horse and cart and pulled over so much onto its wrong side of the road that he was compelled to

Driver Jim Boucher with newly rebodied HTG442, in 1956. Cardiff Central bus station's office block is under construction. It was completed by 1957 after which N&C departures were moved to Bay 7, in pride of place and right next to the exit for quick getaways!

Penny Matthews

stop to avoid a serious head-on collision. He had no chance to signal the coach driver to stop, but managed to see that it was the defendant, who continued on without stopping.

The following Monday, Sergeant Lewis saw the defendant in Neath and reminded him of the incident. Feltham said that there was no need for panic as a result of the manner in which he had overtaken the horse and cart and he denied that the police car had been forced to stop. He said he was travelling behind another bus and a lorry which had just overtaken the horse and cart and he followed them. He was dumfounded when he was later stopped at Bridgend.

Told he would be reported, Oswald said: "I am packing up on Wednesday and it's all because of you fellows. I am going to report you to someone else. If I get fined for this I shall go down."

Mr Wehrle, acting for Feltham, submitted there was no evidence of speed or carelessness and said that it was rather extraordinary that Sergeant Lewis had not stopped the defendant straight away if he was breaking the law. According to police evidence there was a margin of 5ft 6ins to enable three vehicles to pass each other.

In the end Feltham was fined £3 together with an endorsement of his licence, for driving without reasonable consideration for other users of the road.

Trevor Burley joined the company straight from school in 1948 as a junior clerk in the James Street garage. His mentor and boss was Inspector Dai John, for whom Trevor had enormous respect. According to Mike John, his father, Dai spoke highly of his protégé, but then all too quickly Trevor was called up for National Service. He returned to the company in 1951, this time as a conductor.

"The Golden Mile was where we would do our best to make up any lost time," said Trevor. "We always hurried to take the fares leaving Bridgend, so that we could take up look-out duties through the rear window of the coach. It was always the conductor's job to keep an eye out for police patrol cars. Quite often they would sneak up and tuck in close to the boot, and would be invisible to the driver, so we had to always be aware who was following us. Some drivers were on edge and moaned to the conductor if too much time was spent obstructing the aisle, issuing tickets and talking to passengers. It meant an increasing chance of getting caught.

"It was always a game. If a patrol car dared tuck in too close behind us, the driver would sharply pull up the handbrake. There would be no brake lights to alert them and instead they received the fright of their lives. They never tried it a second time.

"There were no penalty points for speeding in those days, but as well as a fine, your driving licence was likely to be endorsed which could lead to a ban if the endorsements built up," added Trevor.

"I used to go to Cowbridge from Laleston to stay with my cousin. My mum would put me on and my aunt would meet me there."

Susan Wells

"It was rumoured that, over time, driver 'Dickie Bach' had accumulated 100 endorsements. That number was exceptional, as the drivers needed to look after their licences, but if you were a union member, you could pay an extra two pence a week to the TGW, who would then pay your speeding fines, so it was never a financial hardship. The company never paid the fines and so the cat and mouse game continued over many years."

When Trevor reached the age of 21, he was allowed by general manager, J J Newbury, to drive the coaches on positioning runs. In those days, the amount of dead mileage needed to take up position was high. There were daily runs up to Cardiff to start the service, and back to the depot at night.

One morning the district MOT examiner was in the yard at James Street and Mr Newbury persuaded Trevor to take his test there and then. He was given one of the AEC Regals, FTX 27, and, despite having had no previous experience driving this coach, nervously drove on test up through Cimla to Cefn Saeson, where he reversed at the crossroads and returned down the hill into Neath.

"Coming down the hill, and with the examiner's face pressed against the screen at the back of the cab, I got into a right pickle and found it impossible to engage third gear of the crash box as we descended," recalled Trevor.

"I had no other option but to drive out of cog, with my left foot on the brake while at the same time revving the engine with my right foot to simulate a lower gear! We reached the bottom and I could see brake smoke in my mirror. The examiner appeared not to notice, and, fortunately, he passed me without question."

Trevor then drove the coaches until 1956, during which time he never felt targeted by the police, but regarded it as a sporting contest with no rules.

"I was fined £2 and my licence was endorsed at Cowbridge Magistrates Court," he said adding: "I defended that one myself because the police officer took his notes on a clip board and mixed the details up. In court I was accused, and convicted, of driving a lorry in the opposite direction! When I challenged this, the chairman of the bench snapped: 'Don't call my police officer a liar, fine £2, licence endorsed, next case please.' I have never driven a lorry in my life, but have a conviction."

Mike John, who began his career with N&C in 1961 as an apprentice coachbuilder, before becoming a conductor and then driver, recalls the day he, too, took his driving test on Cimla Road. "The examiner stopped me on the steep hill outside the Cimla Court

The first underfloor-engined vehicle bodied by Longford was KTX549 which entered service in 1951, a year ahead of two further AEC Regal Mk IVs. Each had pre-selector gears and carried different bodywork styling that was very much in vogue for the period.

Hotel. He poured a coffee and put it on the dashboard, stepped down and jammed his flask under the rear wheels. "Right!", he said with a grin, "don't spill my coffee and my lunch is under the back wheel."

Luckily my mentor, Jock Cross, had given me ample practice on the hill, so there was no flat white. I thought his flask would have landed back by the T A depot at the bottom of the hill, but he had jammed a newspaper behind it. It was a successful day."

Trevor later raised a few eyebrows at the garage by deciding to turn from poacher to gamekeeper. He joined South Wales Police on the beat in Bridgend, then later at Neath. He soon decided his future lay in traffic policing, and underwent training at the force driving school at Bridgend.

The relationship between Neath's traffic division and the N&C was always cordial – many were passengers – but on undertaking his driving tuition at Bridgend, he quickly realised that his new colleagues there had nothing but contempt for the N&C: "It was during darkness that the Bridgend lot used to creep up behind N&C vehicles on their

A coachbuilder's plaque from one of the two Maudslay Magnas which were originally bodied by the N&C Company at James Street, Neath, and entered service in July 1937 and May 1938. *Selwyn Bowen*

side lights. Their Wolseley 6/80s could usually be spotted in time, as their wing-mounted side lights combined with a central illuminated sign high on the bonnet. The resulting triangle of marker lights was normally recognisable to the driver, but could be missed in extreme weather conditions."

Forceful opinions were expressed in a letter by Cardiff driver William Preece when he was summoned for speeding on the dual carriageway at Jersey Marine on 27 July 1956. Preece had driven for 30 years without a speeding complaint and he asked that the Neath magistrates read his letter. He enclosed two pound notes and wrote: "As I know the officer's word is always taken, and if a higher fine is imposed I will send the balance on." The letter was read out, wherein Preece remarked that the company traffic superintendent and passengers attended court in vain because it was a Bridgend solicitor who had reported the matter and therefore "I didn't stand an earthly chance." He continued by remarking that his firm had provided excellent references to his driving, and that he was "seriously thinking of giving it up, as an honest driver doesn't stand a chance on the road with the mobile police."

Mr Toms, the clerk, read out the letter and remarked that it was "Rather a slander on my profession." The chairman, Mr Arnold, said with a smile, "The legal profession and the bench come into this, but it is not going to prejudice our minds." Preece's £2 was accepted, and his licence endorsed.

Certain police traffic officers cut their teeth on the N&C, of that Trevor is certain. He went on to become a fully-fledged Chief Inspector in the traffic division, and yet

An N&C Weymann Fanfare pulls away from its stop in High Street, Cowbridge in days when there was far less traffic and parked vehicles in the market town.
Gerald Dodd.

frequently called into the depot for a cuppa in the staff room and a chat with his former colleagues. N&C's own chief inspector, Dai John, looked forward to Trevor's visits to Briton Ferry depot, and always enjoyed their chats.

Mike John recalled: "Trevor was a really laid back character and always liked a chat about the coaches. The one time I wasn't so keen to see him was when he arrived to speak to me about an accident I was involved in. But being Trevor, he made the interview quite painless."

Harking back to the day Trevor passed his PSV test, Mike quipped: "I never thought you were so devious, Trevor, but full marks for thinking on the spot." Trevor replied: "How do you think I qualified for my later job on the squad cars? You have to look after yourself and yours, don't you."

Police motorcyclist Clive Coulson aboard his 850cc Norton Commando awaiting his next N&C victim!

"He had a nice blue light on his car," quipped Mike. "If a patrol car pulled any of the boys, they all hoped it was Trevor. He would always reason with you — before ending up booking you!"

John Hughes was once pulled over at Swan Street, Baglan, by a patrol car with blue light flashing: "I wondered just what I had done at first," said John. "But the officer had only stopped us to hand the conductor a parcel for his mother to collect at Cardiff."

The speed limit for coaches was raised to 40mph in 1961, and then 50mph in 1967, and this gave much-needed breathing space, but it wasn't until speeding offences were automatically subject to endorsements on the drivers' licences from the late 1960s that things changed. After that drivers were forced to be more accountable for their speed or risk losing their licences. In some cases, drivers whose endorsements had totted up had to go conducting until their earlier endorsements could be wiped clean. That in itself showed a caring attitude by the company, although clearly the writing was on the wall by this time in any event.

Clive Coulson, a retired police motorcyclist fondly remembers chasing the Brown Bombers. Based at the then police mobile headquarters at Glynleiros House, Neath Abbey, his patrol included the main A48 from Pyle Cross to Morriston.

The police regarded the N&C as easy pickings. One of Clive's favourite spots to wait for them was between Pyle and Margam, on the long straight passing the entrance to Margam Park. Many a driver felt a tug from Clive, who was often instructed to specifically target the Brown Bombers. While the N&C had operated Commanders, Clive had a Commando, the first 850cc Norton on the force.

"The speed of those coaches was not just a few miles per hour over the limit. Their speeds were exceptional along that road, even for the N&C. Our targeting of them went on for several months," recalled Clive.

He especially remembers the coaches with centre doors, where the driver had to suffer the indignity of walking past his passengers to reach the door and pick up his ticket. He also remembered the day he booked a driver leaving Pyle heading west, then again later the same day as the driver returned east.

"I also remember several occasions when I clocked the coaches along the old concrete slab Jersey Marine dual carriageway at 80mph plus! They were always the coaches with the doors in the middle. I wondered if they were faster than the rest. "

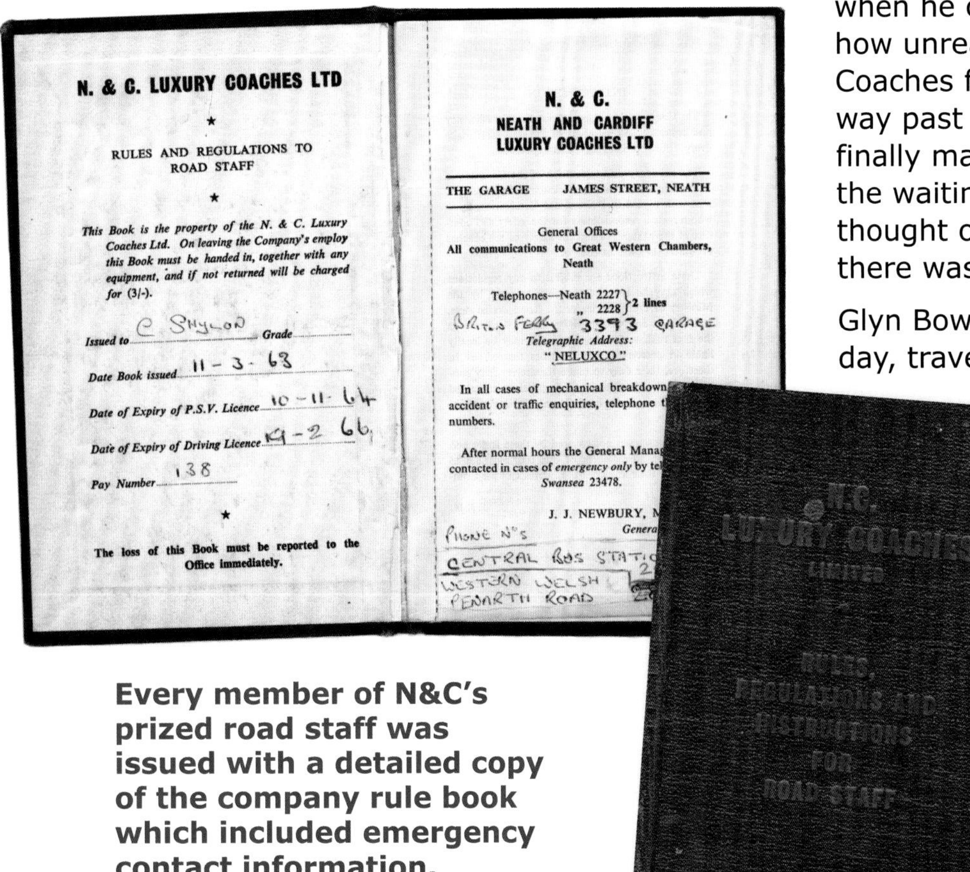

N. & C. LUXURY COACHES LTD

★

RULES AND REGULATIONS TO ROAD STAFF

★

This Book is the property of the N. & C. Luxury Coaches Ltd. On leaving the Company's employ this Book must be handed in, together with any equipment, and if not returned will be charged for (3/-).

Issued to C. Smylon *Grade*

Date Book issued 11-3-63

Date of Expiry of P.S.V. Licence 10-11-64

Date of Expiry of Driving Licence 19-2-66

Pay Number 138

★

The loss of this Book must be reported to the Office immediately.

N. & C.
NEATH AND CARDIFF
LUXURY COACHES LTD

THE GARAGE JAMES STREET, NEATH

General Offices
All communications to Great Western Chambers, Neath

Telephones—Neath 2227 } 2 lines
" 2228
Briton Ferry 3393 Garage

Telegraphic Address:
"NELUXCO"

In all cases of mechanical breakdown, accident or traffic enquiries, telephone t[...] numbers.

After normal hours the General Manag[...] contacted in cases of *emergency only* by tel[...] *Swansea* 23478.

J. J. NEWBURY, [...]
Genera[...]

Phone N°s
Central Bus Statio[...]
Western Welsh
Penarth Road

Every member of N&C's prized road staff was issued with a detailed copy of the company rule book which included emergency contact information.

In 2014, Clive was reunited with several N&C drivers during a get-together at a local hostelry. Old scores were quickly forgotten, although Clive later admitted feeling very uneasy walking through the car park on his way home!

John McDonald never had the pleasure of using the service, but regularly saw the coaches on his way to Porthcawl for his holidays: "When I worked for South Wales Police, I met officers of the traffic division who were great admirers of the Brown Bombers," he said.

Mansel Abraham was another traffic officer, but one who held a grudge against N&C drivers. He always patrolled out of Barry or Bridgend, and may have been one of the few that had a habit of parking their patrol cars at Briton Ferry roundabout to keep an eye on the traffic. Their chosen spot caused an obstruction at the entrance to the depot.

This upset Gerald Truran, who, despite his normally placid disposition, became angered when he could see from the depot how unreasonable the situation was. Coaches frequently had to inch their way past the police cars, and so he finally marched up the drive to tell the waiting officer just what he thought of it. After that occasion, there was no further trouble.

Glyn Bowen remembered when, one day, travelling from Swansea to Cardiff, the conductor told the driver that there was a police motorcyclist right behind the coach. Glyn said: "We proceeded quite a long way keeping within the speed limit and eventually pulled up at a stop. The motorbike passed and it wasn't a policeman. The driver was not happy at all."

Chapter 6

Times of tragedy

There can be no doubt that the N&C company suffered more than its fair share of road accidents, many of which could be classed as serious. This occasionally raised the question of whether the cause could have been a result of the company's hurried lifestyle.

Perhaps this was to be expected, given the express nature of the service and the daily miles the company covered. Timings were tight, and although there was ample turnaround time at both ends of the route, there was little opportunity to recover lost minutes en-route.

The coaches, it must be remembered, were as fast as most cars on the road at the time, so inevitably there was going to be the occasional coming together, particularly when taking the prevailing road conditions into account. In the early days there were no dual carriageways, many three-lane sections including corners and over the brows of hills, and there was little street lighting, particularly on out of town roads. Then there were the vehicles themselves. In the early days they had cross ply tyres and drum brakes which were subject to fade. Combine that with the task of driving on a road network with more than 8,000 fatalities a year and it was perhaps inevitable that accidents would occur. Added to that is the fact that any incident involving a bus or coach was bound to hit the headlines.

One of the earliest incidents occurred in 1931 when a serious collision occurred at Briton Ferry. A coach driven by Hubert John Davies collided with the rear of a Willmore Motor Services vehicle that was stationary at a bus stop. It was alleged that the N&C coach didn't slacken speed sufficiently causing it to collide with the rear of the Willmore bus. Six passengers sustained serious injuries, mostly severe cuts.

Davies pleaded not guilty to a charge of driving his coach in a dangerous manner on the day of the accident, 26 May, 1931 and stated that he was aware of the Willmore bus travelling at about 12 to 15mph when suddenly it stopped dead when he was only 12 yards behind. He said he applied both brakes, but failed to stop. A witness travelling in the second seat of the coach said he did not consider the impact a terrific one. Davies was found guilty and fined £5.

Sadly, in what appears to be N&C's first recorded fatality, the only daughter of a Llandarcy couple, a four-year-old who attended Coedffranc Junior School, was knocked down and killed by a Swansea-bound coach in Skewen, in November 1933.

She was waiting for the bus home to Llandarcy, but had crossed over to the other side, and was returning when the accident happened. A doctor was called to examine the child, who was found lying on a sofa in a nearby shop. She had some marks on both sides of her head, those on the right being more severe. She had bled from the right ear and nose. She had died almost immediately from a fractured skull and damage to the brain.

The war years brought a great number of operational problems for the N&C. Not only were services reduced but duplicates were suspended altogether, and several vehicles were sent away to where they were most needed to transport the many workers required for the war effort. On home ground, frequent blackout conditions meant huge problems maintaining the service. In the hours of darkness, it was next to impossible to provide an express service running on the dimmest of side lights and with all interior lighting extinguished.

Five men were injured and taken to Swansea Hospital on Thursday 19 April 1934, when a coach skidded and crashed into a lamp standard in Neath Road, Hafod. Four of the injured, including the conductor John Niven, were travelling in the coach while the fifth was riding a bicycle following the vehicle, which turned a complete somersault before crashing onto the pavement.

The coach was being driven by Viv Curtiss and was heading for Swansea when it skidded on the wet surface of the road and came into contact with the lamp post, the top of which was snapped off completely.

The worst accident of the war years and indeed N&C history occurred on 31 August, 1940, on the Golden Mile, near Bridgend, when N&C's first AEC, ENY 65, barely a year old, was on a late-night run back from Cardiff, closely followed by a Maudslay Magna of similar vintage. The experimental French grey and red livery of ENY 65's beautiful Strachan bodywork still shone, and its 35 passengers were relaxing in their sumptuous seats when, without warning, a car appeared heading straight for them on their side of the road.

The driver swerved as best he could, and the two vehicles struck a glancing blow. The car didn't stop but carried on at first, towards Cardiff. Shortly afterwards, there was a terrific crash at the back of the coach.

The relief coach, containing 36 passengers, had struck the first coach resulting in several passengers in each coach being injured. The driver of the relief coach, Robert Hawkins, had seen the first coach swerve to the side as it approached Keeper's Lodge and was about to take avoiding action when he saw the car emerging from round its side. The driver of the car, a serviceman, suffered multiple fractures to his arm, but couldn't remember what had happened after the collision. He was fined £1, his licence was suspended for six months, and he was ordered to pay £2 10s costs.

A claim was brought by a Mrs Keenan from Maesteg, who was a passenger in the leading coach. The action before the Judge was to decide whether the agreed damages should be the responsibility of the bus company or the driver of the car.

Mrs Keenan was travelling with her mother and her son in the back seat of the coach when the relief coach crashed into its rear. She was seriously injured, and was taken unconscious to hospital by ambulance. N&C denied liability, claiming the accident was caused by the negligence of the car driver.

The sumptuous Strachan bodywork fitted to N&C's first AEC, ENY65, would have turned many heads in the short time it had before a wartime collision resulted in a replacement utility bus body. This in turn was replaced by a Longford body in 1950. *Strachan & Brown/The PSV Circle Collection*

In turn, the car driver claimed it was the failure of the second coach to keep its distance and that its driver had failed to keep a proper look-out ahead of him.

Mrs Keenan's mother, who had been sitting in the seat immediately in front of her daughter, described how, as they were approaching Bridgend, the coach swerved and there was a terrible crash, with glass flying everywhere. She saw that her daughter had been knocked under the seat and when she got out of the coach, saw that the relief coach had collided with its rear. She also became aware of a saloon car further down the road.

Police Sergeant Ferris stated that he arrived at the scene of the accident at 9.40pm and it was then quite dark. The front luxury coach was on its proper side of the road, and its two front wheels had mounted the kerb and were on the grass verge. The nearside rear wheel was 4ft 8ins from the kerb. The second coach was locked in the back of the first, with its nearside front wheel 10ft 8ins from the nearside kerb, and the rear nearside wheel 9ft 11ins from the same kerb. The leading coach was damaged on the offside front wing, and its rear was extensively damaged, being completely smashed in. There was a saloon car 191ft to the rear of the second coach, and a skid mark extending 66ft, which he considered had been made by the car. The skid mark was on the wrong side of the road according to the way the car had been travelling.

> **"I loved travelling in those N&C coaches. They were so comfortable and with limited stops you were in Cardiff or Swansea in next to no time."**
>
> ***Ann Heatley***

Mr Humphrey Edmunds, defending the company, said: "We suggest the driver of the car came along at a terrific speed on his wrong side towards the first coach, causing it to swerve and stop, and then he collided with it on the offside, and went on 191ft before stopping." When asked if there were any skid marks to show that the first coach had been travelling fast he replied, "None were found."

Mick Williams, the driver of ENY65, the first coach, gave evidence that on the evening in question he was driving along the Golden Mile towards Bridgend with only his sidelights on. He saw two sidelights approaching some distance away on the proper side of the road but they suddenly swerved on to his side, and headed straight for him. There was no other traffic on the road, and the approaching driver failed to return to his proper side, so to avoid a head-on collision, he applied his brakes and swerved his coach on to the grass verge. The oncoming car collided with the offside of the coach, and almost immediately the second coach crashed into the rear of his vehicle.

Robert Hawkins, driver of the relief coach, said he was travelling about three to four lengths behind the first coach, at about 25 miles per hour. "I noticed the front coach easing up and I pulled out to overtake. Then I saw the car coming towards me, so I had to pull back again to avoid a head-on collision, and in doing so I ran into the back of the coach in front."

Addressing the Judge, Mr Edmunds expressed empathy for the coach drivers. "Take the first man. Surely for him it was a little disturbing to find a car being driven towards him on its wrong side of the road in the blackout. No one can say that its driver came to the wrong conclusion. He kept his head and swerved to the left-hand side, so saving the car driver's life, and possibly his own. As to the second driver, it is necessarily more complicated, as he had an unknown situation to deal with and had to act in a couple of seconds. He could see the middle lane was clear and could see the coach ahead was braking. There may

The third of the impressive trio of Longford – bodied AEC Regal IVs, LTX111, is seen at Dispenser Street, Canton, Cardiff, during layover in the early 1950s.
Gerald Truran/The Omnibus Society

have been a dozen reasons why the coach in front was slowing down, and he naturally pulled out into the overtaking lane. He could not have known anything about the car which was coming along on its extreme off-side, which was a surprise to him. Hawkins then had to jam on his brakes and swerve, which was what a normal man would have done in the circumstances. I ask Your Honour to say that my clients are not in any way responsible for this accident."

Summing up, the judge said the saloon car collided with the first coach, and it was the imminence of that collision that compelled the first coach to pull up, and so led the second coach to run into it from behind, but both collisions had to be considered. When the first collision took place, the first coach was on its proper side of the road, and appeared to have mounted the kerb before the collision occurred. It is reasonable to conclude that the driver of the car lost his sense of position on the road in the blackout. Anyone who drove then had a duty laid upon them to see that they kept their place on the road. No blame could be attached to the driver of the first coach. He thought he behaved reasonably throughout.

The judge then said he was sorry he could not take quite the same view with regard to the driver of the second coach. He should have driven within the distance he saw to be clear and with the possibility that there might be some obstruction just outside his vision. Was the driver of the second coach confronted with a situation which gave him no opportunity, or did the driver of the first coach ease-up some appreciable time before coming to a standstill? He thought there was probably a little time between the easing-up and the stopping of the first coach, and the driver of the second coach was given some warning that he was in a sudden emergency. He obviously drove too near the coach in front to enable him to avoid colliding with it, thus his speed and judgement were at fault.

Neath & District Omnibus Proprietors Association.

Support Local Enterprise

All Blue Transport Coy. Ltd.
Abbey Services.
Blue Bird Services.
Johns Bros. Services.
Neath & Cardiff Luxury Coaches Ltd.
Osborne Services.
Richmond Services.
Willmore Motors Ltd.
Windsor Services.

The above Local Companies, operate over 100 modern and luxurious saloon coaches over routes radiating from NEATH to CARDIFF, SWANSEA, LLANELLY BANWEN, GLYNNEATH and intermediate towns and villages.

Cheap return and season tickets are available on all routes, and RETURN TICKETS are INTERCHANGEABLE BETWEEN ALL ASSOCIATED COMPANIES ON THE NEATH LOCAL SECTION THUS PROVIDING A SERVICE SECOND TO NONE.

TWO HUNDRED AND FIFTY LOCAL MEN ARE EMPLOYED, with a Wage Bill approaching £1000 per week, the combined invested capital of the concerns being well over £100,000.

By supporting local companies you will ensure cheap and comfortable travel, and will help to maintain, what is acknowledged to be, one of the finest independent fleet of vehicles in Wales.

During **NEATH SHOPPING WEEK,** the holder of a certain ticket number, purchased on any of the above companies' omnibuses, will be entitled to a 3 months season Ticket free of charge.

The Lucky Ticket Number will be published in next weeks issue of the "Neath Guardian."

"CEFNOGWCH ANTURIAETH LEOL."

'Support local businesses', proclaims the message in Welsh at the bottom of this advertisment from the Neath and Briton Ferry Shopping Week supplement which the Neath and District Omnibus Proprietors Association, including N&C, supported in the Neath Guardian weekly newspaper, probably during the early 1930s.

In conclusion, The judge said, "I find there was negligence on the part of the driver of the car in creating an emergency, and the driver of the second coach who might have avoided the trouble had he taken proper care. Therefore, there must be judgment for the plaintiff against both defendants, which amounted to £82 19s 4d with costs.

The judge said the accident happened through an emergency which was not of Hawkin's making, although he should have been able to avoid it, but the prime cause was the emergency for which he must hold the driver of the car solely to blame. The damages should therefore be apportioned two-thirds to be paid by the car driver and one-third by the coach company.

At Port Talbot Court on Monday 21 April, 1947, as the result of another incident, driver Richard Davies was charged with driving a coach without due care and attention, and alternatively with driving a coach without reasonable consideration for other road users.

The summonses arose following an accident on Margam Road, Port Talbot, on the night of Sunday, 16 March, 1947, when a Mrs Hill, an elderly Margam woman, was knocked down and killed. Mrs Hill's sister said that they had travelled from Sandfields on a local bus on the night in question and Mrs Hill got off near the Eastern Schools, Taibach. She said it was a windy night and she was anxious about her sister, who could only walk slowly.

Wyndham Stevens, a passenger on the coach, said he believed the bus was late, but was travelling at a normal rate. In Margam the coach suddenly swerved, there was a screech of brakes and he heard a scream from outside. They immediately pulled up and he went with the inspector and conductor to see if he could be of assistance to the woman, who was lying alongside the bus, but she was dead.

Police Sergeant C Dando gave evidence of going to the scene of the accident and seeing the body of Mrs Hill lying alongside the bus. When Sergeant Dando spoke to driver Davies, he replied: "She was crossing the road. She hesitated and the near side must have caught her."

Morgan Owen, for the defence, told the court that this was a case where sympathies automatically went to the deceased. But, he said, however great the sympathy, it should not be allowed to influence the decision in the summonses. He then submitted that there was no case to answer, but after retiring, the magistrates decided there was a case to be answered and Mr Owen called witnesses for the defence.

Driver Davies said he was at the wheel of a relief coach which had left Cardiff at 8.45pm. The weather conditions had been bad and had necessitated careful driving. There were some floods on the road after Bridgend, and the coach was running five minutes late. He was travelling at 20 mph through built-up areas. As he approached the Eastern Schools he slowed down as the road narrowed towards a railway bridge. He saw a woman about 15 yards in front of him who was walking across the road in a stooping position and appeared to have a Mackintosh over her head. She was almost three quarters of the way across, and he sounded the horn and swung over to the right. The woman hesitated and started to turn back. Driver Davies immediately applied the brakes and swung hard over to the right. He was convinced that if he had not sounded his horn the woman would have continued on her way and no accident would have happened. Cross-examined, he agreed that to maintain the Cardiff to Swansea schedule he had to average 21 to 22mph even on a non-stop run. John Williams, an inspector with the N&C Company, also gave evidence to the court.

The magistrates dismissed the first charge and on the second, fined the defendant and ordered him to pay costs.

In another sad incident, Eirlys Evans, an 18-year old machinist at the Metal Box Factory, Neath, was killed when leaving the works on 6 October, 1947. She ran straight

Daimler CVD6DD KNY197 at Bridgend bus station in 1959, during its final months of service with N&C. *Alan B Cross*

across the road and was hit by an N&C coach that caught her sideways.

The coach driver, Frank Evans, said he was leaving Neath and driving at 20mph. There was no traffic in front of him, but a number of stationary works buses facing Neath. The girl ran from behind one of these, right in front of his vehicle, about six feet from the radiator. He pulled up within three quarters of the length of the coach, but could not avoid colliding with her.

The Coroner said it did not appear that the girl took as much time as she should have done in looking each way before crossing the road. He had heard of the large number of people who left the factory at the end of each shift, and he felt that some supervising measures should be provided.

A Porthcawl caterer was fined for driving without due care and attention when the car he was driving collided with an N&C coach at the gates of the West Glamorgan Hospital, Penrhiwtyn, Neath, on 19 June 1948. John Crole was fined £3 plus costs, and a further £1 for using indecent language.

David Nevin, a driver employed by N&C, said that on 19 June he was driving his coach from Cardiff to Swansea, and when he got to the gates of the West Glamorgan Hospital he saw a black saloon car coming towards him, travelling at a speed of about 50-60 mph, and swaying from side to side. He thought that it was going to overturn. As the car drew abreast of the coach, it collided with the off-side front wing. He got out of the cab immediately and walked back towards the car. He saw a man standing near it, and when he drew closer noticed that he smelled strongly of alcohol, and tried to pick an argument. Just then another man appeared, and he claimed he was the driver of the car. He also smelled of alcohol.

William Jones, the conductor, said that he was standing at the front near-side of the vehicle, looking through the front window, when he saw the car coming around the corner at an excessive speed swaying from side to side. It then collided with the coach, and he went to phone the police.

Driver Arthur Hughes was in trouble on 7 December 1948, when a collision occurred on the main Neath – Swansea road. At 4pm that day, a cattle truck was being driven along the road between Court Herbert Lodge, Neath and Stan Young's garage. It was being followed by an N&C Luxury Coach and when the truck came to a slight bend in the road, the coach began to overtake. There was a van coming in the opposite direction, and, seeing the coach attempting to overtake the truck, the van driver pulled onto the kerb. The coach ended up being jammed between the cattle truck and the van.

Police Inspector J Grubenman brought driver Hughes to court and for driving without reasonable consideration, he was fined 40 shillings plus costs. Hughes, who had been driving for 16 years, said that he saw the driver of the truck give a signal to overtake, and while doing so he saw the van approaching and braked with the intention of pulling in behind the truck, but it slowed too and he was unable to avoid a collision.

An accident in Margam Road, near Port Talbot Isolation Hospital, on 22 March, 1950, in which an N&C coach and a Glamorgan County Council ambulance were involved, resulted in the drivers of both vehicles appearing before Port Talbot Borough Magistrates. Charges against Gwilym Gwynne the ambulance driver were dismissed, but Evan Davies, the coach driver, was fined £5 together with 12 shillings costs, and his licence was endorsed.

Davies stated that he was driving a coach from Neath to Cardiff. He left Neath at 10am, and at 10.17am left the bus stop in Port Talbot. He drove along Margam Road at between 23 and 25 mph, and there was no traffic in front of him. He was on his correct side and approaching the Isolation Hospital on Margam Road, when an ambulance overtook the coach and at the same time put out its nearside indicator. "We were pretty near the hospital entrance, and I braked and turned the coach up over the pavement, trying to avoid a serious accident." Both vehicles came to a stop side by side and Davies found he was unable to get out through the door, as the ambulance was against the cab. He climbed through the window and found that none of his passengers were injured. The roads were wet and greasy due to the rain.

Conductor Robert Harris said that after collecting fares, he took up a position on the steps, facing the front of the bus. He had a clear view of the road ahead. There was no traffic except for an ambulance on the off-side of the coach. As they neared the isolation hospital, it seemed to shoot across in front of them.

Gwynne, the ambulance driver, told the court that at no time did he pass the luxury coach. While 200 yards away from the hospital entrance, he put his near-side indicator out. He saw the coach in his driving mirror. He pulled out in the middle of the road to enter the hospital as it had a difficult entrance. The coach came up on the inside and the accident occurred. A number of independent witnesses said that at no time did the ambulance overtake the coach.

“The N&C company ran the coaches for the convenience and benefit of the travelling public, which is more than you can say these days.”

Stanley Williams

On Saturday evening, 15 December 1951, Mrs Margaret Axworthy was travelling home to Neath after visiting her daughter, a patient in Sully Isolation Hospital, who was recovering from tuberculosis. The coach on which Mrs Axworthy was travelling came to a halt in Briton Ferry Road, Neath, opposite Mile End Row from where she intended climbing School Road to reach her home at Evans Road. A long wall stood along this stretch of road, edged with the narrowest of pavement, enough only to keep traffic away from brushing the wall itself. Telegraph poles situated at regular intervals take up its full width. The coach came to a halt with its centre door directly aligned with one such pole, barely allowing it to slide open. In her confusion, Mrs Axworthy, standing in the stairwell, pressed the bell, intending that the driver should move on. She believed that he would do so slowly, having realised her dilemma, and would come to a halt a few yards further along. However, being unable to see Mrs Axworthy on the steps, the driver moved off briskly, causing his passenger to fall through the open doorway, where the post squeezed her against the coach, whereupon her own body weight pulled her down and under the vehicle. Before the driver realised what had happened, Mrs Axworthy had fallen under the back wheel and suffered catastrophic injuries.

Hedley Picton, Mrs Axworthy's grandson recalled the night of the tragedy. Together with his father and mother, they were making their way home to Evans Road, when they stopped and knocked on her door to say goodnight.

"My dad was knocking at the door when a neighbour, roused by the noise, called down from his front bedroom window to reveal the terrible news," said Hedley.

"We hurried down to Penrhiwtyn Hospital to find my uncle beside himself, swearing he would murder the poor innocent driver. Hardly five years previously, Uncle George had been fighting Japanese in the jungles of Burma, and the 39-year-old would doubtlessly have done as much again.

"Granny underwent extensive surgery, and I saw her briefly being wheeled to the ward swathed in bandages. She passed away in the early hours of the morning without regaining consciousness."

The subsequent inquest concluded, that her death had been a misadventure, and the driver was not to blame."

A verdict of accidental death was returned at the inquest into the death of 68-year old Mrs Marjorie Wyatt of Baglan, who was killed on the night of Saturday, 13 December 1952 after being knocked down by an N&C coach near her home.

On the evening of her death, Mrs Wyatt had gone to Briton Ferry in a private bus to sing with the Port Talbot Women's Choir. She came back on the same bus, and sometime after 10pm it dropped her near her home. People on the bus saw her walking alongside the wall at the edge of the road, and she then disappeared from view.

A witness said that at 10.15pm on Saturday he was travelling in an N&C coach through Baglan on the way from Cardiff to Neath. He had a clear view of the road, and suddenly a woman appeared in the roadway. She walked right in front of the bus. "Everything happened so quickly," he added. "The coach braked sharply, but the driver had no chance of avoiding her. I went and summoned help, and when I came back I saw the woman lying on the road with her feet about a foot from the off-side wheel of the coach."

The driver, Gordon Lewis, said he was travelling at about 27mph at the time, and had to dip his headlights because a car was approaching from the direction of Neath. As he was about to put his headlights back on he noticed a shadow about 20 feet in front of him moving quickly across the road. He immediately applied his brakes, but hit the woman before he could pull up.

In evidence, Lewis said that someone had suggested the deceased had been wearing her reading glasses and not her outdoor glasses at the time. He added that he thought the lights on the coach were working well and were exceptionally good lights.

William Phillips, the conductor, said he felt a bump and found Mrs Wyatt lying on the road. Questioned by the Coroner, he said the road was very dark as a gas lamp a short distance away was not lit.

PC Edwards said the accident location was very dark, and the street lamp was not lit at the time. There was a fine drizzle of rain when he was called to the scene.

A Wales Gas Board engineer inspected the lamp near the scene of the accident and found that it had gone out because of a fault

The second of the three Longford bodied AEC Regal Mk IVs, LTG226, parked up at James Street, around 1960. The sign on the wall survived intact well into Neath town centre redevelopment in the 1980s.

in its mechanism. The timer had been running fast and had turned out the lamp early. Before the war, lamps were lit all night, but the local council's ruling at the time was that lights should be extinguished at 11pm. One light out, he said, would make a great difference to the road.

The jury exonerated the driver of the coach from blame, and recommended that all possible precautions be taken to see that street lamps were in good working order.

When it comes to accidents it seems that the Longford-bodied AEC Regals introduced in 1951/52 were particularly prone to mishap. some believe this may have been on account of their heavy weight, and their pre-selector gearboxes which could be difficult to master. Also, frontal damage was greater on these vehicles as their underfloor engines led to greater crumpling of the thin front panels without a radiator to offer protection. There were many minor accidents that looked worse than they actually were, yet resulted in vehicles being taken out of service awaiting new front or rear ends.

Roy Wilcox, who began his apprenticeship with N&C in 1943 at the age of 14, recalled those heavy Regals. "In 1952 we had a very bad accident with KTX549 at Peniel Green, Llansamlet," he recalled.

"It was on a private hire when a puncture caused the coach to swerve off the road and hit a concrete lamp standard. The collision caused the front part of the coach's roof to collapse on to the seats and a number of passengers were injured. The driver, Glyn Hoskins, spent several days in hospital before he was able to return to work."

Passengers travelling from Cardiff to Swansea in another Longford-bodied AEC Regal escaped serious injury when it skidded and crashed through a wall at Peniel Green, on Tuesday 28 June, 1955. Some 10 people in the bus were shaken, but only one was slightly injured.

Witnesses said the accident occurred while the coach was being overtaken by a lorry whose driver, apparently unaware of what happened, continued on his way. As the coach crashed through a wall another lorry struck it in the rear and ripped off the vehicle's back panels.

Mike John recalled the hazards of the three-lane sections of the A48: "I had a big fright one day bombing down the middle, making up a bit of time. Just passing the St. Hilary TV mast by the petrol station, a low loader with a huge digger on board trundled around the corner towards me. He could go nowhere, and I was a bit too far past the vehicle I was overtaking to drop back. So, I had to go flat out to pass and then quickly swerve to the nearside before straightening the back. With Cyril Shackson muttering "Ooh! tic-tic-tickets!" in the footwell we just got through. Near misses were quite commonplace in those days, but it shook me up a bit and I don't think I ever tried to pass a vehicle near that spot again."

Such near misses, or witnessing a road accident in the course of duty, could be unnerving for a driver. He could be badly affected by the experience and remain shaken for many days, during which there would be no heroics in his manner of driving.

A 12-year-old Cardiff schoolgirl — Beryl George — lost her claim for damages at Glamorgan Assizes in November 1955, for personal injuries received in an accident where she was knocked off her bicycle by an N&C coach. Cyril Salmon, QC, gave judgment with costs for the coach company in an action in which Mr F W George, claimed damages on behalf of his daughter.

The coach driver, Ken Daniels, said that the girl appeared from behind a lorry about 3ft in front of him and he had no time to take any avoiding action. The court was told that Beryl received serious injuries from which she was making a good recovery and which she was bearing with fortitude.

"She is a very charming and intelligent child and one cannot but feel the greatest sympathy for her," said Mr Salmon, adding that it would be very difficult to say that the driver had been negligent or in any way responsible for the accident.

On 6 April the following year, the Western Mail reported that traffic was held up at Cowbridge when an N&C Coach was involved in a collision with a lorry loaded with gas cylinders at the foot of Darren Hill. Fortunately no-one was hurt.

In July 1958, a collision on Baglan Road, Port Talbot, involving a car, lorry and an N&C coach, led to proceedings at the town's Magistrates Court on 20 November that year. The lorry driver, and the car driver, whose vehicle was not damaged in the collision, appeared to answer charges of driving without due care and attention or driving without reasonable consideration for other road users. Both pleaded not guilty.

The car driver, Rev. Leslie Shaw, was travelling towards Cardiff when two cyclists pulled out into the road and began to ride alongside one another. He told the court: "I braked and pulled out, but while overtaking, I saw in the corner of my eye the N&C coach swerve. I heard a bang and saw that a lorry had collided with the rear of the coach and the car following me."

The coach driver, Percy Gates, said he saw the cyclists coming towards him when proceeding along Baglan Road and noticed a green car pull over to the crown of the road to overtake them. "I realised the car was coming head on towards my coach. I swerved out of his way and my nearside, front wheel mounted the kerb. I applied my brakes to avoid going through a privet hedge and heard a terrific crash at the back of the coach. I then saw the lorry, which had been following me, go across the road and collide with the other car."

The lorry driver, Peter McCutcheon, said that when he was driving behind the coach, "Without warning, it swerved and stopped. I swung right to try and avoid it but collided with its rear."

The driver of the other car, told magistrates he was travelling behind a small green car driven by Rev. Shaw. This vehicle tried on two or three occasions to overtake the cyclists and was swinging out to do so. The green car finally started to overtake the cyclists while an N&C coach was approaching, and the coach just managed to pull up and stop to avoid a collision. A lorry travelling behind it struck the rear of the vehicle, and then slid across the road to collide with my car. "I received seven stitches in my head, suffered an injured shoulder, and my car was a total wreck," he added.

At the end of the hearing, Rev. Shaw and the lorry driver were each found guilty of driving without due care and each fined £2 7s 0d.

In November 1959, two middle-aged women and a man were rescued by passengers travelling on a passing Swansea-bound N&C coach after their car had overturned near the Tair Onen forestry plantation, St Hilary. The three were unconscious when taken from the car, which police believe skidded on the icy road. The coach driver, Peter Talbot of Cardiff, said he saw a hand hanging out of the window of the car. Passengers helped them out and kept them warm until the ambulance arrived. All three were detained at Bridgend General Hospital.

On another occasion, Jock Cross was driving his coach along Station Road, Port Talbot, at 7.30am on 13 October, 1960, when he was accused of pulling out into the path of a following local Thomas Bros bus, causing its driver to take avoiding action which resulted in an injury to its conductress. Jock Cross was accused of driving without reasonable consideration for other road users. It seems the Thomas Bros service to Margam had stopped at Bethany Square to pick up passengers, and two N&C coaches overtook it and pulled up at their stop a short distance ahead. The Thomas Bros driver then moved off and as he neared the second coach, it pulled out from behind the first forcing him to brake suddenly and causing his conductress to fall. She sustained an injury to her head, which required stitches. In a statement made later that day, Jock said he had no passengers on his coach that morning for Bethany Square and as the accompanying coach could cater for the passengers at the stop, he had no intention of pulling up.

"As the first coach slowed down," he said, "I saw the local bus following close behind so I gave a signal with my flashing indicator that it was my intention to overtake. I was not able to overtake at the time owing to oncoming traffic, but did so when I saw it was clear". He stated that he had only become aware of the incident later that day.

Mr Neville Walsh said that it was very unfortunate that the conductress sustained an injury that morning but submitted that it was not the fault of his client. The Magistrates were satisfied there was a doubt in the case and Jock was granted an absolute discharge.

Eleven-year-old Ruth Tallamy of Briton Ferry was injured when she came into contact with an N&C coach driven by Terence Hackshaw, at the junction of Neath Road and Regent Street East, Briton Ferry, on Monday, 22 October 1962. Ruth, a pupil at Neath Girls' Grammar School, was taken to hospital where her condition at the time was described as fairly comfortable.

It wasn't a happy New Year for driver Ivor Thomas, described as having 'an exemplary driving character,' when on New Year's Day 1964, he blotted his clean 27-year driving record. Port Talbot Borough Magistrates found him guilty of careless driving despite his denial of charges of driving without due care and attention, failing to stop after an accident and failing to report an accident.

A Mr O'Connel was driving a Land Rover along the A48 towards Pyle, when he felt something scrape the back of his vehicle. "I was forced up on the pavement to avoid a serious accident," he said. "The next thing I saw was an N&C Luxury Coach heading in the direction of Port Talbot. I didn't give the bus chance to forcibly hit my Land Rover and swung off the road." He later reported the incident at the N&C depot at Briton Ferry. O'Connel's two passengers said they felt the vehicle slowing and then saw the coach swerve in front of them and carry on without stopping. No one was injured but there were scrape marks along the whole length of the Land Rover.

In court, Thomas, who had 17 awards for good driving, said he didn't remember coming into contact with anything. "If I had, I would certainly have stopped," he said.

Witness William Allen told the court he was driving a workmen's bus behind the N&C coach and said he saw its indicators flashing. The vehicle pulled out to overtake the Land Rover and just as it appeared to draw level the bus swung in. The Land Rover was forced off the road. After checking to see if the occupants of the Land Rover were hurt, the witness said he continued on his journey and caught up with the coach at Taibach. He got out of his vehicle when the coach was at the bus stop and noticed a large scrape along the side of the coach. He was on his way to speak to the driver when the bus pulled away. He took the number of the coach and passed it on to the driver of the Land Rover.

Driver Thomas said there were around 40 passengers on the coach and none had been aware of any incident. In cross-examination, he said he remembered overtaking the Land Rover on the three-lane stretch near the RAC box on the Bridgend side of Margam Castle. "I pulled out into the centre lane when it was clear and began to overtake. A small car travelling in the opposite direction pulled into the middle lane after I did, and to prevent a head-on collision I was forced to take slight evasive action." He added that he thought he completed the overtaking manoeuvre safely and blamed the overtaking car for the incident. He said that he did not consider on that day he had driven without due care and attention.

Mr Maurice Sheehan, defending, said Thomas had been driving for 27 years without an accident. A public service vehicle driver for 18 years, he had a number of safe driving awards. "Can you imagine a man with such driving knowledge and experience to be so careless as to drive on after an accident?" he asked the bench. He added that the three-lane traffic system had often been described as 'suicide' and claimed the small car that pulled into the middle lane heading for the coach was the cause of the accident.

The magistrates found Thomas guilty of careless driving and imposed a fine of £5. The second charge of failing to stop after an accident was dismissed, but the defendant was fined £2 for failing to report the accident. The bench ordered two driving licence endorsements.

A particularly nasty accident occurred in Station Road, Port Talbot, on the morning of Monday 2 March, 1964. Conductor William Brayley left his coach in slow moving traffic, to deliver a parcel, and left the door open. A number of passengers alighted as the vehicle continued slowly to the bus stop. Unfortunately an elderly woman attempted to alight, slipped and fell, and the wheels of

The N&C monogram was designed by a Neath signwriter, cast in aluminium and carried on the front of coaches until 1958. It stood the test of time and was also applied in transfer form to the sides and boot of vehicles. This one was proudly displayed up front on Guy Arab LCY783 and now takes pride of place in the author's office.

Conductor Herbie Gibbon inspects the damage to one of the former Sheffield United Burlinghams at Briton Ferry after it collided with a lorry on the Bwlch Mountain road during rail replacement work, 1969.

the coach ran over her legs causing serious injury. The incident led to the appearance of the bus conductor before Port Talbot Justices, where he pleaded guilty to failing to take all reasonable precautions to ensure the safety of passengers entering or alighting from his coach. Before Brayley left the vehicle, he instructed the passengers not to leave until it had reached the official stopping point. He told the driver he was getting off the bus and alighted, leaving the door open. As the coach moved slowly forward, several passengers jumped off, but the elderly lady slipped and fell. Brayley, who had nothing to say in court, was fined £3.

The author recalls a bleak winter's morning, when the rain was lashing down and in the pitch black, driver Eddie Owens had brought his coach, Commander CTX985C, onto the A48 at Stalling Down, having climbed Primrose Hill.

We were just gathering speed when there was a loud bang, and a large chunk of metal, maybe a ball joint, shattered the windscreen and dropped on to the dash. We stopped, looked back and could see that there had been a serious multi-vehicle pile-up on the westbound side just as we passed.

Eddie didn't hang around. He put on his uniform greatcoat, cleared the remains of the windscreen with his elbow, turned up his collar and carried on. Eddie never hung about and that morning lost no time despite the conditions. Upon arrival at Cardiff the driver partition screen was as wet as the nearside remaining windscreen. Poor Eddie was soaked to the skin and in desperate need of a cigarette and a coffee in Astey's.

Sister vehicle CTX986C came to grief when still quite new, and sustained rear end damage at Penllyn dip, near Cowbridge. When it was repaired and repainted, it became the first coach to feature the Briton Ferry garage address in Harrington-style script on the boot, in place of the original monogram.

Stock
debris
the ro
tion o
and Ha
Cardiff
careere
of a
early
people
hospita

Two in hospital after dance bus crashes

SIX PASSENGERS AND the driver o[f] ... carrying people home from a dance were taken to Cardiff ... after the coach crashed into a shop ...

Firemen and police released three passengers trapped inside the vehicle.

The coach driver, Mr. Philip Evans, of Heol Pen Lan, who received chest injuries, and Mr. Robert Carol, of Maes Glas, with concussion, both of Whitchurch, Cardiff, were detained in hospital.

A hospital spokesman said later they were both in a satisfactory condition. The other five passengers were allowed home after treatment for shock and minor injuries.

The shop window was completely shattered in the accident and the wall of a flat above collapsed on top of the bus.

On wet road

The bus—touring the city after the annual dance of the

Baldwin, of He... Arthur Blannin, ... wydd; Victoria Ma... Ogmore Road, all ... diff, and Cherida... Cowbridge Road V...

Eric Jones, a... Splott Road, C... rushed to the cr... father, uncle an... other men, descr... of "complete ... youngsters still ... shouting and sc...

Mr. Jones sa... got there, we w... bus and got o... people trapped ... chap sitting i... the bus was tr... lot of falling ... lifted those an... men got him...

"Afterwards, ... of the boys a... our house fo... They were ve... up and one of the girls was having hysterics."

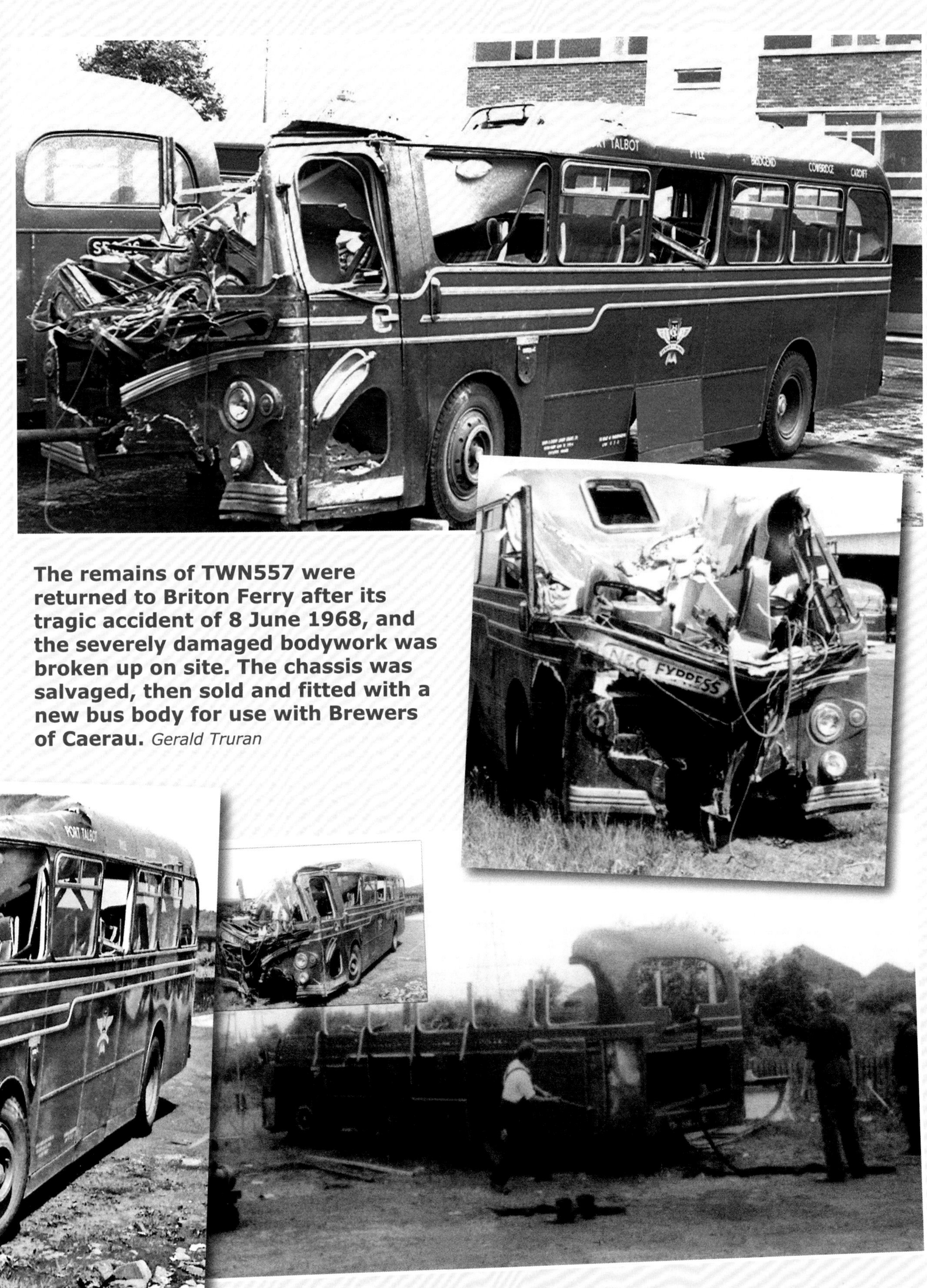

The remains of TWN557 were returned to Briton Ferry after its tragic accident of 8 June 1968, and the severely damaged bodywork was broken up on site. The chassis was salvaged, then sold and fitted with a new bus body for use with Brewers of Caerau. *Gerald Truran*

In the 1960s, one of the worst accidents involved TWN557, which skidded on a wet road and ploughed into a shop front in Splott, Cardiff when on a late night private hire. Driver Philip Evans had to be pulled from the wreckage and was lucky not to have sustained broken ribs. The body of 557 was recovered to Western Welsh's Ely works before being subsequently broken up at Briton Ferry. The chassis was sold to the Brewers bus company of Caerau, Maesteg, for rebodying as a service bus.

There were many unusual incidents too. A Dalmatian dog ran out and went straight under the wheels of a coach at Cowbridge one afternoon. Its driver, Selwyn Bowen, was very subdued when I returned with him from Cardiff. We stopped at the town's police station on the return journey where he reported the accident.

One wintry evening, a fully laden Commander, CTX985C, was unable to leave Cardiff, as the starter motor had jammed. Driver John Hughes couldn't budge it, but help willingly came from the passengers, myself included. Around 10 of us took up position at the rear and gave a push. The result was almost instant success and no cancelled service, no delay for the next available coach, no call to the fitters for a recovery vehicle, just very grubby hands! Our reward according to John: a CDM — Cadbury's Dairy Milk — medal would be on its way!

Tudor Davies, an ambulance paramedic stationed at Cowbridge recalled an horrific accident which involved an N&C coach: "I remember in the early 1970s attending a fatal road accident at the top of Crack Hill involving an N&C coach and an Austin Allegro car. Ironically, two brothers were returning to Cowbridge after attending a funeral. At around 4.30pm the bells went at the Ambulance Station to inform us of the accident. In fact, it was an N&C coach & two cars. One chap had been thrown from the Allegro and the nearside front wheel of the N&C had gone over his head. Aberkenfig Ambulance Station backed us up, they took the corpse and we took two injured to the old Bridgend General Hospital. I don't recall what coach it was as I was too busy dealing with casualties, but the colour scheme stood out straight away."

Old and new type of cap badge, all part of history that will never be repeated.

Despite the horror stories recalled here not a single N&C passenger was killed in any of the accidents that involved their vehicles. The last words on the subject of accidents go to Trevor Burley. "When you consider the road and traffic systems of that era," said Trevor, "It's amazing there weren't many more collisions. Although I only drove for a few years before joining the police in 1958, we knew that the principle cause of accidents was overtaking, particularly when you consider there were no motorways or dual carriageways, just those death trap middle lanes. The design of the half-cab coaches meant poor nearside mirrors and there was an element of motorists who didn't like to be passed by a bus and accelerated while in the blind area.

"We also ran through a heavily industrialised area which meant a huge lorry presence. Add to that the many pre-war cars in poor mechanical condition, with no MOT test requirement and no breathalysers.

"As a Chief Inspector in the 1970s, I processed the reports of around 65 - 70 fatal road accidents a year in West Glamorgan alone, with a national figure exceeding 7,000 annually.

"In that context, N&C had an awesome reputation throughout its existence, and I loved my time there."

Chapter 7

Behind the scenes

In 1932, with business booming, N&C moved its depot from Burrows Road to James Street and a ramshackle collection of masonry buildings which had once served the Neath Canal Company before seeing use as a depot for Neath Borough Council.

Despite its larger area, the James Street premises was no great improvement over Burrows Road. It was cold, dark, often wet and as the company continued to expand, soon became seriously cramped. All in all, it demanded the utmost resolve from the company's engineering staff to keep the fleet adequately maintained. Their skills in these austere surroundings produced many miracles during the 30 years that followed.

George Matthews was the garage foreman at James Street and Trevor Burley remembers the daily routine under his rule: "George placed a notice allocating each vehicle and driver for every shift, and on completion of their duty the coach was washed and fuelled immediately it entered the garage.
The driver and conductor would make a written entry listing any fault on the vehicle that had developed during its turn of duty. Even the most minor fault would be brought to George's attention this way, and every report was examined to ensure no vehicle left the garage until absolutely everything was signed off as remedied."

Norman Dewitt worked on the vehicles for many years and proudly recalled the reliability and presentation of the fleet as being second to none. However, Norman also recalled how primitive things were in the early years: "Conditions at the garage in James Street could have been better. Lighting and heating was poor, there were only two pits, and every morning water had to be pumped out of one," he said.

"We were forever crawling under the vehicles in those conditions. Coaches would return to the garage after every journey for refuelling, and this was done with a hand pump which could only release five gallons at a time.

Steam chassis cleaning was one of the worst jobs at the garage and required sturdy waterproofs, a sou'wester and wellington boots. On this occasion CTX986C is receiving attention at the back of the depot in 1968.

Everything was labour intensive but we loved the job and knew the service we provided was something special.

"We dismantled and overhauled the engines on site, and nothing was left to chance: axles, gearboxes — they were all stripped, cleaned and replaced. We were proud of our work, and when a coach was returned to service, all the drivers knew it was our own work, done properly and to precise standards. They could go out safe in the knowledge that the vehicle could be relied upon to perform its role."

In an urban environment such as James Street, there was inevitably the occasional vandalism, even during the war. In 1942, magistrates at Neath Police Court fined 18-year-old John Evans from the town's Mackworth Lane £2 and ordered him to pay costs totalling £5, or an alternative of one month's imprisonment, for causing malicious damage to a glass window at the garage.

A painter there said that at 8.30pm on Friday, 8 May, he heard stones falling on the roof of the garage, and on examination found that a pane of glass measuring 7 feet by 2 feet and valued at £5 had been smashed. On the opposite side of the canal he saw three boys running away, one of them with a limp, and on going in pursuit, caught the defendant in Bridge Street.

When Evans was told he would be reported, he said "I don't care, I won't pay. I've been down twice and I will go again." When Sergeant Jenkin Hopkin asked who the other two boys were, Evans is reported to have said: "Find out, I'm not telling you." Inspector William Hopkins reported previous convictions against Evans, who had already been sent to an approved school on two occasions, the last time, in 1939, for breaking and entering.

A year later, in April, 1943, two 10-year-old boys were summoned at Neath Borough Juvenile Court, again for damaging windows at the garage. Both sets of parents were ordered to pay £2-10s-0d each towards the damage and costs, although cost of repairs had amounted to £7-3s-0d.

A rogue employee got into trouble in 1954. A cleaner at the garage caused damage amounting to £98 when attempting to drive a coach around the yard without permission. William Hendra pleaded guilty at Neath Borough Magistrates Court and was fined £1 for each of four summonses for taking away a motor vehicle without the owner's consent; driving without reasonable consideration; driving without a licence and driving a public service vehicle without lights. He was also fined £3 for driving without insurance, and disqualified from obtaining a driving licence for a period of 12 months.

Inspector Hedley Onions told the court that at the time of the offence, 118

Hendra had been employed by N&C Luxury Coaches for one week as a night cleaner. He had been told that he was on no account to drive any of the vehicles without authority. On the night of 6 January, Hendra reported for duty at the company's garage in James Street.
The foreman cleaner later found one of the coaches half way out of the yard gates into the street. The rear of the vehicle was in contact with the gates and Hendra was still in the driving seat. The engine was running and the coach lurched forward several times. Hendra had no excuse to offer.

In a statement, Hendra said he was cleaning the bus and went inside the cab to put on the lights. He thought he would run the engine because it was frosty, and when he pressed the starter, the vehicle moved forward through the gates, and although he applied the brakes, it came into contact with a wall. The coach was damaged to the extent of £81 and the gates to the extent of £17.

Returning to life working at the garage, Mike John began his career there in 1961 as an apprentice coachbuilder. His interview for the job was held at James Street by the then chief engineer, Bert Beddoes: "I remember Bert well," said Mike. "He had his own little office with a lovely view of the canal. He gave me the job, and it may have helped that my father already worked there as an inspector. He was a really pleasant and knowledgeable man and knew everything there was to know about the coaches. I used to fetch his favourite Capstan Full Strength cigarettes

NEATH & CARDIFF LUXURY COACHES LTD.
VEHICLE
COACH BUILDER
REQUIRED
Good working conditions. Free Travel Pass.
Apply:
CHIEF ENGINEER,
NEATH & CARDIFF LUXURY COACHES Ltd.,
BRITON FERRY, Glam.

N.C. LUXURY COACHES, LTD.

SWANSEA, MORRISTON, LLANSAMLET, NEATH, BRITON FERRY, BAGLAN, PORT TALBOT, BRIDGEND, **CARDIFF** AND BARRY

Get our Quotation for your Private Party — **TIME TABLE** — **Travel by N.C. Express**

	WEEK DAYS.															SUNDAYS.					
	X																				
SWANSEA (Alex. Rd.	a.m.	a.m.	a.m.	a.m.	a.m.	a.m.	p.m.	p.m	p.m	p.m	p.m	p.m.	p.m.	p.m.	p.m	a.m.	a.m.	p.m.	p.m.	p.m.	p.m.
op. Free Library) dep	6 15	7 15	8 5	9 20	10 30	11 45	1 0	1 40	3 0	4 20	5 35	6 40	8 0	9 20	10 30	9 20	11 45	1 40	5 35	8 0	8 45
Morriston (Cross).....	6 23	7 23	8 13	9 28	10 38	11 53	1 8	1 48	3 8	4 28	5 43	6 48	8 8	9 28	10 38	9 28	11 53	1 48	5 43	8 8	8 53
Llansamlet (Star Inn)	6 26	7 26	8 16	9 31	10 41	11 56	1 11	1 51	3 11	4 31	5 46	6 51	8 11	9 31	10 41	9 31	11 56	1 51	5 46	8 11	8 56
Neath (Alfred Street)	6 45	7 45	8 35	9 50	11 0	12 15	1 30	2 10	3 30	4 50	6 5	7 10	8 30	9 50	11 0	9 50	12 15	2 10	6 5	8 30	9 15
Briton Ferry (Lodge)...	6 50	7 50	8 40	9 55	11 5	12 20	1 35	2 15	3 35	4 55	6 10	7 15	8 35	9 55	11 5	9 55	12 20	2 15	6 10	8 35	9 20
Briton Ferry (Villiers Street).....................	6 52	7 52	8 42	9 57	11 7	12 22	1 37	2 17	3 37	4 57	6 12	7 17	8 37	9 57	11 7	9 57	12 22	2 17	6 12	8 37	9 22
Baglan (Bungalow)......	6 56	7 56	8 46	10 0	11 11	12 26	1 41	2 21	3 41	5 1	6 16	7 21	8 41	10 1	11 11	10 0	12 26	2 21	6 16	8 41	9 26
Port Talbot (Beth. Sq)	6 59	7 59	8 49	10 1	11 14	12 29	1 44	2 24	3 44	5 4	6 19	7 24	8 44	10 4	11 14	10 1	12 29	2 24	6 19	8 44	9 29
,, (Empire)	7 1	8 1	8 51	10 3	11 16	12 31	1 46	2 26	3 46	5 6	6 21	7 26	8 46	10 6	11 16	10 3	12 31	2 26	6 21	8 46	9 31
,, (Taibach Pol Stn)	7 3	8 3	8 53	10 5	11 18	12 33	1 48	2 28	3 48	5 8	6 23	7 28	8 48	10 8	11 18	10 5	12 33	2 28	6 23	8 48	9 33
Margam (Co-op).........	7 5	8 5	8 55	10 7	11 20	12 35	1 50	2 30	3 50	5 10	6 25	7 30	8 50	10 10	11 20	10 7	12 35	2 30	6 25	8 50	9 35
Bridgend (The Green)	7 30	8 30	9 20	10 35	11 45	1 0	2 15	2 55	4 15	5 35	6 50	7 55	9 15	10 35	11 45	10 35	1 0	2 55	6 50	9 15	10 0
Ely (Culverh'se Cross)	8 0	9 0	9 50	11 5	12 15	1 30	2 45	3 25	4 45	6 5	7 20	8 25	9 45	11 5	12 15	11 5	1 30	3 25	7 20	9 45	10 30
Cardiff (Victoria Park Tram Terminus)	8 10	9 10	10 0	11 15	12 25	1 40	2 55	3 35	4 55	6 15	7 30	8 35	9 55	11 15	12 25	11 15	1 40	3 35	7 30	9 55	10 40
,, (Neville Street) ...	8 13	9 13	10 3	11 18	12 28	1 43	2 58	3 38	4 58	6 18	7 33	8 38	9 58	11 18	12 28	11 18	1 43	3 38	7 33	9 58	10 43
,, (Westgate St) Arr. outside C'diff Arms Pk	8 15	9 15	10 5	11 20	12 30	1 45	3 0	3 40	5 0	6 20	7 35	8 40	10 0	11 20	12 30	11 20	1 45	3 40	7 35	10 0	10 45

	a.m.	a.m.	a.m.	a.m.	a.m.	p.m.	p.m.	p.m	p.m	p.m	p.m	p.m.	p.m.	p.m.	p.m.	a.m.	p.m.	p.m.	p.m.	p.m.	p.m.
CARDIFF (W'gate St) (outside Cardiff Arms Park) dep.	7 5	8 25	9 30	10 10	11 30	12 40	2 5	3 10	4 20	5 15	6 30	8 0	9 0	10 10	11 25	11 30	2 10	4 20	8 0	10 10	10 50
,, (Neville Street)	7 7	8 27	9 32	10 12	11 32	12 42	2 7	3 12	4 22	5 17	6 32	8 2	9 2	10 12	11 27	11 32	2 12	4 22	8 2	10 12	10 52
,, (Victoria Park T'm Terminus)	7 12	8 32	9 37	10 17	11 37	12 47	2 12	3 17	4 27	5 22	6 37	8 7	9 7	10 17	11 32	11 37	2 17	4 27	8 7	10 17	10 57
Ely (Culverh'se Cross)	7 17	8 37	9 42	10 22	11 42	12 52	2 17	3 22	4 32	5 27	6 42	8 12	9 12	10 22	11 37	11 42	2 22	4 32	8 12	10 22	11 2
Bridgend (The Green)	7 50	9 10	10 15	10 55	12 15	1 25	2 50	3 55	5 5	6 0	7 15	8 45	9 45	10 55	12 10	12 15	2 55	5 5	8 45	10 55	11 35
Margam (Co-op)........	8 15	9 35	10 40	11 20	12 40	1 50	3 15	4 20	5 30	6 25	7 40	9 10	10 10	11 20	12 35	12 40	3 20	5 30	9 10	11 20	12 0
Port Talbot (Taibach Pol. Stn.)	8 17	9 37	10 42	11 22	12 42	1 52	3 17	4 22	5 32	6 27	7 42	9 12	10 12	11 22	12 37	12 42	3 22	5 32	9 12	11 22	12 2
,, (Empire)	8 19	9 39	10 44	11 24	12 44	1 54	3 19	4 24	5 34	6 29	7 44	9 14	10 14	11 24	12 39	12 44	3 24	5 34	9 14	11 24	12 4
,, (Bethany Sq)	8 21	9 41	10 46	11 26	12 46	1 56	3 21	4 26	5 36	6 31	7 46	9 16	10 16	11 26	12 51	12 46	3 26	5 36	9 16	11 26	12 6
Baglan (Bungalow)......	8 24	9 44	10 49	11 29	12 49	1 59	3 24	4 29	5 39	6 34	7 49	9 19	10 19	11 29	12 54	12 49	3 29	5 39	9 19	11 29	12 9
Briton Ferry (Vill'rs St)	8 28	9 48	10 53	11 33	12 53	2 3	3 28	4 33	5 43	6 38	7 53	9 23	10 23	11 33	12 58	12 53	3 33	5 43	9 23	11 33	12 13
Neath (Alfred Street)...	8 35	9 55	11 0	11 40	1 0	2 10	3 35	4 40	5 50	6 45	8 0	9 30	10 30	11 40	12 55	1 0	3 40	5 50	9 30	11 40	12 20
Llansamlet (Star Inn)...	8 54	10 14	11 19	11 59	1 19	2 29	3 54	4 59	6 9	7 4	8 19	9 49	10 49	11 59	...	1 19	3 59	6 9	9 49	11 59	12 39
Morriston (Cross)......	8 57	10 17	11 22	12 2	1 22	2 32	3 57	5 2	6 12	7 7	8 22	9 52	10 52	12 2	...	1 22	4 2	6 12	9 52	12 2	12 42
Swansea (Alex. Rd) arr	9 5	10 25	11 30	12 10	1 30	2 40	4 5	5 10	6 20	7 15	8 30	10 0	11 0	12 10	...	1 30	4 10	6 20	10 0	12 10	12 50

X—Starts from Swansea Mondays only (other days from Neath)

All Return Tickets are available for any length of time

FARE TABLE

From	To	Single s. d.	Return s. d.
Swansea, Morriston and Llansamlet	To Baglan Bungalow	1 2	1
	Port Talbot	1 2	1 6
	Bridgend	2 6	3 0
	Cardiff	3 9	4 6
	×Barry	3 9	4 6
Neath	To Baglan Bungalow	1 0	1 0
	Port Talbot (Empire)	1 0	1 0
	do. (Taibach Police Stn.)	1 0	1 2
	Bridgend	1 9	2 6
	Cardiff	3 0	3 9
	×Barry	3 0	3 9
Briton Ferry	To Baglan Bungalow	1 0	1 0
	Port Talbot	1 0	1 6
	Bridgend	1 9	2 0
	Cardiff	3 0	3 9
	×Barry	3 0	3 9
Baglan Bungalow	To Bridgend	1 4	1 8
	Cardiff	3 0	3 9
Port Talbot	To Bridgend	1 3	1 6
	Cardiff	3 0	3 6
	×Barry	2 10	3 6
Bridgend	To Cardiff	2 0	2 6
	×Barry	1 11	2 6

× For Barry, change into White's Buses at Culverhouse Cross. Tickets to Barry interchangeable with Western Welsh Omnibus Co., Ltd., over the route Neath to Culverhouse Cross.

Make use of our Express Parcel Service to Swansea, Neath, Briton Ferry, Port Talbot, Bridgend, Cardiff. We have agents in each town. Twelve deliveries daily. Ask for your nearest Agent. Parcels must be prepaid

Rates—Not exceeding 6 lbs : 4d. 10 lbs : 6d. 16 lbs. : 9d. 36 lbs. : 1/-. 56 lbs. : 1/4.

Parcels are accepted at Owners' Risk. Insurances can be effected at Owners request at Low Rates.

Parcel Service Agents—

Swansea	Mrs. Jones Confectioner and Tobacconist, Alexandra Road
Neath	Mr. H. Fraley, Hairdresser, Alfred Street.
	Mr. T. H. Davies, Newsagent, Windsor Square
Briton Ferry	Mr. Jones. Newsagent, The Lodge.
Port Talbot	Mr. David Wilde, 125 Station Road.

R. G. LLEWELYN, Managing Director

No passengers can be accepted at Swansea, Morriston, Llansamlet or Neath for any fare short of Baglan Bungalow, and no Passengers can be accepted for a WESTERLY DIRECTION (i.e., SWANSEA DIRECTION) after leaving Baglan Bungalow

The comprehensive 1937 timetable for what was still described as the N.C. Luxury Coach company. Such a regular and tight timetable showed that the company's engineers had to be on their game at all times. They were, and as a result of their dedication, breakdowns were few and far between.

A group of engineering staff take time out from their labours in the gloom of the James Street garage, mid-1950s. From the left: David 'Dai Dai' Davies, electrician; Graham Isaac, fitter; Malcolm Davies, coachbuilder and Peter Jones, Graham's apprentice.

from the corner shop. You could always tell if Bert was in his office as there would be more smoke coming out of his window than the exhaust of a Guy Arab ticking over awaiting its driver!

"I was under the wing of Dai Watkins primarily, but worked a lot with Malcolm Davies. These two were fantastic tradesmen and I learned so much from both of them. They must have joined N&C many years earlier, and talked about the Longford days, so they must have done some time there also. Both had very powerful operatic voices that could be heard the full length of the depot. That was a fair distance, and even the air compressor in full flow couldn't compete with them! Dai used to race his Norton Dominator on the Oulton Park circuit. While in James Street he made a lovely plywood case for my guitar, fitted it out with foam and painted it in a watered-down N&C red. He really was a great guy!"

During his apprenticeship, Mike assisted painter Reg Bevan with bodywork repairs, filling and rubbing down: "Rubbing down was a lousy job and I always marvelled at Reg's patience while doing it, then painting, then starting again with the second coat. Then he had to apply all the transfers. The whole process probably took about a fortnight. There was no spray painting in those days, just a paint pot or two, three-inch brushes and a keen eye for any runs in the paint. I vividly remember him crawling along the roof of the coaches with a rag, a brush, and a pot of N&C brown. With no safety harness, it was scary to watch him. He ended up with quite bad eczema through constantly washing his hands and arms in paraffin."

Mike also kept a keen eye on coach trimmer Dai Clements, whose son Keith worked in the stores: "I spent many hours watching him with his mouth full of tacks and a magnetic hammer, re-covering seats and cushions at machine gun speed after a coach had been in dock for refurbishment," he recalled.

"The problem was I had to install all the seats when he had finished, and that was a back-breaking job. Dai was a short little character, and great fun to be with. I think Keith eventually left for a job in the ambulance service."

Norman Dewitt was held in great esteem by Mike: "He was pretty much a laid back character who was considered to be a top mechanic, although he never asserted his authority unless absolutely needed. I would marvel at the way he and his apprentice dropped the massive engines onto a trolley with a minimum of heavy equipment. This was usually done over a pit containing a couple of inches of water. He would drag the engines out, then start the long process of stripping, cleaning and replacing any worn parts. I once asked Norman how he remembered where everything went back. His reply was that it was all guess work!"

John Vessey was another character who Mike remembers well: "John was a weasel of a character. He was a very good fitter but a bit of a loner. His boots had metal tacks in the heels to save on wear. Most of the time, John wore a smirk on his face when approaching you, and made you wonder what he had been up to, as he was a bit of a practical joker. Although not the tallest of people, he had a very long stride and when he clip-clopped through the garage like a horse in a stable yard, I swear he lost another eight to 10 inches in height!

When the company was preparing for the move to the new depot at Briton Ferry, Mike worked there for a few weeks preparing for the official opening. "I was busy installing signage on doors, and machinery in the body shop. Most of the staff were unhappy with the move out of James Street. We were content at the old depot, despite the poor conditions. It was so central for Neath, and I enjoyed escaping up to the shop near Cow Lane or running errands to get cigarettes for Bert Beddoes." Following the move to Briton Ferry, the James Street premises stood empty for many years before eventual demolition and redevelopment.

Mike admired the protocol involved behind the scenes at Briton Ferry to ensure the right

The rear of the Briton Ferry garage could become quite congested with vehicles receiving or awaiting mechanical attention. The steam chassis cleaning apparatus was outdoors and working conditions were not always pleasant. *Gerald Truran/The Omnibus Society*

A driver observes rebuilding work being carried out by N&C engineering staff on the chassis of underfloor-engined AEC Regal IVs KTX549. The offside chassis member in the picture had to be completely replaced after an accident. The rebuilt body was fitted at Longford Coachworks.

coaches were allocated for their respective duties and could leave the depot at the drop of a hat when needed: "Drivers knew every coach by its number, for example 778, 779, 780 were Guy Arabs, 828, 829, 830 the latest Plaxtons, and so on. The Duty Inspector placed the coach number next to the driver's name on the noticeboard just inside the sliding doors of the main garage. The drivers just had to glance out to the yard and could spot their coach at once. The remaining coaches were constantly moved around as others disappeared up the ramp and into service. They were usually parked up by the garage hand, so sometimes I would help out and practice reversing at the same time. I always thought they looked their best if parked in order."

Phil Williams, as a keen schoolboy observer looking down from the road, was aware of the coaches parked up in this way, and wondered if it was company policy, and if so, why? "Mike has just solved a question I thought about regularly back in those days. Now I know the reason behind it," he said.

ITS QUICKER TO SEND YOUR
PARCELS
by
N. & C. EXPRESS
★
PARCEL AGENTS
IN ALL TOWNS ALONG THE ROUTE

Behind the scenes at the depot, Norman Dewitt, by now senior fitter, recalled an extraordinary character who worked alongside him during the night shift: "The staff at the depot included garage hand Bill Morgan, a severely disabled man whose job it was to wash and fuel the coaches, and arrange them ready for the following day's duties. Come rain or snow, he would be there, manoeuvring the coaches to the fuel pump, hauling himself in and out of their cabs in all weathers, then washing them down, sweeping out the interiors and finally parking up in the yard. He never complained once. Incredible that, for someone so badly disabled, he did the work of three people."

"I conducted and drove those lovely coaches. I remember touching 95mph on the newly-opened Cowbridge by-pass."

Jeff Bunce

Mike John recalls that Bill's overzealous approach to the job could sometimes be a problem: "He got my hackles up one day when I brought an ailing Guy Arab in for a change of coach, due to brake fade. I nipped in to the staff room for a drink of water, and looking out to the yard, watched Bill jump into the Guy, rev up, then drive a few yards and slam on. My father — Inspector Dai John — who was on duty and watching, went over and Bill said something to him. My father returned to me and said Bill reckoned the brakes were OK. I told him for goodness sake he was doing 10 mph with five passengers on board. I just came over Stormy Down with a standing load and nearly went through the railway bridge!

"I went to have a little word in Bill's ear, but Dad stood in the way and told me to leave it there, and to take anything bar the first two coaches parked in the row. Job done!

Weyman Fanfare RCY 803 being given a thorough chassis cleaning at Briton Ferry yard.

One of the trio of 1960 Harrington Cavaliers gingerly peeps out of James Street garage in the early 1960s. The three were kept back for tours and private hire work for many years, with the later 36ft Cavaliers forming the backbone of the express service.

"Twice a week we had a visit from Len the tyre fitter. He shared his duties around other companies. Len was a bit of an extrovert, and a very strong man, although there was more meat on a skewer. He would march around singing 'She Loves You YEAH! YEAH! YEAH!' at the top of his voice, then stop in his tracks and start doing the twist! It did look funny, especially with his ski jump nose and Marty Feldman eyes. To see him change a tyre with only levers and a 7lb sledge hammer was amazing. No power seal breakers then, just pure strength and skill. It might take him an hour to do one wheel – no Formula One with four wheels in 2.4 seconds for Len. I had to admire the guy for his tenacity though."

Remembering the behind the scenes staff at both James Street and Briton Ferry, Mike's observations may on occasions be tongue in cheek, but as he explained, no offence is intended: "They were my friends and colleagues and were a pleasure to be around for most of the time at least."

Mike later transferred to the road staff, briefly as a conductor then behind the wheel. "When I got my PSV, my first day driving was on a very busy and wet August bank holiday," he recalled.

"Four trips Swansea to Cardiff on a double shift. It nearly finished me off, but at age 21 the excitement saw me through!"

Fitter Graham Isaac was thrilled to be given the job of collecting one of the 'baby' Harringtons, WWN189, from the factory in Hove and delivering it to Neath. To be allocated a delivery run meant a welcome change of scenery and the driver was his own boss for the day. It usually meant a night in digs prior to collecting the coach from the factory. A nice dinner and a full English breakfast before the journey back to base in a new coach — perfect! Graham was so excited at the thought of all this high-living though, that he completely forgot his false teeth!

Mike John remembers Graham fondly: "He was a cool customer who had a lovely, gleaming, 500cc motorbike – BSA or AJS, I think. He had it tuned to perfection. Graham was always ready for a long chat, and took an interest in helping all the apprentices. Later at Briton Ferry depot, he found out I had got engaged and asked me what my fiancé's job was. I told him she was a nurse, and he told me his wife was a nurse, you can't go wrong there! He wore brown overalls which were unusual then, so was instantly recognisable."

Richard Sanders was a fitter based at the Western Welsh depot at Penarth Road, Cardiff, at the time when the depot served as N&C's Cardiff outstation.

Richard recalled receiving a call from an N&C driver who was out on a private hire in PTX830F. He had stopped at traffic lights in Newport Road and when he tried to pull away, discovered he had no drive at all.

"I went out and played around with the clutch," recalled Richard. "but could not persuade it to engage, so I towed 830 back to Penarth Road depot. A little later on, after it had been parked in the yard for a while, I went to have another look, anticipating having to get some of the team to push it on to the pit. On starting, it engaged gear and drove perfectly, so I put it over the pit and checked it out, but couldn't find a single problem. I took it for a road test and all was fine. It returned to traffic and never gave any more trouble. Weird!"

A group of garage and road staff proudly gather around the latest addition to the fleet, WWN191, at James Street, Neath, in the early 1960s. *Gerald Truran*

Chapter 8

Payroll personalities

The N&C earned itself the contrasting nicknames of the Flying Bananas and the Brown Bombers. Not surprisingly, many of the colourful characters among its ranks, both on and off the road, also gained some wonderful nicknames.

Those with the most contact with passengers were of course the drivers and conductors who made sure that against all the odds timetables were adhered to and their travelling clientele looked after.

Among them, two personalities of particular note were long serving drivers 'Spaceman' Jim Boucher and Tom Jones, both popular with the passengers they carried. Jim in particular could spin the tallest of yarns and wasn't shy about expressing his forthright views on many vastly differing topics. Tom on the other hand would take everything in, driving with one eye on the road and the other in the living rooms of passing houses! He also had a habit of referring to everything as 'wha'sname', which always caused some amusement when used for the umpteenth time in the same sentence. Both were good company and if either was your driver for the week, you also knew that you wouldn't be late for work during that time.

In later years Jim would proudly tell of his love of going to work each day saying: "They were good coaches, maintained well. Everything was checked and prepared for you in the morning. In the winter they would be warmed up, and warm they would stay. There would often be a standing load coming out of Cardiff, as the passengers would rather stand with us than catch the Western Welsh service behind."

Darrrel Edwards meanwhile, was a conductor with South Wales Transport who found himself on loan to the N&C company for a number of weeks to cover a staff shortage. He was teamed up with Jim Boucher and recalled having two particularly memorable trips to Cardiff. "What an amazing experience it was," said Darrel. "Jim would stop on top of Stormy Down and look into the night sky, pointing out all the stars. I realised then why all his colleagues called him Spaceman."

Conductor Harry Jones, a slightly built man, was notorious for creating a fuss when a passenger offered a banknote for their fare. He would bite on his pencil and mutter some almost obscene remark, often jumping up and down in temper. It wasn't unknown for him to run down the aisle in a rage and wave the pound note at his bemused driver. His colleagues never understood the reason for his behaviour, and unsurprisingly perhaps he became known as Harry Pound Note.

Harry was nevertheless a good mate to have as a conductor, and John Hughes recalled the time when Harry, having pre-booked the Sunday evening Flyer to Cardiff, chose to stay on board for the ride, instead of jumping off at the garage to finish.

"Some friends had asked me if I knew of a way to bring a bed back from Cardiff," said John, "I knew I'd be on the Flyer and returning light to the garage. It was arranged that the bed be brought to the bus station in Cardiff. It arrived on the roof of a car, and without hesitation Harry gave a hand to load it into the boot of the coach. We dropped it at the friend's house and together we had it installed upstairs in no time at all!"

Harry's son, Basil, was also a conductor. He followed his father's slight build, and appeared a gaunt, humourless character who enjoyed a pint at the end of each run. It was rare to see Basil stood at the door, instead he would find an empty seat in which to

An impressive panoramic 12 vehicle line-up of N&C rolling stock in the Briton Ferry depot yard on a rainy day in 1967. *Gerald Truran/Omnibus Society*

enjoy an alcohol-induced doze between the more distant stops.

He was on service with Jim Boucher one day when he was given instructions to drop off a parcel at The Twelve Knights Hotel in Margam. The hotel manager was stood there waiting, and when Basil looked into the boot he discovered the parcel was a large box of fish, perishable goods which, strictly speaking, shouldn't, under any circumstances, have been aboard.

"Would you mind carrying it over?" asked the hotel manager. Basil was having none of it.

"I'm not carrying it," he replied. "I'll be stinking of fish for the rest of the day. Carry it yourself!"

"I can't carry it, I'm in my best suit," said the manager to which Basil retorted: "Well, you'd better arrange for your twelve knights to

Driver Doug Thomas and conductor Basil Jones bring Weymann Fanfare RCY803 to journey's end in Cardiff Central bus station in 1968. *Chris Stanley*

carry it over when we come back!" On the return trip, the manager was waiting again, along with five other members of staff.

"We were well and truly on the carpet when we got back to the depot," recalled Jim, "Mr Newbury gave Basil a right telling off, but when I turned to leave, I could see he was smiling."

Helping to keep things running smoothly was Cardiff-based Inspector Archie Hutchings. Archie was very efficient, but often seemed on edge and worried about everything, yet he was the master of organising smooth running at the busiest of times. Drivers and conductors regularly had to pacify him to curb his worrying.

The more cynical crews wound him up terribly, yet through his furrowed brow he was still popular. There was no-one more capable during busy times at Cardiff to organise the relief crews, who would dash at short notice to their coaches over on the perimeter road and bring them round to the stand at just the right time to relieve the fully laden service coach. This could then be sent on its way, often ahead of schedule.

Bill Drury was another of the company's characters. Always immaculately dressed he was known for his dry wit and wicked sense of humour. Bill had been promoted to inspector but considered himself unsuitable for the role, so returned to driving.

Long serving employee and by this time Senior Inspector, A J H 'Mick' Williams casts a critical eye over one of the newly delivered, and final, N&C vehicles, August 1970. *Gerald Trurany*

The wringing of hands and weird gestures that drivers used when passing each other on the road was down to Bill. His favourite prank was to stand at the door of his coach staring into the sky, and pointing up at something that really wasn't there at all! To those in the know it was hilarious to see him in action and witness the reaction of passengers. Occasionally he would flash an approaching coach on the A48, flagging it down as if to report a problem. Then, just as the unsuspecting driver slid his window open, he would shout a tirade of nonsense and drive off, to the embarrassment of the other driver and within earshot of the shocked front seat passengers.

N&C's Traffic Superintendent, Ron Gallanders, was another who put in sterling service for the company over many years. He was a fearsome looking man, especially to a mere teenager, as I discovered when first visiting the depot to ask his advice about hiring a coach. He certainly commanded respect, and you wouldn't call him Ron to his face until you really got to know him. During all the time I knew him, I never heard a bad word said against him.

Mike John recalls his days working with him: "He was a real gent and kind to me when I transferred from the role of coachbuilder to driver. He was also a great friend of my father, inspector Dai John.

"It was the same with senior inspector Mick Williams," said Mike. "Considering some of the characters he had to deal with on a daily basis, he was never anything but fair, and once you got to

Inspector Archie Hutchings looks pensive as he supervises operations at Cardiff bus station in 1967.

With driver Selwyn Bowen at the wheel Weymann Fanfare RCY805 has arrived in good time at Cardiff Central bus station during the summer of 1969. The preceding service with Plaxton Panorama LTX829E has yet to depart.

know him was a man with a wicked sense of humour and great company.

"He was a lovely, friendly, jovial guy who teased me rotten when I started as a 16-year-old apprentice. I can still picture him and hear his voice."

Peter Jones, one of Mick's many grandsons, enjoyed spending time at Briton Ferry during the school holidays. He lived near me in Bridgend in those days, so it was crucial that we became best of friends! He was my golden ticket to the depot and ensured my access and acceptance, all of which played such a big part in building my enthusiasm of all things N&C.

Richard Davies, better known as Dickie Bach, was the shortest man ever to wear the N&C uniform. It was amusing to see him struggling to adjust the drivers' seat to its lowest setting when he climbed aboard, and even then, his feet would barely touch the pedals. Dickie had problems with the 90 degree turns that were necessary to enter Bridgend bus station. His lack of height affected his ability to grapple with the steering wheel, and so he would have to leave his seat, and spin the wheel from one lock to the other as fast as he could.

Mike John recalled conducting with him once in a Guy Arab with a standing load of passengers. "We were negotiating the cenotaph at Bridgend when Dickie called me from the back of the coach to give him a pull with the steering," he said. "He often stood up to steer around corners, and at Bridgend there were several 90 degree turns to get onto stand 18 at the bus station. Until I started driving myself I didn't really appreciate how heavy some of the coaches without power-assisted steering could be to manoeuvre.

"Dickie hated the 36ft long vehicles, and thought they were too big for the job.

He was often in a strop about something or other, and his squeaky voice seemed to suit his short temper. But Dickie Bach could fly, and there was no holding him back once he'd eased the coach into top gear. It didn't seem to worry him when he occasionally picked up speeding tickets. How he managed with the poor brakes on those Guys is a puzzle."

Another driver lacking in height was Doug Thomas, who for obvious reasons was known as Teapot. He smoked Woodbine Full Strength cigarettes and when he laughed, it sounded like somebody was tuning an accordion. The first thing Doug did on entering a coach was pull the blackout blind down allowing him to cough and spit out of the window without being seen by the passengers sat behind him. The regular burst of fresh air and slamming shut of the cab window gave the game away, however.

> **"They had a completely different feel from all the other buses – they hummed rather than chugged or rattled."**
> ***Marilyn Harris***

All of these characters had their own individual tales, Tudor Reynolds among them. On one occasion he was conducting on a Guy Arab and moving forward from the centre of the vehicle, collecting the fares. He approached a well-dressed woman who had earlier fought hard for the front seat, issued her a ticket and charged a shilling for her dog. "I haven't got a dog," the woman said indignantly. Tudor looked again and realised she was wearing a mink scarf!

Mike John and John Hughes both remember Tudor for always thinking of ways to supplement his wages. "He wanted me to partner him to buy a flatbed truck and haul boulders down to Aberavon Beach for the sea defences, but we couldn't even buy a single bed on our wages in those days, leave alone a flatbed," said Mike.

The venture went ahead, however, with Malcolm Davies and Dai Watkins from the body shop. John Hughes recalls them fitting sheet metal over the vehicle's floor. "It still came back with a dip in it. Nonetheless it was a nice little earner at the time," said John.

N&C's Cardiff-based operations consisted of five or six coaches along with around a dozen drivers and conductors based at Western Welsh's Penarth Road depot, where paying-in facilities were provided.

The most fondly remembered was a snowy-haired conductor by the name of Gwilym Williams, who was extremely well-spoken, and who also served as a JP. He used to sit and entertain his passengers with stories of when he worked on the Greyhound network in the United States and Canada. He didn't like to see passengers having to stand, and he positively hated people calling his vehicle a bus. When he arrived at Bridgend he would slide open the door and, with his wispy hair catching the breeze, lavishly announce: "This is the N&C luxury coach for Cowbridge and Cardiff only."

Every syllable was given his own unique emphatic treatment. Gwilym always went that extra mile and was highly thought of by the passengers. A true ambassador for the company, he would never ring the bell to signal the driver to start, but instead would shout up the coach, "Right-o, driver, bang! bang!" Even on a front entrance coach he would close the door and give the driver this unique right away call. Then he would repeat his passenger announcement for the benefit of all: "Can I have your attention, ladies and gentlemen. This is the N&C luxury coach stopping at Cowbridge and Cardiff only." You could imagine him in an earlier time saying 'Phoenix, Albuquerque and Santa Fe!'

Tudor Davies recalled his uncle's journeys on the N&C with Gwilym as conductor: "He was Deputy Head of Coedffranc Primary School in Skewen, and travelled from Bryntirion in

Presenting a contrast in style, WWN191 and RCY803 await their next turns of duty, July 1968.

Bridgend every weekday during term time, said Tudor.

"He knew Gwilym well, and remembers him calling out 'Little Houses' instead of Taibach, continued Tudor. "He insisted on calling out 'Dodge City' on arrival at Pyle Cross too! "One day he rang the bell unexpectedly, much to the concern of the driver, who quickly pulled over — "It's ok, driver," called Gwilym, 'bell test!'

Gwilym's announcements always delighted the passengers, and brought many smiles when shouting 'bang! bang!' up the aisle of a centre-entrance coach. Not surprisingly, he earned the nickname 'Bang! Bang!' not only on account of his announcements, but also because at Bridgend bus station he would bang his hand twice on the rear panel of the coach to indicate it was safe for the driver to reverse off the stand. This meant seeing that the bus manoeuvring area was clear, then standing at the offside rear of the coach, beckoning the driver back until a further bang on the panel signalled him to stop.

On a coach with the door at the front, he would then run around the front and hop on. It wasn't quite as simple on a centre entrance coach because he had to run around the rear and up to the centre door, and couldn't be seen by the driver. On one occasion the coach moved forward a little prematurely, and Gwilym lost his footing and landed flat on his back. The next 10 minutes was spent picking up the coins from his satchel that had been sent flying, scattering the day's takings across the yard. There was little thought for risk assessment or health and safety in those days.

On rare occasions, conductors got left behind, as indeed happened to Gwilym one day when a parcel needed delivering to a nearby shop. His coach left without him, but as soon as the driver realised, he turned back. But by this time Gwilym had flagged down a passing car and was in chase. Whether or not he ever managed to become reunited with his coach is not known. He probably did at some point though.

Another fondly remembered Cardiff conductor who was warm and friendly, was a silver-haired man in his sixties called Alwyn. His wife worked in the Western Welsh booking office at Cardiff. He was another who epitomised the spirit of the N&C

company and it was always a pleasure to see him in charge of your coach.

Ray Dukes, known as Noddy, was a young conductor based at Cardiff, who had terrible eyesight and a habit of nodding his head. His tie was rarely straight, and to check a ticket, he had to hold it at the end of his nose and squint to focus on the detail. If you approached an oncoming coach when out on the road, and you saw the conductor perched on the dash with his nose against the windscreen, you knew it was Ray, nodding away as usual!

I'm afraid I had an unfortunate falling out with one Cardiff conductor — Eddie Lewis — at the time Bellgraphic ticket machines were replaced by the Setright type in 1970.

Weekly tickets had always consisted of two Bellgraphic tickets, one endorsed with 'from' and 'to' details and the other with expiry date and fare paid, and all neatly written by hand. They were clipped in their respective pre-printed boxes on the back for each forward and return journeys.

When the Setright tickets were introduced, two of them were still issued, the fare printed from the machine in decimal pence, but requiring holes to be punched twice, one per ticket, for each single journey. Half way through the first week grumpy Eddie refused to accept mine, as he claimed I had exceeded the number of permitted journeys. I tried to explain the new procedure to him, but it was no use as he wouldn't accept my explanation. If it wasn't for my travelling companions telling him how ridiculous he was being, I think I would have had a long walk home that night. I never liked Eddie, not because of his ignorance, but because of his audacity not to accept his regulars' explanations — even if led by a long-haired upstart whose journey through life had barely begun! By this time, a weekly ticket was valid for 12 single journeys in a month, and would last me most of the month in any

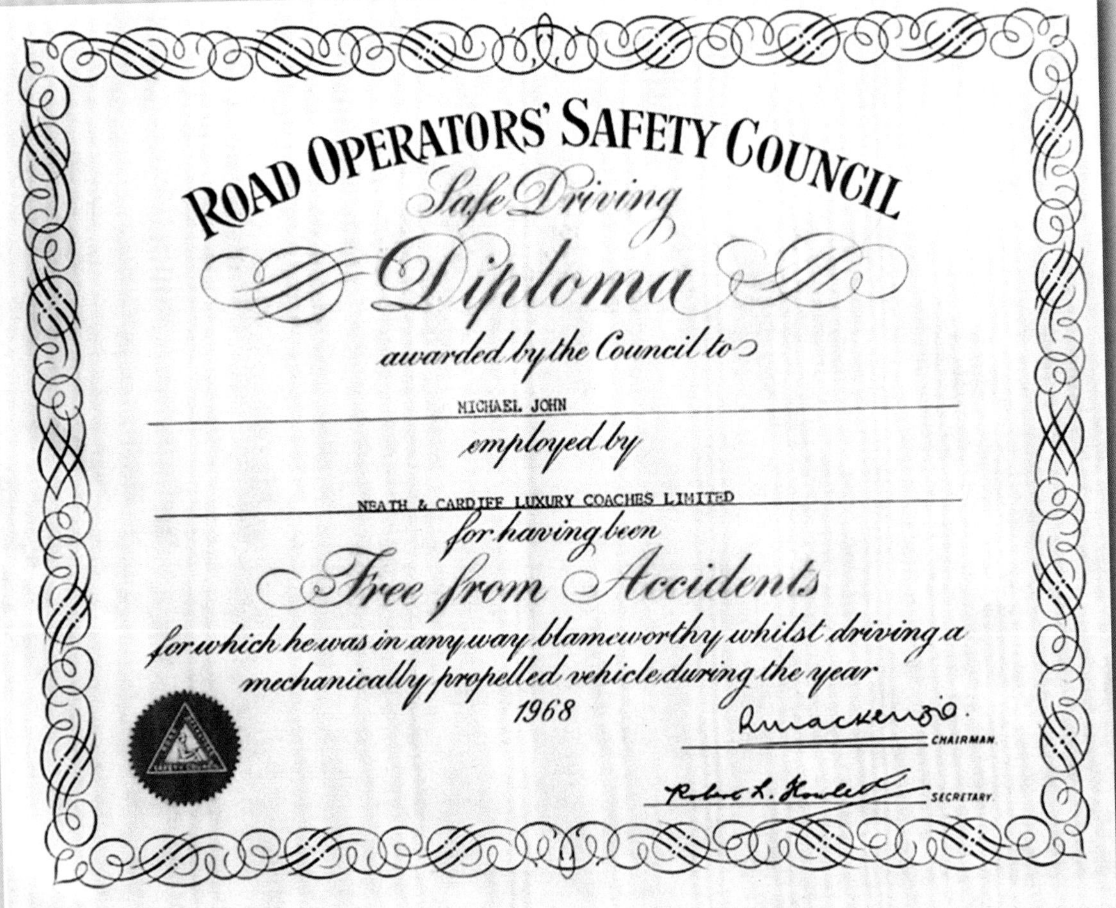

ROAD OPERATORS' SAFETY COUNCIL

Safe Driving

Diploma

awarded by the Council to

MICHAEL JOHN

employed by

NEATH & CARDIFF LUXURY COACHES LIMITED

for having been

Free from Accidents

for which he was in any way blameworthy whilst driving a mechanically propelled vehicle during the year

1968

CHAIRMAN

SECRETARY

A Safe Driving Diploma awarded to driver Mike John in 1968.

event, as many conductors who I considered good friends simply pretended to clip the ticket but missed the target deliberately.

The 17:30 Bridgend Flyer presented the opportunity for a quick sprint home, with its driver being on what was referred to as a 'relief after turn.' The service was pre-booked and the driver returned light to Cardiff to clock off and go home for his dinner. It also served as an opportunity for conductors aspiring to become drivers, as they would come for the ride then drive the coach back under L plates. Dai Goodland and 'Big' Roger Williams spring to mind.

Later, once Dai had passed his test and was driving officially, he demonstrated a cunning little trick to an ever-observant regular. By depressing the clutch while climbing Tumble Hill out of Cardiff, it gave the coach a brief surge of revs and made for a better ascent, or so it seemed at the time! Dai certainly had lead in his boots. Roger was another one with the same condition, and

AEC Regal 1 FNY556, affectionately known as Fanny, negotiates its way along Station Road, Port Talbot, in the early 1950s. Its original Burlingham body was replaced by Longford Coachworks in September 1949.

prone to what is now referred to as road rage — although the term had yet to be invented. If a car was parked at a bus stop, even if meeting a passenger, woe betide its driver as Roger pulled up an inch from its bumper and leaned on the horn!

Vic Greenwood was another of the Cardiff-based drivers, and one of the best. He was known as 'The Man from Uncle' because of his resemblance to the actor David McCallum. His style of driving was never less than exemplary, and he certainly knew how to handle his coach always driving according to prevailing conditions and with due regard to timekeeping. When required, he could turn up the gas and yet his passengers would be blissfully unaware of the speed they were travelling. He was a 'cockney sparrow' with a twinkle in his eye, and it was obvious to all that he took great pride in his driving, ably handling any vehicle in his charge. John Hughes remembers letting Vic take a spell behind the wheel one day when he was travelling as a passenger, and being very impressed with his style. If Vic was on the Bridgend Flyer you knew you were in for something special. He stayed at Penarth Road under Western Welsh, then became a full-time officer for the General and Municipal Workers' Union, based in Porth.

One evening in August 1969, returning from Cardiff on the Flyer, we had one of the Plaxton Panoramas and Vic was at the wheel. He stood on the step, welcoming everyone aboard, and then as soon as the conductor had pre-booked, we were off in his usual flamboyant style. Just 30 minutes later we were gliding down the Golden Mile, minding our own business in the inside lane, when a car coming towards us in the centre lane was forced to swerve to avoid another car that pulled out from the line of traffic being overtaken. At the time, there were recently completed roadworks, and positioned every 50 yards were wooden signposts advising motorists to keep off the soft verge. With all three lanes occupied by oncoming traffic, Vic had very little time to think, and swerved off the road, between posts, slid around on the soft grass, then regained the road without hitting a single post.

Drivers Doug 'Teapot' Thomas and Richard 'Dickie Bach' Davies.

Jimmy Vaughan, one of the Cardiff drivers, sold fish in his spare time. Off duty, but still in uniform, he often brought his van to the perimeter road at Central Bus Station to sell his wares.

Margaret Truran, wife of chief engineer Gerald Truran, remembers the custom of bringing a large box of fish, and sometimes chicken portions, on the last service out of Cardiff on a Friday night. These were to be distributed among the staff for their weekend dinners. Jimmy, not surprisingly, became known as Jim the Fish, and this may have been the reason for the hand sign greeting as coaches passed on the A48. A clap of hands and fingers held under the nose signified the smell of fish. It was always gamely taken by Jimmy.

Back at Briton Ferry, conductor Cyril Shackson joined Bill Drury in this system of sign language and gobbledegook. He perfected his art with his passengers with a call of "Are they off?" when they had all disembarked.

Stanley Unwin and Cyril would have made a great double act. Mention of rusty spindles, ballcocks and gushing water were all part of his dialogue, which was usually accompanied by the fluttering of fingers and blinking of eyes. His passengers loved him for it.

Reg Hoare was another charismatic driver who, through failing health, had to give up driving and become a conductor. It was in this role that I got to know him. He was always cantankerous and yet downright funny with it. When he looked at you through his piercing Tommy Cooper-like eyes, you knew you were going to burst out laughing any time soon. Everybody loved Reg, he had a nickname for everyone he knew — mine was Aubrey — and he had an effortless rapport with the ladies. A journey to work with Reg on board was like an adults-only pantomime, a giggle from start to finish!

A gathering of N&C management and staff for what may have been a skittles tournament, 1966.

Reg, along with Eddie Jones and Herbie Gibbons, were conductors who really looked after me, not only on my daily commute, but at other times too. If they were on Turn 1 for the week, it was possible to gain an extra five minutes in bed and board at the Coach & Horses in Bridgend, as they would sit in the front seat and move aside for me before they began collecting the fares.

Herbie was a dear, rotund man who loved to chat, so much so that often all the words would jump out of his mouth at once, rather than flow at the normal rate. He may have been broad in the beam, may not have been able to fasten all the buttons of his uniform jacket, and may have struggled while passing down the aisle, but he was one of the friendliest and a pleasure to have known.

The crew that turned up on a Monday morning could make the difference between a fun week, a week of early arrivals, or a week of dashing madly across Cardiff to arrive at my office before the signing-in book was removed. Sometimes many weeks could go by without any punctuality problems, even to the point of having a few minutes to chat before leaving the bus station. Then, a rookie driver or a steady one would mean a battle to be first off the coach and then a mad dash across to Greyfriars, swerving through the arcades, and using every available short cut. A few ignorant drivers seemed oblivious to the existence of the sixth gear. This was an overdrive gear improvement that came about as a result of Gerald Truran's liaison with AEC. Eventually it was fitted to all of N&C's 36ft vehicles.

Some drivers who were aware of its existence were engaging it at 30mph and wondering why the engine was struggling. Ken Arthur springs to mind, which was particularly annoying as he had come to N&C from Black & White Motorways, and should have known all about driving express services. Sometimes, it was not unknown for him to be overtaken by the following service, the morning Flyer which left Bridgend 20 minutes after us and was often right behind as the routes merged at Stalling Down near St Hilary. For me, it became a difficult decision as to whether to switch to the Flyer for the rest of the week.

N&C's drivers collectively joined forces to provide the express service that its customers never forgot, and talk about even to this day. But they were individuals who came from differing backgrounds. They had learned to drive, passed their PSV tests, had driven many vehicles in a range of environments and developed a variety of differing styles of performing their art.

Driving up and down the A48 at high speed was as demanding as driving along Oxford Street in London, or through Cornwall's narrow lanes. There were drivers for whom it was considerably more arduous. There were those who had lead in their boots while others kept time with gentle, steady driving, and some who always seemed to struggle. On the 17.30 Flyer, there were those who would knock the coach out of gear coming down the Cowbridge by-pass; while others, once out in the outside lane, would stay there and overtake everything!

One busy Saturday, dropping down from St Hilary in NCY886, we were overtaken by Commander CTX986C with Selwyn Bowen at the wheel, complete with cigar clenched between his teeth, just like Clint Eastwood's Man With No Name. All that was missing was a poncho! He had appeared from nowhere, swept past us then around the gentle bend,

Selwyn Bowen at the wheel of Plaxton Panorama 1, LTX828E on a private hire to Cheddar, March 22, 1969.

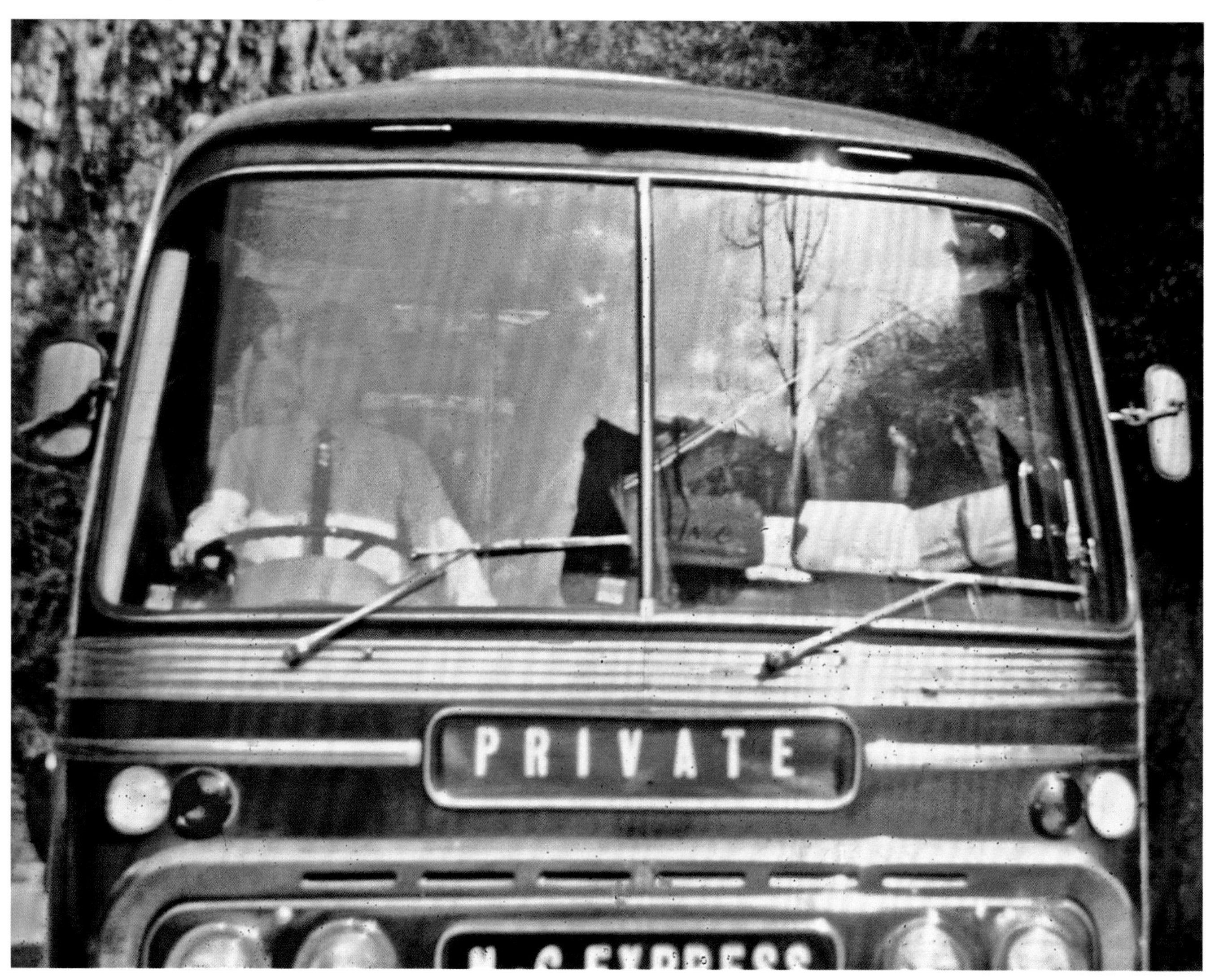

staying out in the centre, even though there was no centre lane. Coach 986 could be seen over the top of the hedgerow approaching Bonvilston, and it was rocketing along!

Graham Colwill, Alan 'Concorde' Williams and 'The Revered' Derek Parry were three conductors who were relative latecomers. Graham was good company and soon became a driver. Later, he had his own company based in north Gower. Alan, it seemed, hero-worshipped the fastest drivers, much the same as I did. He was a lanky six-footer who amazingly fitted into his Mini Cooper with no obvious discomfort. Derek was less flamboyant, mild-mannered and a little shy. It is believed he became a clergyman when the N&C came to an end.

John Friend was another conductor who stood out from the crowd. He joined N&C when the Western Welsh garage at Margam Terrace, Port Talbot, closed. He was a straight-laced West Walian, regimental in stature, officious and not easy to get to know. He wore dark glasses and when he took them off he was constantly blinking hence his nickname of Colonel Blink.

One day at Cowbridge, he left his centre door coach to place a woman's suitcase in the boot. Mike John, the driver, must have mistaken the thump of the boot for the saloon door and moved off leaving Johnny behind at the roadside.

Inspector Archie Hutchings happened to be aboard and as soon as the mistake was realised, flagged down John Hughes at Pentre Meyrick, as he approached in the opposite direction. Archie returned to Cowbridge and found Johnny outside the police station, stood to attention. Archie flagged down an approaching Blue Circle cement lorry and hitched a lift, but there was only one spare seat in the cab. It was here that seniority went out of the window. John bagged the cab seat to keep his uniform clean, while poor Archie sat outside in the dirt and dust! There was a history of liaison between N&C and Blue Circle, for reasons unknown, and they would always acknowledge each other on the road.
On this occasion it paid off, and the coach was waiting for them at Waterton.

On another occasion, Johnny was enjoying a break with John Hughes at Cardiff, when he announced he was going ahead to board the coach and make up his waybill. John duly followed and pulled away, and as he gained speed along Wood Street he realised he could not see his conductor. A woman in the front seat confirmed she hadn't seen him either. John returned to the bus station after a lap around the block, to find Johnny waiting there — he had been to the toilet and forgotten the time!

Johnny Friend was an excellent companion and was always the first to intervene if a parked car was causing an obstruction, or if another driver was causing problems.
When he left the N&C, he continued as a special police constable. He was forever the pinnacle of officialdom. One of Johnny's former colleagues, Mike John, summed him up perfectly: "Who could forget Johnny?
His eyelids were like butterfly wings. You had to be careful not to find yourself copying him inadvertently," he said.

"He was a real fun guy to have as your conductor. He was always on the lookout for someone acting outside the law. I have some great memories of him."

Regular passenger William Williams agreed, adding: "He was not only a conductor but also a special police constable. There would sometimes be a police car waiting at Briton Ferry garage to take him to Port Talbot police station for duty.

"On one occasion, so the story goes, as a second officer in a patrol car, his driver booked an N&C driver for speeding.
The following day Johnny turned up for work and much to his misfortune, was paired with that very same driver."

Another conductor at Briton Ferry, who had better remain anonymous, often arrived for duty with a rolled-up blanket under his arm. He considered himself to have a special gift for attracting women, and if luck went his way, the blanket would be useful inside the boot of the coach at the end of his shift.

One evening at the depot, some of his colleagues noticed the boot of one of the coaches open. Realising what was going on, they crept up and quietly closed the boot door on its amorous occupants. It was a cold night, and as the hours ticked by, they would certainly have needed the blanket for warmth! They were locked in all night, and in the morning, when the door was opened, the girl quickly ran off, but the intrepid conductor on the other hand calmly rolled up his blanket and with a smile on his face simply said "Morning, boys."

Another member of the road staff for whom anonymity is again called for, wasn't all he appeared to be. An amicable character with a Somerset accent, he joined N&C as a driver in 1969. He would always stop and chat outside the coach during his break at Cardiff when I was at lunch. In fact, he chatted so much the coach would often leave five minutes late, which bothered me, and I couldn't look the passengers in the eye.

He didn't stay long with N&C, and he returned to the West Country which was a shame as he appeared to be a good driver. I remember him saying his goodbyes one lunchtime outside Astey's cafe and feeling genuinely sad that he was leaving.

It was many years later however, that I became aware of the anger he had left in his wake. He had been collecting the funds for the staff Christmas party, and allegedly when he left, the funds went with him. I was really saddened to learn of this, and realised for the first time in my life that some people aren't always what they seem.

There were many groups of fathers, sons, brothers and cousins who made up the N&C family over the years. The Bowen and Hughes families were the biggest N&C dynasties during the late 1960s and together with their families they also represented a sizeable portion of the population of Skewen.

Arthur Bowen was a first generation driver who, as late as 1970, performed a number of jobs around the depot and even took a turn behind the wheel if required.

Mike John recalled times when, back at James Street, Arthur would supervise him to drive down from the top yard and reverse onto the square piece of land nearby.

"I was only 17 at the time, and this was a great thrill for me, although very naughty," recalled Mike.

"I thought I had come unstuck one day when a police car came towards us, stopped and waited until I had parked up. Arthur just kept whispering 'don't panic' and gave the officers a cheery wave."

Trevor Burley also recalls being impressed by Arthur, when he arrived at James Street, straight out of school. "He was hugely helpful and always displayed a loyalty to the firm and fellow employees alike," he said.

"It was not just a place of work to Arthur. He lived near the garage and was always Foreman George Matthew's right hand man. It wouldn't surprise me if he sometimes came in on his day off, happy to help out. He was a delightful man to know and an ideal workmate."

Mike John agreed adding: "I would have worked there for nothing, even though the James Street depot was hardly the Ritz. Even the mice seemed to have fun there. Arthur and George had red and brown blood running through their veins," added Mike, "Often, George could be heard muttering to himself whilst wandering about in his long dust coat, hands behind his back. Occasionally, you would hear him repeating a registration number, so I think his mind was focussed constantly on N&C."

Arthur's two sons Selwyn and Peter followed him onto the coaches. Peter conducted for a while before leaving to launch his own building business. Selwyn, of course, was that macho young driver whose trademark cigar gave him the look of Clint Eastwood or, depending on the length of his hair, Jason King.

Selwyn could be featured in a book devoted entirely to himself: he was as fast as he was

Drivers Vic Greenwood and Selwyn Bowen at the wheel, during a stop at Oxford during a private hire to Woburn Abbey on May 24, 1969.

flamboyant. In fact, he was very fast, which scared some of the elderly conductors who just wanted a quiet life. Most were happy to work with him and he certainly enhanced N&C's reputation of speed. The more nervously disposed avoided him, however, swapping shifts to earn their wages more sedately.

On another occasion, Jeff Phillips was driving his United Welsh double-decker along the dual carriageway at Jersey Marine when he saw an N&C coach in the distance, travelling slowly. He caught the coach up and drew alongside, in readiness for his right turn to Elba Crescent. With that Selwyn smiled, lit his cigar and put his foot to the floor.
His passengers laughed as they left Jeff for dead. Such were the daily antics of life on the N&C!

Selwyn was married to the sister of Mel and Dai Hughes, both conductors and the most easy going brothers you could wish to meet, although in looks they differed considerably. Mel was slim with shoulder length straight hair and Dai was of average build with curly hair. When N&C finished, Mel went to work as a railway freight guard based at Margam, and Dai launched a taxi company in Bridgend. Other brothers included Jack and Joe Magness. Mike John remembers working with them at Briton Ferry.

"Jack was a lovely guy, always cheerful with a wicked sense of humour. He got on well with the passengers and never complained. He was a small man, with a hunched back caused by an accident as a baby. Joe meanwhile, was a dapper figure with a moustache. He was always smartly turned out and reminded me of an RAF officer."

Joe retired in 1972, after enjoying two careers: one in the Royal Navy for 23 years, and another in public transport for 24 years. He rose to the rank of Chief Petty Officer in the Navy, and saw something of the Spanish Civil War at first hand when aboard HMS Newcastle. He also served on HMS Renown at the outbreak of the Second World War and was torpedoed in Corsica harbour — "but the majority of us got away with it," he said.

He left the Navy in 1948 and became a bus conductor, joining United Welsh Services. Then in 1955, he switched to N&C, where he enjoyed every moment of his life on the road. Of all the incidents during his 24 years as a conductor, one in particular brought a smile to his lips. "It happened when I was on the Cardiff run," he recalled. "A lady got on the coach and put a shawl down on the seat beside her for her dog. Impressed by her apparent consideration for other passengers, the inspector told her: "That is very thoughtful of you, madam." Her reply, which took him completely off guard, was: "Yes, you have to be careful. You don't know who has been sitting there."

Driver Tom Jones at Briton Ferry depot, 1966. *Philip Curnow*

Joe's daughter, Janet agreed: "My dad was always a joker, but always kind to people. He often told us funny stories about some of the things his passengers said. I know I'm biased, but he was a genuinely lovely man."

One tale that has probably done the rounds in many a bus company canteen reached my ears during a conversation with former N&C driver, John, or 'Jack' Cole. He was the typical comedian, and one day he was asked during his break in Cardiff, to pick up a new AEC steering wheel from the dealers.

Returning west in his Guy, he noticed his two female front seat passengers were dozing, so he raised his legs over the dash to cover the steering wheel, and, descending Crack Hill, grabbed the new steering wheel and held it up, waving it around and yelling 'help!'

The two women woke with a start, and screamed in fright at what they deemed a terrifying sight. They left the coach at Bridgend, but news of the incident travelled fast that day and on returning to Neath, John was hauled over the carpet for his efforts.

Cyril Knight left school in 1916 and started as a conductor on the Neath Tramways. When the trams ceased in August 1920, he was further employed at Court Herbert Colliery, Melyn Sheet & Tinplate Works, and he was a part-timer with Neath Borough Police Fire Brigade. In 1940, he volunteered for full-time duty in the National Fire Service, and became Station Officer in the Skewen and Jersey Marine area. When the National Fire Service was disbanded in 1946, he joined N&C and served 23 loyal years with the company, being promoted to inspector in 1949.

Inspector Knight's retirement was marked by a gathering of management and staff at the King Edward Hotel in London Road, Neath in March 1969. The social evening was the culmination of a varied and hard-working life, and all at N&C joined in wishing him and Mrs Knight a long and happy retirement.

Arthur Bowen in his driver's uniform at N&C's James Street, Neath depot in 1960.
Gerald Truran collection

Peter Parker joined N&C in 1969, from City of Oxford Motors, which immediately earned him great esteem in my eyes. Peter was a fiery character who began his career with South Wales Transport, before driving in London for a while, where, as he put it, he was taught to drive properly.

With N&C Peter lost his temper one day while leaving Bridgend bus station. The manager of a furniture shop was in the habit of displaying his wares on the road outside his Market Street premises, leaving an ever-decreasing margin of error for coaches leaving the bus station. Both Peter and the manager were so incensed after the coach made contact with this unofficial street furniture that they would have come to blows in the road had it not been for the intervention of Inspector Mick Williams.

Peter remembers driving PTX830F, containing a large proportion of N&C management, staff and wives, to Mick's retirement event near his home in Aberkenfig: "When we got there," he said, "there was no sign of him. There were a few family members including a tall, attractive blonde woman in an evening dress. We were all wondering when Mick was going to appear for his presentation. As I walked to the gent's toilet I was confronted by this same woman, who, in a deep familiar voice said "Hello Pete, everything alright?" It was only then that I realised Mick had been there all along, convincingly disguised by his drag costume!"

Last but not least, among N&C characters has to be Shandy, the depot cat.

Margaret Truran recalls the beautiful marmalade-coloured Persian cat who decided she liked life among the N&C coaches and so made her home there.

"Shandy decided to make herself comfortable at the depot. The women in the office would look after her all year round and

A group of road and office staff alongside newly rebodied Gloster Gardner 6LW WN6536, late 1940s. *Margaret and Helen Truran*

that was fine until everything stopped for Christmas. Gerald and myself lived in Bryncoch then, and we used to go away for Christmas. But the cat needed feeding and so we always had to return early on Boxing Day to make sure she was fed. When the depot closed, we took her in at home, but not long after, despite all those years among the coaches, the poor thing was hit by a car and we lost her."

It cannot be denied that the N&C company had more than its fair share of personalities on its payroll throughout its 40-year history. There were extroverts and introverts, ranging from formula one contenders to those more suited to driving a hearse. There were the philosophers and the after-dinner speakers; sergeant majors and unforgettable stand-up comedians.

All of them provided the life and soul of an excitingly vibrant operator. From the Casanovas to the market traders, they all had one thing in common: the desire and determination to provide a sterling service to all who wished to travel in style, comfort and speed between Swansea and Cardiff.

One thing is certain: the N&C company was remarkable in every respect, it was many things to many people and the mark it left on the travelling public of South Wales is still very much remembered.

Once again, Mike John sums it up: "They were good old days. There were some real characters about then and even to this day I still get the yearning to bomb up and down the A48, trying to catch Selwyn!"

Chapter 9

Delivering the goods

In the heyday of the N&C company, passengers were not the only cargo to be transported from one place to another aboard its fast and luxurious vehicles. Parcels also had an important part to play in the generation of income.

In the post-Second World War years the reliability of N&C's service meant that for many businesses it was an unbeatable method of sending parcels between Cardiff and Swansea as well as towns between.

"What a service that was," recalled Dennis Preston, who was employed by Halfords in 1949. "One of my duties was to meet the N&C coaches and collect parcels which had been sent from the company's Cardiff branch. At the time it was really remarkable to have such a same-day express delivery service."

Norman Chinnock had a similar job as a 15-year-old parcel boy at Western Welsh's Bridgend depot. He remembers one of his duties was to collect parcels from the N&C coaches as they entered the bus station. He also recalls times when things didn't quite go according to plan.

"On one occasion, one of my colleagues went to meet a centre door coach, and as was the custom, the conductor threw the parcel out. Unfortunately, he failed to catch it and it fell under the rear wheels of the coach," remembered Norman.

"The parcel contained numerous sets of dentures, and as you can imagine, there was quite an uproar. There were false teeth all over the road, and all the intended recipients eventually had to be called back to their dentist's. After that we had to walk to the bus station's Bay 18 to collect parcels."

Alan Roberts remembers being out with his mother, when she was speaking to one of the drivers: "She mentioned something about being a bus driver. She was immediately corrected with 'coach driver, madam, coach driver,' which certainly put her in her place.

"Another time, while walking along the road to Briton Ferry an N&C coach went flying past. 'Too fast', muttered my father. A minute or two later a Western Welsh Tiger Cub went by. 'That's better!' he said. I knew which I preferred though."

Bill Price was very interested in the transport scene in his home town of Cowbridge, and recalls the impressive sight of the N&C coaches as they travelled through the town, stopping at the Town Hall on their way to and from Cardiff and Swansea.

"I couldn't work out why the vehicles we travelled on to Swansea were known as the N&C coaches. Surely they should have been called the S&C coaches," said Bill.

"In my youth, it was always a thrill to travel to Swansea on the N&C, to visit my like-minded cousin. Those were the days when there was usually a hold-up in the centre of Port Talbot where there was a railway level crossing. The journey via Morriston was a bit of a drag too, until the Briton Ferry Bridge and Jersey Marine link road was opened in October, 1955.

"The speed of the coaches seemed incredible compared with the plodding rural bus services of the Western Welsh company that I was more familiar with. Better still, on many of the older N&C coaches there was the opportunity to ride in the front seats alongside the driver.

"Sadly, in 1964, for me the character of the fleet suffered with the withdrawal of the six handsomely rebodied AEC Regal III Park Royal half-cab vehicles. The following year two 36ft AEC Reliances appeared with striking Duple Commander bodywork. Another three arrived in 1966, but to brighten things up a bit, a new private hire livery of light fawn and deep red was applied

From top brass to rank and file, N&C was one big happy family as this gathering from around 1960 shows.

to these three vehicles. By this time, the 12-year-old Guy Arabs were beginning to wear out."

The N&C was the entrusted provider of many things to many people. Commuting to work or for attending appointments, journeys for pleasure or in search of romance: it was all in a day's work for the boys in brown. Phil Williams used the company's vehicles for getting to school, and found even at that young age he was already developing an interest in the Brown Bombers:

"In the mid-1950s I lived in Dinas Baglan Road, Port Talbot, near The Elms bus stop which was one of N&C's limited stops, although I could never understand why that stop was deemed important enough to be one of theirs," said Phil.

"My mother worked at the National Union of Public Employees office in Swansea and I went to school there so we both travelled back and fore daily by N&C.

"At this time, the coaches in service included some AEC and Daimler half cabs plus the company's fleet of Guy Arabs and the three new Burlingham Seagulls. My firm favourites were the Guys and Burlinghams with their centre entrance doors, because, with that body style, if the front seats were available, it meant I had a great view, sitting alongside the driver.

"Standing at The Elms bus stop each day, it was possible to hear the magnificent AEC engines working hard climbing Pentyla Hill before the road levelled out, then rounding a bend and sweeping down to The Elms. There were two coaches that ran together at that time of the morning, one which I used would go via Briton Ferry Bridge, the other the long way round via Neath.

"Peering through the gloom and drizzle of a winter's morning, trying to read the small destination blind to select the right vehicle was no mean feat. However, most of the drivers knew their regular passengers and which coach they wanted, so even when I put my arm out for the wrong one, it would be met with a beep on the horn and the driver waving his thumb backwards to indicate that ours was the one behind.

"In the early 1960s NUPE decided to relocate to Porthcawl, and my mother's job moved with it. Fortunately, I was now of an age where I could travel to Swansea on my own. Occasionally, I'd get to Swansea and instead of going to school I would board the next N&C service for the long way round, purely because I never went on that route. I didn't do it often though, so my parents never got wise to it.

"By this time, the dwindling number of half-cabs were no longer providing front line service, and used only as an occasional relief coach or as a replacement in the event of a breakdown. I fondly remember the last half-cab I travelled on. The new garage at Briton Ferry had opened and my coach from The Elms one morning was a particularly sick Guy Arab. We limped into the garage to change vehicles and I could hardly believe my luck that we were given AEC Regal III EWN 556 to complete our journey. Despite the driver protesting loudly it completed the journey without incident and continued to run faultlessly all day. I know it did for a fact, as I had decided on the way to Swansea that this was going to be one of my 'sickie' days and my lunch money would be spent on several tickets travelling the day on this beauty!

"New, modern coaches began arriving, and when passing Briton Ferry garage each morning, I would glance down and admire the sleek new Harrington Cavalier coaches

"It was an ultra-good coach service. How they managed to keep up with the timetable was amazing."

Dennis Preston

parked in the front yard. They looked so modern compared to the Guy Arabs, but the Guys, Burlinghams and occasional Weymann Fanfares were still the mainstay of the services I used to catch. The newer coaches were generally being used on excursions and private hire work at the time.

"I don't remember many of the names of the drivers and conductors. I worked with a few of them later in life, in the employ of British Rail either as freight guards or as drivers on the staff buses. I remember a tragic incident one morning when, having travelled to school as usual, I learned on my return journey that the morning driver, feeling unwell, had gone for a lie down on the back seat before his next run, and while there he had sadly passed away.

"It was always a pleasure to board the N&C coach in the morning. It felt a very special way to start the day, and for me, travelling to school in this way was most acceptable. I'm not sure what speeds these coaches actually reached but one morning, I'm guessing around 1962-63, only the 'via Neath' coach approached The Elms.

The cab of UNY832G, newly delivered at Briton Ferry, March 1969. The wonderful smell of a brand new Plaxton could never be forgotten!

The driver tooted and signalled that the other one was behind, but it was a good 10 minutes later before it appeared.

"It was a Burlingham Seagull, the front seat was empty, and I was in it in a flash! We positively flew along Baglan Road and over Briton Ferry Bridge in a bid to make up some time, and once on to the Jersey Marine road the driver really went for it, and he called me across to look at the speedometer needle which was hard against the stop, absolutely flat out! From memory, I believe the AEC speedo read as far as 80mph, where the needle stopped, but what our true speed was, I don't really know. That road in those days had a concrete slab surface punctuated every few yards with an expansion joint, and the tyre noise as we passed over the slab joints at this speed was horrendous. The driver kept laughing and making 'Yee-Haa' sounds, like a cowboy rounding up steers! Our arrival at Swansea was almost right on time, and our passengers commended the driver on making up the deficit. Luckily, there were no traffic police around that morning!

"Travelling home each afternoon, I would arrive at the coach with plenty of spare time before its departure. It would be parked in the street, open to all, the driver and conductor having gone for their break. Sometimes I would be the only one sitting on there for about 20 minutes or so. On numerous occasions the next passenger to arrive was a large woman travelling home to Cardiff. She looked quite fearsome with long black hair and heavy make-up, but she was very quietly spoken with a foreign accent. She would chat to me while we waited, and ask me about school and my homework, and what I wanted to be when I grew up. I don't know where the thought came from, but one day I answered her saying I wanted to be a solicitor. 'Oh,' she said, 'my son is an up and coming lawyer and soon to be a politician. Mark my words,' she replied adding 'One day he will be famous in Westminster and will own the biggest law firm in Cardiff. His name is Leo Abse.' How right she was!"

"As my school days continued, and I was growing older, I was taking an interest in girls. By this time, the 36ft Harringtons were appearing on my service home, and I was describing these ultra-modern coaches to a group of friends in school. One of the girls, who lived near the Clarence Street terminus, didn't believe me and said she had never seen a modern N&C coach there, so a bet was made, and after school she accompanied me to see this modern coach. It was a safe bet really, because if there was a new coach there, I would get a long kiss from her. If there wasn't a new coach there, she would get a long kiss from me. A win-win situation! When we arrived, there she was — a shiny 36ft Harrington, gleaming in the afternoon sun and looking beautiful. We both climbed aboard the empty coach and the bet was duly paid. She was so impressed with the feel and the smell of the coach that she stayed on it with me and the bet was paid several times over! We chatted until it was time for the coach to leave. Who would have thought an N&C coach could have that effect on a young girl?

N&C's general manager Captain J J Newbury welcomes a civic visitor on the occasion of the opening of the new Briton Ferry depot, November 1962. *Caroline Newbury*

"With my interest in girls rapidly gathering pace, I had noticed an attractive girl around my age who was already on the coach each morning as I got on at The Elms. She wore a Mynyddbach school uniform and, instead of making for the front seat, I would now walk down the coach to find where she was sitting, and try to get a seat nearby, smiling as I caught her eye. Eventually I got into conversation with her, found out her name and that she caught the coach at The Twelve Knights Hotel in Margam. After a week or two of travelling together, we arranged to meet a couple of evenings a week, one of us catching the N&C to the other's home to listen to records. A few weeks of this and we were firmly boyfriend and girlfriend. After school we would get to the empty N&C as quickly as possible and cuddle up together in the back seat of Harrington Cavalier 568 ECY which became etched in my memory as my favourite of the entire fleet!

"I remember one Saturday around August-September 1964 I was travelling from Port Talbot to Cardiff for the day. The coach was 567 ECY. With these new vehicles now running frequently it was quite unusual to even see, let alone catch an older half cab AEC any more.

"As we pulled into Cowbridge, I was amazed to see one pull up on the opposite side of the road. I left my coach and abandoned my Cardiff trip, deciding to catch the old half cab instead. I can't recall the number of that coach for certain but I think it may have been EWN 556, just before it was withdrawn for the second time. I paid for a ticket to Swansea but at Briton Ferry the driver pulled into the garage saying she was losing power and we would have to swap coaches. Maybe that was the reason it was withdrawn soon after. We left the depot in one of the TWN Park Royals, 556-558. I could never look upon these three coaches as 'real' Brown Bombers.

"Sadly, my days of daily commuting by N&C came to an end after taking my GCE exams, and I moved to a Port Talbot school for a short time before starting my first job. Missing the Brown Bombers, I started cycling to the depot on Saturday mornings, just to keep an eye on the fleet and see the comings and goings. I was nearly 17 by now, and although my trips on the N&C became fewer, I became very friendly with some of the depot staff. With Saturday mornings being fairly quiet at the garage, I was allowed to help out washing coaches and doing a few menial tasks. One morning, a Harrington I had just washed was to be taken from the back yard to be parked up in the front yard, and I jumped aboard for the short ride, as I usually did. This time, though, the driver asked me if I wanted to have a drive. Did I? I couldn't believe it! It was just a slow speed crawl in 2nd gear, and obviously I wasn't allowed to park it in the line-up in case I got it wrong, but just that short drive was beyond my wildest dreams.

"This continued on Saturday mornings with more and more short drives being offered to me until eventually I was trusted to shunt them around on my own to where they were required to be parked. My one regret is that I never got to drive a Guy Arab or Burlingham Seagull, but I will be forever thankful to the staff who gave me that great experience.

"Sadly, around six months later, work commitments with my first job put an end to those visits to the depot. I passed my driving test four weeks after my 17th birthday, the success of which I'm sure was helped by my time spent shunting and parking those N&C coaches. Unfortunately, I cannot recall travelling by N&C during the final 12 to 18 months of the company's life. My last trip was on a private hire early in 1970, when my employers organised a staff and partners' night out at a medieval banquet in Cardiff Castle. I was delighted when I saw Plaxton Panorama Elite UNY832G arrive at the pick-up point and whisk us off to Cardiff in true N&C style. It was a fitting end to my time spent travelling on the Brown Bombers.

"It's very sad how and why the great N&C company ended, but I have my memories. No one can take those away and I am so thankful that I travelled on the Brown Bombers for such a long period of time when they were kings of the road."

There is no doubt that N&C coaches played a big part in the long cherished growing up memories of so many people.

For me as this book's author, I have to admit that as well as my interest in transport, I

The Park Royal rebodied AEC Regal IIIs were reaching the end of their days when the move from James Street to Briton Ferry came. Here, HNY22, HTX407 and HNY913 await their fate in 1964.

considered myself to have a sense of rhythm, and like many other teenagers in the 1960s, sought fame and decided to have a go at playing the drums in a band.

It was possibly a forerunner of 'garage' music, because that's exactly where we played! The first step was to create a set of drums from buckets tightly taped with tracing paper, together with a range of kitchen pots and strung-up baking trays. Then I gradually bought a few proper drums as my pocket money — anything left from my N&C ticket money — would allow.

Then, in 1970, and now earning a living in Cardiff, I made an initial sortie to Grimwades of Canton, and made plans to buy a range of better drums and cymbals. My friends Alan Old and Dave Clements came up from Bridgend to assist in bringing the new kit home — by N&C of course!

The first essential task was to work out who would be on the exact N&C turn out of Cardiff that evening, so that we could ride home with the drums stored in the boot and therefore delivered free.

The day duly arrived, I walked over from Greyfriars to Canton, met the boys off the coach at St David's Hospital, and strolled along to Grimwades. Once there I began putting several mismatched drums to one side, just like selecting items from the 'beyond their best' shelf at a supermarket.

The thought had occurred to me to stop the coach at Neville Street and load up there, but it would be embarrassing in front of a full complement of passengers, so instead we allowed time to struggle over to Central Bus

Station, with frequent stops to regain our composure. We eventually made it, although our arms felt a foot longer. On arrival there we found our unique courier in the form of Duple Commander CTX985C. With the assistance of its crew — driver Selwyn Bowen and conductor Alan Williams — the drums were duly loaded.

After the usual lively run home, we disembarked at The Coach and Horses, and I ran to the back and opened the boot doors. I was surprised to find the drums had shifted the entire length of the boot, a considerable distance which involved climbing inside to retrieve them. After a slap on the side panel, Selwyn pulled away and we struggled the final quarter of a mile home. I was hot, sweaty and covered in dirt from deep inside the boot space of that coach.

Ironically, within a year, this second scratch set of drums was replaced by a sparkling new Premier set from Grand's in Cardiff, which were delivered by the sales manager on his way home, without the hassle of a struggle across Cardiff and the need for a change of clothing!

Barbara Genery worked in the Western Welsh booking office at Cardiff's Central Bus Station, and although issued with a pass for that company, preferred to travel to and from Bridgend by N&C coach.

"I started travelling in September 1969. On my first day at work I met my first proper boyfriend," recalled Barbara. "There was one seat left on the coach, so I sat in it and the young man sitting next to me started chatting.

"Then, for the rest of the week, he would keep me that seat. I thought he was never going to ask, but by the end of the week he asked me out. We stayed together a number of years and got engaged, but I broke it off with him as I wanted to go and have some fun. Sometimes I think 'silly me.'

"The clearest memory I have is being put off the coach in Canton because the N&C conductor wouldn't accept my Western Welsh pass. I wasn't going to pay extra so had to leave the coach. He was a miserable conductor whose name escapes me now, but Selwyn Bowen was driving that day and was quite sympathetic to me although he didn't intervene."

There would usually be an inspector on duty at Cardiff, either Archie Hutchings or Gwyn Hare, although Gwyn retired during this period. He bought a greengrocery in Cowbridge, located on the High Street, presumably so that he could still keep an eye on things! There was often an inspector or two — Dai John or Mick Williams — to oversee crew changes at the depot, and sometimes one of them would have a spell of duty at Swansea or Bridgend. It was fairly rare to see an inspector jump on your coach, and I never witnessed any problems which led to disciplinary action. The presence of such activity was quickly relayed on the N&C grapevine, so everything was usually ship shape by the time the inspector boarded.

As a teenager, Charles Smith remembers a younger conductor who was happy to charge him and his friends the child fare without question. "Unfortunately every now and then we'd be told 'Sorry, lads, full fare today.' Then a couple of stops later an inspector would board. There was obviously a jungle telegraph warning the crews when this was likely to happen."

There is no doubt that the thousands of miles I travelled up and down the A48 between 1967 and 1971 and experiences gained during those journeys played a big part in the creation of this book. I could work out the distance exactly, but it would involve mathematics, never my strongest subject.

Chapter 10

All weather challenge

Constantly battling to meet timetable pressures, coping with stressful congestion and dealing with awkward passengers were all part of the daily challenge that N&C crews faced. There was however one further adversary in the struggle to stay on top of the express game — the weather.

That was something the company had no control over. It was also a factor which could produce the biggest challenge, and without warning. Despite that, everyone's attitude was to clock on for duty, turn out, and run the service. It was always the aim to show up Western Welsh and South Wales Transport at any cost, and that's exactly what they did. Time and again.

Situations such as poor night-time visibility could often delay services, and winter smogs were common at the time, contributed to by the heavy industry which was prominent across the South Wales seaboard were a driver's worst nightmare. These often occurred in the heavily industrialised lower Swansea valley between Llansamlet and Morriston, one of the most heavily polluted areas in the whole of the United Kingdom.

Combined with this, the headlamps on the early pre-war fleet, left a lot to be desired and their power and beam bore little or no comparison to those of the vehicles used by the company in later years.

In the early days, conditions could be so bad that it was not uncommon for the conductor to sit on the vehicles nearside mudguard, alongside the cab, and keep the driver informed of their proximity to the kerb.

Wales is also renowned for its unrelenting rainfall and at any time of year there is a possibility of flooding. Not surprisingly there were many places along the route between Cardiff and Swansea that were prone to flash floods. Such incidents ranged from a huge pool of water on the road to more serious affairs over a far larger area. Each of these would present their own problems.

Back in the 1960s many winters saw heavy snow which sometimes led to problems for N&C in providing the usual service. This Christmas card scene from the winter of 1965-66 suggests there may be a few problems for drivers even before they reached the top of the ramp out of Briton Ferry garage. *Gerald Truran/The Omnibus Society*

I left school early in 1969 and was delighted that my travels would now include a daily commute from Bridgend to Cardiff. It turned out that these would be the final years of what to me and a great many others was the beloved N&C company. I had become a junior member of a travel elite and enjoyed every minute of it, come rain or shine.

I rode on the Brown Bombers from the mid-1960s, travelling as far and as often, as my pocket money would allow on weekends and during school holidays. Little did I know however, when I pulled back the curtains on the freezing winter's morning of Friday, 19 December, 1969, the adventure that was about to unfold. It would culminate in the most exciting and memorable trip I ever undertook on the N&C and unexpectedly happened on one of my journeys to work.

It was in the run up to Christmas and there had been a spell of very cold weather. For the third night running it had been snowing.

On the Wednesday and Thursday it hadn't presented much of a problem, but on the Friday conditions were much worse. So, it was with some trepidation that I set off for the bus station for my coach, the first of the day, at 7.30am. After a tricky walk into town, I was amazed when the Duple Commander CTX985C, pulled in on time, with Selwyn Bowen behind the wheel, and conductor Derek Parry taking the fares. Selwyn, who had become a good friend, had been on the 8.00am Flyer all week, non-stop to Cardiff, but today had thoughtfully turned up for work early in anticipation of problems with other drivers being unable to get to the depot. At this time, a relief coach ran up to Bridgend then turned back to form the 7.45am to Swansea, but on this occasion it had turned back at Stormy Down. Its driver, Ken Arthur had consideried it unwise to continue. But Selwyn Bowen was a much braver man, so the scene was set for an epic trip to Cardiff.

The classic lines of the Burlingham Seagull body on NCY887 are evident in this fine study at Briton Ferry in 1969. *Richard Evans*

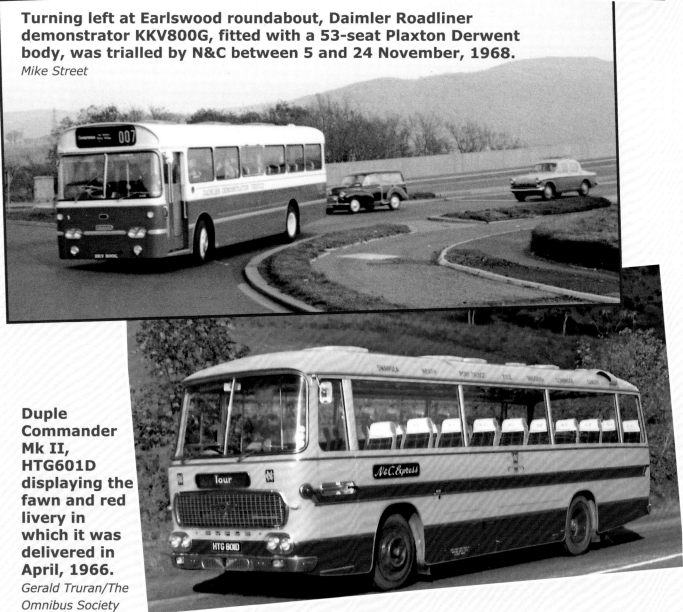

Turning left at Earlswood roundabout, Daimler Roadliner demonstrator KKV800G, fitted with a 53-seat Plaxton Derwent body, was trialled by N&C between 5 and 24 November, 1968.
Mike Street

Duple Commander Mk II, HTG601D displaying the fawn and red livery in which it was delivered in April, 1966.
Gerald Truran/The Omnibus Society

It soon became obvious how Selwyn had managed to get through. Where there was a queue of vehicles, Selwyn simply overtook them, ploughing through the virgin snow in the centre of the road. We overtook a line of cars stretching from the Coach & Horses pub in Cowbridge Road, to Waterton Cross, and again from St Nicholas to the top of Tumble Hill. If this sounds a bit reckless and foolhardy, nothing could be further from the truth. Extreme caution and intense concentration were the order of the day and the fact that the journey to Cardiff took 85 minutes instead of the scheduled 45 indicates the slow but steady and skilful progress that was made.

We picked up the usual passengers at Cowbridge then gleefully passed the early morning Western Welsh Atlantean double decker on service 301 which was stuck at the lights on the hill! We crawled steadily up the hill in low gear and as we passed the Atlantean, Selwyn remarked with some determination: "If the lights turn to red now, I'm still going through!" Several more abandoned vehicles were passed as we continued up Primrose Hill, then the going became a little easier until we met another long queue of cars at St Nicholas. These we simply left standing, to the sheer astonishment of their occupants, peering out through misted windows at the sight of our coach. The middle of the road was snowbound to everyone except ourselves, and in any case, nothing was getting through from the Cardiff direction.

We paused briefly at the approach to Tumble Hill as a few cars were pushed clear, and then as we began our descent, everyone was told to sit in the nearside seats. Our progress was painful, inch by cautious inch through the softest snow, Selwyn instructing the passengers to change sides as we progressed at various angles to the direction we ultimately wanted to go. Round the right-hand bend, and eventually the left-hand bend at the bottom, then we cheered and breathed a sigh of relief as Culverhouse Cross came into view. Along Cowbridge Road West from Culverhouse to Ely roundabout was a line of vehicles awaiting progress in the opposite direction. The Cardiff-based coaches were among them, their crew showing a mixture of expressions from disbelief, amazement and pride that one of their own had been the first to get through. But Selwyn wasn't finished yet: we actually overtook one of the Cardiff coaches returning to base as we ran down through Ely, causing utter astonishment to driver Danny Vaughan, who was never renowned for his bravado.

We arrived at the Central Bus Station at 08:55, 40 minutes late, and upon reaching my place of work discovered that I was signing in a lot sooner than many staff living locally. By lunchtime I was beginning to consider my plans for returning home and picked my way over to Central Square.
I need not have worried: there was 985, still on the stand, still with fog and spot lamps blazing and with Selwyn and Derek cosily ensconced in Astey's supping their coffee. What I hadn't realised was that they had returned to Swansea after the rigours of the first trip up, and had battled all the way back again, totally fulfilling their duty and making up time into the bargain.

Don't think that the story of N&C always unfolded in bad weather however. There were sunnier times too and lots of them. For me though, while it was a thrill to take a journey by N&C coach at any time of day, there was always an extra magic about travelling in the early morning as the skies lightened, or at the end of a summer's day when the lights began to twinkle and the roads quietened down.

Through the worst of winter conditions, N&C always did its utmost to provide the advertised service to the best of its ability. This was in no small way due to the military background of those at the helm.

They instinctively recruited the right calibre of employee as a prerequisite for their proud little company to succeed. It was a feature that was tangible with N&C almost to the end, and was something that rarely existed in other transport undertakings.

Sylvia Hawkins used to commute between Bridgend and Cardiff in the 1960s. A sudden, late snowfall on 14 April 1965 led to a six hour journey home: "I left the Welsh Office at 17:00 just as the snow began to fall, and by the time I'd got to the bus station it was coming down quite badly. My coach was due out at 17:30, but hadn't turned up. A growing crowd waited for ages and we were told the coach was having trouble getting down Tumble Hill, just outside Cardiff. Eventually it turned up, and those that could, piled on. We left Cardiff slowly but surely, until the coach returned to 'that hill' again. We were stuck there for ages, and my boyfriend (now husband), and a couple of the other lads, left the coach to walk to the nearby pub and ring home to explain why we were so late.

> **"My husband and I used to catch them at the bottom of Alfred Street to go to Cardiff. Lovely coaches."**
> ***Daphne Winter***

"Not long after they left, the coach started to move. Of course, we all shouted that they weren't back, but the driver said he couldn't stop as no one would be able to get past him on the hill. So, we left them behind and slowly made our way to Bridgend. I'm not sure how late we were exactly, but I got home at 23:30 that night, having walked to Tondu, as there were no buses or anything else moving on the roads. The boys managed to get back by thumbing a lift, the driver being glad to have their extra weight in the car to stop it sliding on the hill.

"Despite that night, I loved the N&C coaches, and got to know the drivers and conductors over the years. It was a huge shame when they finished.

"My husband still mentions it, especially as he walked all the way to my house, knee deep in snow, to make sure I was OK. I lived with my grandmother, who opened the door and said to him 'Yes, she's home safely, thank you', then closed the door on him! Poor thing, he had to walk two miles back home again. Still, we've been married over 50 years, so it didn't put him off!"

Jim Boucher recalled just how tricky it could be in the days when the volume of traffic was simply not enough to spread the salt and keep the roads clear. "I was coming down the Golden Mile during a snowfall. We had about 30 passengers aboard when suddenly the coach started spinning. It spun three times before it stopped on the grass. I looked around and could see that six or seven of the passengers had fainted!"

To be sat in the comfort and warmth of your coach, with just the crew and a handful of passengers for company was fine by me, and with that tuneful AEC orchestra gently playing away beneath your feet, life somehow appeared far better. It all added up to an intense sense of security and of being at peace with the world.

One of my many memorable journeys came on a summer's evening, returning home from Swansea on 568ECY. It was in the earliest days of my interest in the N&C, probably the summer of 1967. We had left Swansea and the crew had no need to hurry, even though they were due to finish at the garage and be relieved by Cardiff men. As we ambled along the Fabian Way dual carriageway, the sun was setting over Mumbles Head, darkness was slowly descending, and yet we were driving just on our sidelights. The gentle, repeating rhythm of the joints along the concrete road — 'bo-boom, bo-oom' — caused me to float away into a wonderful relaxed and sleepy state. It was a journey that, for no other reason than that, will stay in my mind forever.

Unfortunately, the idiosyncrasies of the human race meant that late night journeys could not always be enjoyed to the full. Peter Parker recalls a troublesome couple who caught an evening service home after

A busy time at Cardiff in the mid-1960s. Harrington Cavalier 568ECY is in as-new condition complete with wheel trims. The vehicle had low-profile seats in yellow and green check moquette.

spending the day in a pub. "They were regulars, but would cause a disturbance to the other passengers with their frequent swearing and arguing," recalled Peter.

"This became too much one night and so I stopped the coach at Taibach police station. A police inspector boarded and gave them both a clout round the head, and to everyone's relief all went quiet. As he left the coach, the inspector winked and removed the truncheon from up his sleeve!

"Another regular passenger, a dentist, would use the last service out of Cardiff at the weekend. He would board the coach at Ely Bridge for his journey home to Port Talbot after work, but not before visiting the pub. He always carried a half-empty glass of beer, and as he took his seat, would place the glass on the floor of the coach, and announce to both driver and conductor that they would receive a half-crown tip if his beer remained in the glass when he arrived at his destination of Bethany Square, Port Talbot, a distance of around 30 miles. A tip of that amount was not to be sneezed at, and many times the journey was completed with the beer intact, if a little flat. As soon as the dentist had planted both feet on the pavement he would raise the glass and gulp down its contents as the coach disappeared into the night."

Colin Williams often caught the last coach from Bridgend, returning home to Pentyla, Port Talbot. The service was always lightly loaded at that hour, but the few passengers that were aboard were going to be disappointed if they expected the usual speedy journey.

"It was the slowest I have ever known the N&C to travel," recalled Colin, "but there was a reason: they would let the Western Welsh service pass them so that if they had no passengers left on reaching Baglan, they could go straight to the garage for an early finish.

"On one occasion a lady was sitting behind the driver, who had his blind pulled down. Apart from her, I was the only other passenger left on board, and the conductor, who shall remain anonymous but was also a special constable in Port Talbot, as well as a traffic warden, was winding the driver up wickedly. This caused the driver to swear at him profusely. The lady left the coach at Pyle and commented to the driver that she was unaccustomed to such foul language. He was very apologetic to her, and her reasoned reply as she made light of the situation was that it was better to hear than be deaf. The conductor had hell from the driver after she had left. They would often stop at Pentyla for me to save the walk from either Bethany Square or The Elms, as my local stop was not recognised as a limited stop."

Fay Chick fondly remembers her journeys to work by N&C: "I used to travel regularly on the coaches. I worked at the Ford Motor Company in the early 1970s, and used to fall asleep on my way home. The conductor would wake me up at my stop. It was a great service."

Dennis Preston recalled how his wife Nan used to travel on the N&C coaches every day from Scurlock's Garage in Bridgend to Penrhiwtyn in Neath.

Even from the rear, the ultra-modern styling of the Plaxton Panorama Elite was impressive. Newly delivered UNY831G shows this off to advantage at Briton Ferry garage in March 1969.

"She was a nurse at Neath General Hospital. It annoyed her when, falling asleep after a hard day's work, she would hear the Inspector calling out: tickets please."

On hearing this story Colin Williams, said: "She was lucky. One night a passenger fell asleep on the journey back to Port Talbot. He missed his stop at Stormy Down and woke up in Margam. He was not amused, as he had to pay for a taxi to get home."

I experienced a particularly memorable journey to Swansea, in November 1968. It was a gloomy Sunday, and what better way for a transport enthusiast to while away the afternoon than a trip on the N&C. A stroll down to the bus station to await whichever coach ran in first, and soon enough, with five minutes to spare, in came Commander HTG602D on a Swansea service with Cardiff-based driver Vic Greenwood and conductor Philip Evans in charge. Philip had been a driver until the recent serious accident in the Splott area of Cardiff, when his coach, on a late evening private hire, skidded into a shopfront and trapped him in the cab. Happily, he made a full recovery but was on conducting duties either by personal request or on compassionate grounds in view of the trauma he had suffered. Vic, as previously mentioned, was one of the steadiest drivers, capable of high speed driving but only if and when necessary. On this day, despite a typical quiet Sunday afternoon on the roads, this ability to 'turn up the gas' was soon to be tested.

We headed steadily west through Laleston and over Stormy Down. Traffic was light and we waited time for a minute or two at Pyle. As we continued towards Port Talbot a problem suddenly became evident.

Seen on service at Cardiff on 27 October, 1969, HTG601D had finally lost its fawn and red colours and received standard livery. It was unusual to see antimacassars on seats when on scheduled daily service. *Mike Street*

Roadworks alongside Margam Park had necessitated single-line traffic and to make matters worse, the temporary traffic lights were badly phased, resulting in a long tailback of traffic heading west. As we moved forward by only a few car lengths at a time, it soon became obvious that this badly balanced traffic control was going to seriously hinder our timekeeping.

As the minutes ticked by, any hope of making up lost time was abandoned, and the crew were now worried that they would miss their return working which they were booked to take over at Briton Ferry depot after a short break. Philip checked the duty roster against the timetable and, sure enough, they were by now overdue at Briton Ferry and should have been waiting to take over the return part of their shift, which had already left Swansea and would soon be waiting outside the depot. Eventually we cleared the bottleneck and immediately Vic straightened up in his seat and put his foot to the floor. As the revs built up we flew through Margam and Taibach, ignoring the speed limit and leaving the many Sunday drivers bewildered in a way that only a Brown Bomber could. On arrival at Bethany Square it was half-expected that the Cardiff service would be waiting, having been brought forward by a spare driver or the duty inspector. In those days, it should be remembered that there were no mobile phones or ship-to-shore radio which is commonplace today, so no-one knew for sure what was happening. There was no sign of the Cardiff service, but just in case it was on its way, Philip jumped out and ran up High Street along the incoming one-way system as Vic hurried 602 around the narrow streets of the old town centre.

The Park Royal bodywork on the 1959 intake — TWN556-8 — was box-like and lacked the style of earlier deliveries, but the vehicles gave many years of sterling service. They were nicknamed 'The Furniture Boxes' by the staff, for understandable reasons. Here TWN556 calls at the depot for a crew change, during July 1969. *Geoff Morant/The Transport Library*

We picked up our breathless conductor at the bottom of Pentyla before screaming up the hill, the vibrations of the AEC engine through the lower gears being felt through the seats. Vic coaxed more out of the normally sluggish 602 than anyone had achieved before or since. Once on to the Dinas Baglan Road we steadily rolled through the parked cars and hurtled down to Baglan. Then there followed the mile-long dash along the dual carriageway, during which we must have reached 80mph as Briton Ferry garage came into view. Across the road in the layby was a Harrington coach and outside its crew awaiting relief, together with those who were waiting to relieve us, all accompanied by two inspectors. All had their eyes pinned to the horizon searching for our long overdue appearance. On board the waiting coach sat a dozen or so bewildered passengers wondering why they were unlikely to be home in time for tea. With typical panache, Vic knocked 602 out of gear as we approached the layby, pulled the handbrake up and was out through the door before the coach stopped!

We were around 40 minutes late and had caused the Cardiff service a delay of about 20 minutes, but knowing Vic, the day was not yet done and no doubt most of that time would have been safely made up before his arrival at Cardiff.

Two months later, in January 1969, I took another Sunday afternoon joyride to Swansea. It was an unforgettable day out, but for all the wrong reasons. I caught the 2:45pm Swansea coach, CTX985C with Bill Phillips and Philip Evans, and came back at 5:15pm, HTG602D with 'Jock' Cross and John Friend. We climbed out of Pyle and as we gathered speed at the top of Stormy Down, a blue Austin 1100 overtook us, then went into a series of swerves, each with increasing severity. The car was all over the road, then mounted the central reservation and crossed the westbound carriageway at the only point where both carriageways run level, before flying into a deep ditch at the far side.

I was sat in the front and, along with Jock, had a grandstand view of it all. Johnny Friend was up the back of the coach. We all jumped out, and signalled other vehicles to stop. Fortunately, a police dog van was one of the first. We then went over to find the three female occupants of the car half in, half out, upside down in the ditch, shocked but mercifully without serious injury. We got them out eventually, then about 15 minutes later police, fire engines and ambulances came, bringing the total number of vehicles on the scene to 10 or 11, including 602.

We ran into Bridgend about 35 minutes late. I was flustered by the experience, which was only to be expected, I suppose. Could I have done better? At least I gave my name as a witness, the only local one, as it happened.

The following day two women constables arrived at my home in a Land Rover and took my statement over a cup of tea. A few months later, I returned home from work to find an official looking brown envelope had arrived. Worryingly, I had been summoned to attend court as a witness in the case of 'SW Police v B Rowe'. Now the odd thing was I had no idea what this was about. I knew of a Brian Rowe, but what had he done and how had I witnessed it? I had to make a nervous phone call to discover the defendant was in fact a Beryl Rowe, who was being prosecuted for dangerous driving following an accident at Stormy Down. The accident of course! But what would I say, and what about Jock, would he be there too?

I looked everywhere for Jock over the next few weeks, as I badly needed a calming voice to tell me 'leave it to me, everything will be ok', but there was no sign of him. On the day of the hearing, I had the day off work and nervously went down to the court, but I found nothing was going on, and there was no sign of a familiar face from the N&C. The case had been adjourned and no-one had told me. When it finally came to trial again I refused to attend, citing some pre-booked holiday as an excuse. I was quite adamant that the Crown wasn't going to waste any more of my time!

I enjoyed the privilege of being a regular passenger from March 1969 until the takeover by the National Bus Company led to N&C's rapid demise during 1971. In the greater scale of it all. It was but a mere flash in time, but it was the swansong of the company and it was an honour to have been there amongst such a 'gallant band of men' - to quote an obituary to the company which appeared in the press at the time.

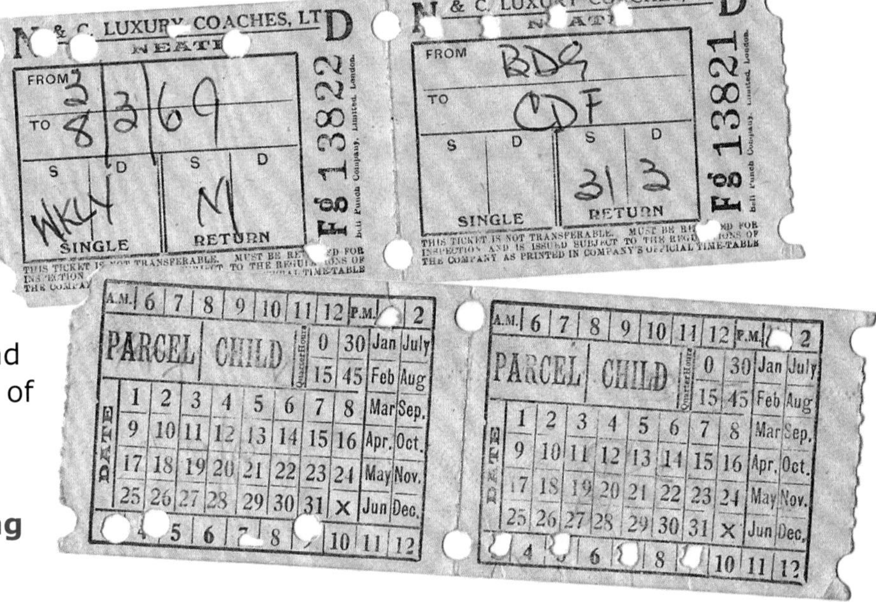

The weekly ticket issued on the author's first working day, 3 March, 1969.

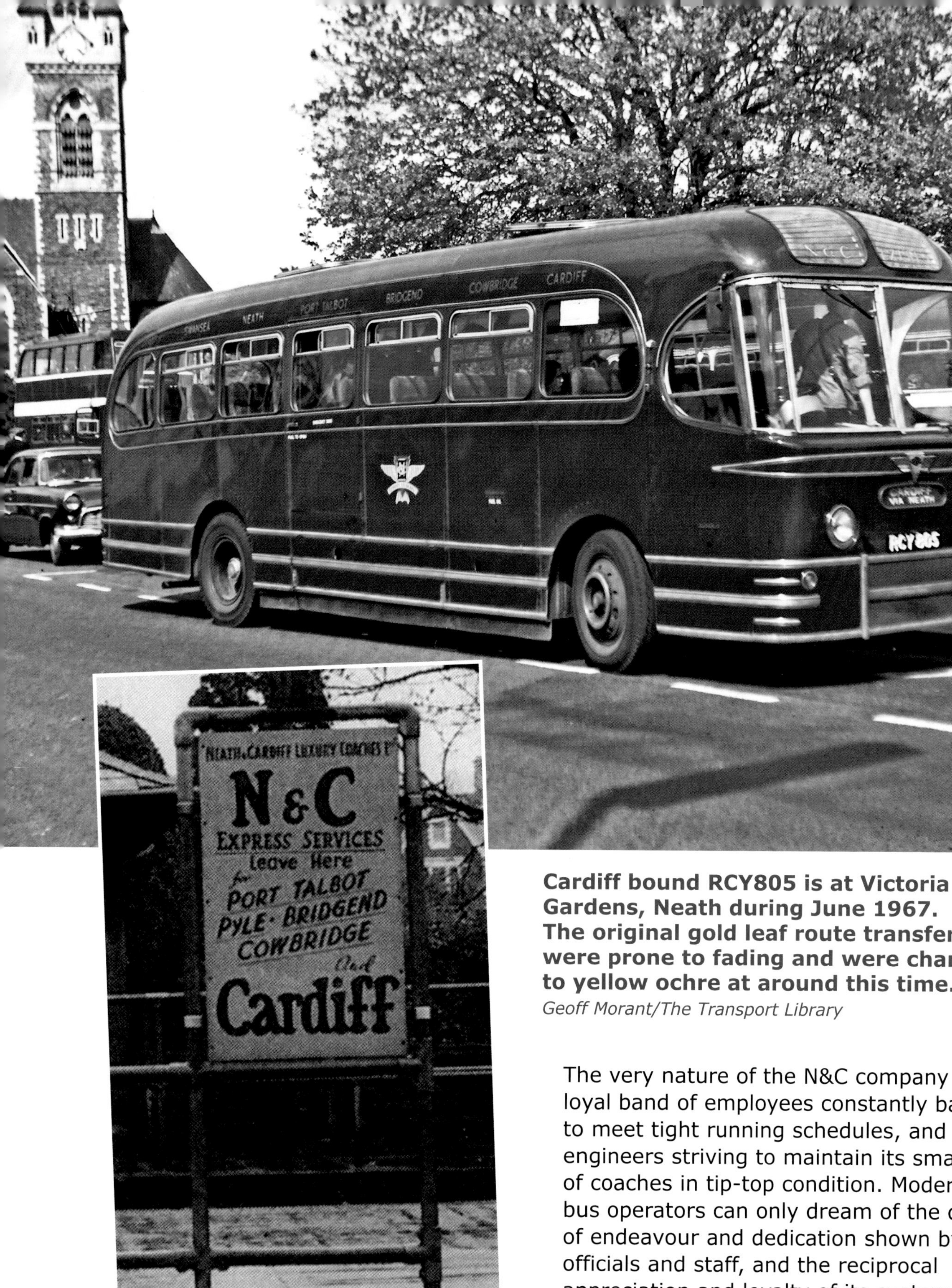

Cardiff bound RCY805 is at Victoria Gardens, Neath during June 1967. The original gold leaf route transfers were prone to fading and were changed to yellow ochre at around this time.
Geoff Morant/The Transport Library

The very nature of the N&C company saw its loyal band of employees constantly battling to meet tight running schedules, and its engineers striving to maintain its small fleet of coaches in tip-top condition. Modern day bus operators can only dream of the degree of endeavour and dedication shown by N&C's officials and staff, and the reciprocal appreciation and loyalty of its customers.

It was a joy to go to work on the N&C and to be in such good company getting there.

The N&C departure board at Victoria Gardens, Neath.

At weekends I would continue travelling for sheer pleasure: Swansea, Cardiff, often both in the same day. I knew most of the road staff and would choose when and where to go depending on who was on duty, or the coach that was on the service. I preferred the newer coaches rather than the classic centre-entrance Guy Arabs and Burlingham-bodied AECs, a fact which is now a major cause of regret.

The newer coaches, in turn, have now also become classics and are a far cry from the vehicles that came along later, whose body styling had all the charm of giant chest freezers — a far cry from the stylish Harringtons, Duples and Plaxtons of the 1960s. Now however, 21st Century styling, and ever-improving vehicle graphics mean that modern coaches are turning heads once again, just as in the days when N&C ruled the road.

The killing-off of such a successful and highly regarded company by its successors appalled and disgusted just about everyone who knew it. In the eyes of the faceless new directors and managers, who were not true busmen, it was pay-back time for all the occasions when they had been shamed and left wanting by this upstart company. They were hell bent on replacing the luxury coaches with slow saloons which would be one-man operated, observe extra stopping places and lengthen journey times. It was totally wrong thinking and an unacceptable replacement which drove away the many loyal regulars, never to return.

Bus operators today can only dream of the degree of endeavour and dedication shown by N&C's officials and staff, and the reciprocal appreciation and loyalty of its customers — something that was evident throughout N&C's life, but now non-existent.

As N&C gained its enviable reputation along the Swansea to Cardiff corridor, the comfort, speed and style of its operations attracted a number of celebrities of the time who were not averse to being seen using its services. It has even been suggested that the celebrity status that the Brown Bombers enjoyed may have been sampled by certain members of the Royal Family. This is impossible to verify, so mention will be made of a mere handful of personalities that were definitely known to have travelled by N&C.

Among these are a number from the world of entertainment. It is said that Shirley Bassey and Bonnie Tyler were just two of the stars that sat on N&C seats on various occasions, albeit in their younger days. Popular Welsh broadcaster and celebrity Roy Noble is another who used the N&C whenever he could. "I lived in Brynamman and during my college days in Cardiff, I caught a South Wales Transport bus and changed at Gwaun-Cae-Gurwen.

THE GUARDIAN, FRIDAY, SEPTEMBER 6, 1957 15

NEATH & CARDIFF
LUXURY COACHES LIMITED

IMPORTANT NOTICE
CHANGE OF BOARDING POINT
AT NEATH

On and after MONDAY, SEPTEMBER 9th, this Company's Services will operate from the

Victoria Gardens Bus Station

The use of Alfred Street as a Boarding Point for Passengers from Neath will be Discontinued

J. J. NEWBURY, M.B.E.,
General Manager.

A newspaper notice proclaiming an up-coming change for the company's passengers boarding at Victoria Gardens, Neath on or after 9 September, 1957.

"This was my 'Check Point Charlie', and from here I would board the Western Welsh limited stop service to Cardiff," recalled Roy. "Sometimes at Neath, I would break the routine by getting off this bus and jumping aboard the N&C for a little more luxury for the long final leg into Cardiff."

Doctor Charles Smith recalled how he had often heard Rhodri Morgan address audiences in Swansea: "He nearly always started with an anecdote about how he and his brother, when young boys, would be sent from Cardiff to Swansea as unaccompanied minors to stay with relatives for a while during the summer holidays. They would, of course, travel on the N&C — via Neath in this case — and the conductor would ensure they alighted by Hole's newsagent's at Morriston Cross. A master politician - creating a warm glow in the home audience, recalling steadier and safer times. I expect he had similarly suitable stories for most districts of Wales, but how significant that he chose the safe and reliable N&C to help him evoke warm memories of Swansea in the not so distant past."

Bus industry tycoon Dawson Williams' name hit the headlines in the 1990s for all the wrong reasons. He had risen to great heights as the colourful boss and major shareholder of British Bus, the UK's largest privately owned bus company, but at the height of his fame got into serious trouble over dubious financial activities. Many people rise to great heights through innovation and a large dose of self-motivation, and Dawson Williams was no exception. His notoriety began in humble surroundings — as a fitter with the N&C.

Mike John remembers him well: "Mr Hot & Cold I called him. Being around him was like treading in a pool of 20/40 engine oil. He was up one minute and down the next, depending what job he was allocated. Dawson was not someone you wanted to upset if at all possible. With a Dolly Parton waist and a coconut mat chest, his great love was weightlifting, which obviously turned him into a very strong spanner man.

An immaculate 231BWN, in original condition with 'dustbin lid' wheel trims and red around the windows, stands proudly in its prime spot at Cardiff's Central bus station, in the mid-1960s.

The experimental fawn and red livery was aimed to provide a separate identity for the tours and charter fleet, and WWN190 was the first vehicle to display this in late 1965. The idea was soon dropped, apparently due to complaints by passengers who failed to recognise their approaching coach when the vehicles were used on normal service. Just as the experiment was abandoned, the three Duple Commander Mk IIs arrived in these colours in April 1966, and looked striking in the already redundant livery. *Gerald Truran/The Omnibus Society*

"His party trick was to sneak up behind one of the apprentices, grab them by the collar and an ankle and do a few overhead bench presses. He would roar with laughter and dump you back down to earth, all embarrassed. We hoped he would turn and fall down the pit!

"One day when I got on his wrong side, he chased me around the garage shouting 'I'll kill you when I catch you, you little so and so!' I hid in the toilet until he calmed down a bit, and Malcolm the coachbuilder warned him off. Half an hour later we were mates again."

It was while at the height of his success in 1997 that Dawson Williams was accused by the Serious Fraud Office and the City of London Police of a number of offences.
He was found to have taken a series of interest-free loans with his former bank manager and was charged with eight counts of alleged or attempted bribery with the aim of obtaining favours for his company.
A figure of £1.2 million was involved.
Upon being charged, he resigned from his position as chairman of British Bus immediately, and was later sentenced to two years in jail for corruption.

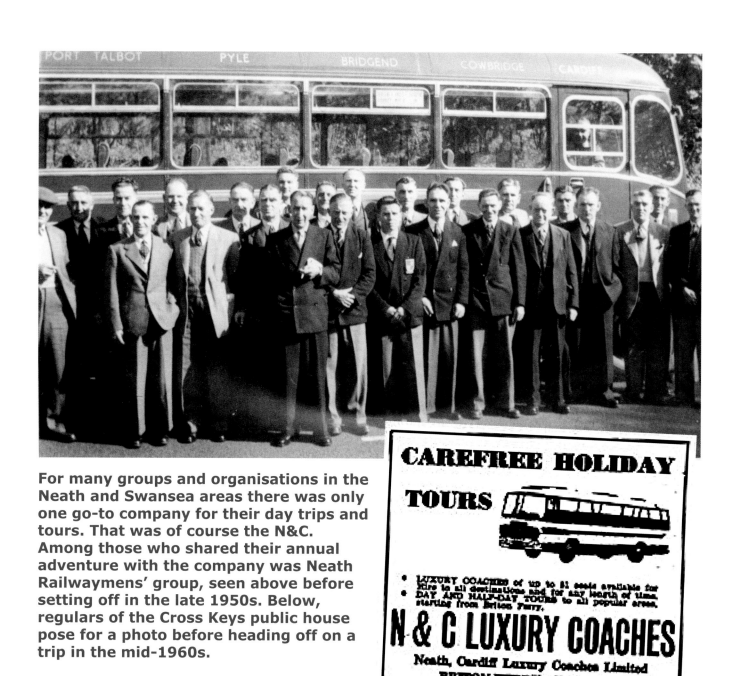

For many groups and organisations in the Neath and Swansea areas there was only one go-to company for their day trips and tours. That was of course the N&C. Among those who shared their annual adventure with the company was Neath Railwaymens' group, seen above before setting off in the late 1950s. Below, regulars of the Cross Keys public house pose for a photo before heading off on a trip in the mid-1960s.

Chapter 11

Away day adventures

As the N&C company began to establish itself on the South Wales passenger transport map it was inevitable that it would at some point engage in private hire and tour operations as a useful way of boosting the revenue it needed to survive and grow.

From the very early days of passenger transport, vehicles had been used to ferry communities on what at the time would have been regarded as adventurous days out. In the earliest such travels the conveyance of people would have often been in open vehicles offering little comfort.

After the cessation of the hostilities of the First World War, servicemen returning home wanted work and a surfeit of lorries that had been used in the conflict combined for a resolution in the form of makeshift passenger carriers. Lorries became buses.

Former War Department vehicles could be bought cheaply and hastily converted with a bus body and rudimentary seats. At the time there was little requirement for licensing and almost anyone could set up a bus service.

The development of charabancs mainly followed the slowly growing demand for private hire vehicles and day tours. Often bus wars would be waged with a no-holds barred ethos between unscrupulous firms on routes where the pickings were rich.

Fortunately all this eased significantly with the passing of the 1930 Transport Act though there were often hints of dubious actions if the tales of many of those early days road staff are to be believed!

After the Second World War which had brought more than five years of hardship and containment for the population, people were desperate to enjoy their freedom and 'getting away from it all' travel exploded.

Private hires boomed as groups, including churches, chapels, streets, friends, social and sports clubs all arranged their own adventures. Works outings went by coach as did groups of pub regulars.

Popular destinations included Gower beaches or outings across the border to places like Weston Super Mare, Gloucester or Hereford. More regularly, destinations such as Barry, Tenby or Porthcawl would be targeted as everyone revelled in their new found and much valued post-war freedom.

Look at any seaside coach park across the region at this time and you would more than likely have spotted an N&C coach among the many others visible. Days out by coach had become a way of life for a large proportion of the population.

By the early 1950s, N&C which had carefully capitalised on the trend as it unfolded had built up a highly profitable and thriving private hire and tours business. All the tours had to be registered and as a result a list of popular destinations and routes was published, and widely advertised in local newspapers which informed potential day trippers of what was on offer and also provided ideas for private hire organisers.

Lots of people will recollect heading off for the day to some exciting destination aboard an N&C luxury coach. Some will recall returning to N&C year after year for their own special day out. Others among them would have become fans of the company's short breaks which took them further and lasted longer, often three or four days.

Many group leaders preferred to choose the N&C for all their outings because they knew they would receive the best treatment, from coach to accommodation, and often with a regular driver who would be treated like one of their own. Regular customers included choirs, among them the Morriston Orpheus Choir; sports clubs, including Cimla Cricket Club, Neath, which even preferred the same coach each time and of course, my own personally arranged day trips during the final years of this unique company. For me, they, more than any other, always produced memorable moments and demonstrated why many of those arranging trips specifically asked for certain vehicles and specific drivers.

In the late 1950s, Linda Feltham lived in Cimla and recalled some of her neighbours running trips to the Gower beaches on sunny summertime Sundays.

"Bank Holidays would mean trips further afield, and this would mean a full day to Tenby. We would watch for the coach coming into our road, and always used to hope that it would be the N&C one that came along, and it was. Memorable days!"

Phil Williams meanwhile, recalled a childhood holiday that brought a surprise but familiar twist: "My parents loved Scotland for our annual holidays," he said.

"One year, in the early 1960s, we were staying in the Deeside Hotel in Ballater, in the Scottish Highlands. It was a lovely summer Sunday evening in this quiet village. We had just finished our evening meal and were sitting in Church Square waiting to see the Queen's Dragoon Guards bagpipe band march through the village, when way in the distance a familiar droning sound broke the still air. I hadn't realised I was attuned at that age to the music of a diesel engine. Suddenly I jumped up and exclaimed: 'There's an N&C coming!' I was told not to be so silly, but a few minutes later two Brown Bomber Guy Arabs, LCY781 and KCY489, with a party of holidaymakers aboard swept into the square and glided to a smooth stop outside the Glenaden Hotel.

"My parent's faces were a picture as I strolled over to the coaches. The drivers were first out to attend to the luggage and when they saw me standing there I was greeted with comments such as 'What the hell are you doing up here? You're going to

> **"I really loved going to Swansea on the N&C coaches. Those were the best years."**
> ***Nicola Carter Wells***

be late for school in the morning!' I took a photo of the pair of coaches parked there in the evening sun, but I don't remember ever seeing the developed print. Such a shame really, I wish I had that photo now of the two Guys, so far from home.

"From memory, I only ever saw one other N&C coach outside Wales, and that was in 1969 when I was working for the Borg Warner company at Kenfig, near Port Talbot. Their head office was in Letchworth in Hertfordshire and I travelled there to meet the engineering department staff. As I left the office at 1:30pm, I was met by a line of coaches from Stevenage Travel bringing in the afternoon shift, and there in the line was Guy Arab LCY782, but now in Stevenage Travel's livery. It was like seeing a long-lost friend, and I recall thinking how much smarter she had looked when painted brown and red."

Robert Thomas played cricket for Cimla and recalls the team charters to Ebbw Vale in September 1969 and August 1970, when HTG601D was provided for both trips. Also, in August 1970, they enjoyed a four-day tour of Devon based in Barnstaple, and on this occasion RRC238 was the coach supplied.

One of the more unusual contracts the company was awarded was that of the rail replacement service between Cymmer Afan and Treherbert, when geological conditions forced the closure of the Rhondda railway tunnel under the Bwlch mountain in the late 1960s.

The contract, which was originally awarded to Thomas Bros (Port Talbot), required coaches to meet the trains either side of the mountain, and whilst the train would have run through the tunnel in just a few minutes, the coaches had to tackle the mountain pass which took a lot longer and would become particularly treacherous in bad weather.

It was usual to find the oldest vehicles were used on this contract, in complete contrast to what one may expect today where rail replacement vehicles are needed. It was perhaps a wise move by the company, knowing that it was a very steep and winding route that climbed to 1,476ft.
This placed a huge demand on the coaches. Collisions were not uncommon on the twisting road, and the railway guards, who had to ride on the service, were not the most calm and relaxed of passengers!

On one occasion I was invited to take time off and spend a summer's day on the mountain service, and bitterly regret that I never did take advantage of the offer.

Driver John Hughes and a BR Guard await the next diesel railcar at Cymmer Afan station in 1968, during operation of the N&C's Rhondda Tunnel rail replacement service. This ran over the Bwlch mountain road, and could be a hair-raising journey in bad weather.
John Hughes

Former Trent Motor Traction Weymann Fanfare RRC238 has received a fresh coat of paint and is awaiting a call for relief work at Swansea, 15 July, 1970. *Robert Thomas*

SWANSEA EXPRESS SERVICE CARDIFF

N. & C. LUXURY COACH

Manager :
D. N. FLOWER

NEATH & CARDIFF
LUXURY COACHES LTD.
BRITON FERRY, NEATH, GLAM.
Telephone : BRITON FERRY 3393/4 (2 lines)

Directors :
B. GRIFFITHS, (C
J. T. E. ROBIN
Sir JOHN GUTCH, K.
G. CARRUTF
R. C. HILTO

18th April, 1969.

RJG/GMJ.

Mr. C. Scott,
"Fort Erie",
32 Jubilee Road,
BRIDGEND.

Dear Sir,

We thank you for your esteemed enquiry of the 15t
1969, and our price for a 51 seater coach from Briton
Woburn Abbey, proceeding via Porthcawl and Bridgend, i
The suggested route would be via Gloucester, Oxford Py
Aylesbury and Leighton Buzzard. Travel time should b
approximately five hours each way and we estimate the
mileage to be approximately 360 miles. It would be r
for us to provide two drivers on this occasion.

Should our quotation be acceptable we shall be p
make a firm booking.

Yours faithfully,
p.p. N. & C. LUXURY COACHES LTD.,

R. J. Gallanders,
Traffic Superintendent.

It could be reasoned perhaps that the N&C was like a travelling repertory company. Wherever they were appearing, for every performance, the theatre-goers took to their seats and watched the plot unfold centre stage. The cast would vary; sometimes there was a stand-in, and sometimes there was a twist in the plot that differed from the previous performance. And there was always without fail, a liberal sprinkling of ad-libbing.

In my case, using a similar analogy, it was an honour to occasionally be invited back-stage, not only to the dressing room of the stars themselves — the coaches in the garage — but to that magic place where the production team, from directors to stage hands, made sure the show was ready to hit the road. One peep here and you'd instantly realise the characters that lurked there were just as flamboyant as the leading players!

Many regular passengers looked upon the N&C family as familiar friends. They acknowledged each other in the nicest way, and looked out for each other at all times. There were a great many people who, like me, were accepted into the fold and taken under their wing. You felt safe, valued and ppreciated — an unforgettable time.

During 1969 and 1970, I hired N&C coaches myself. They were trips for the youth club, the school model railway club and anyone else I could find to help fill the coach. I finished school at that time and, having embarked on a career in local government, was enjoying a daily commute to Cardiff by — you've guessed! — N&C coach.

I could think of nothing better to do with my weekends than to carry on riding, but to somewhere a little further afield than Cardiff. I kept doing it with alarming frequency: my

SWANSEA EXPRESS SERVICE CARDIFF

N. & C. LUXURY COACHES

Manager :
D. N. FLOWER

NEATH & CARDIFF
LUXURY COACHES LTD.
BRITON FERRY, NEATH, GLAM.
Telephone : BRITON FERRY 3393/4 (2 lines)

Directors :
B. GRIFFITHS, (Chairman)
J. T. E. ROBINSON
Sir JOHN GUTCH, K.C.M.G., O.B.E.
G. CARRUTHERS
R. C. HILTON

RJG/GMJ.

5th May, 1969.

C. Scott, Esq.,
"Fort Erie",
32 Jubilee Road,
BRIDGEND.

Dear Sir,

re: Party P.46.

We thank you for your letter of the 30th April, 1969, confirming that you will be boarding our coach at approximately 0720 on Saturday, 24th May, 1969, on the occasion of your outing to Woburn Abbey. Mr. S. Bowen will be your driver and arrangements will be made for Mr. V. Greenwood to be picked up at Cardiff and act as co-driver.

Yours faithfully,
p.p. N. & C. LUXURY COACHES LTD.,

R. J. Gallanders,
Traffic Superintendent.

SWANSEA EXPRESS SERVICE CARDIFF

N. & C. LUXURY COACHES

TELEPHONE: BRITON FERRY 3393/4 (2 LINES)
TELEGRAMS: NELUXCO

NEATH AND CARDIFF LUXURY COACHES LTD. — HEAD OFFICE: BRITON FERRY
SOUTH WALES

ALL COMMUNICATIONS TO
BRITON FERRY

GENERAL MANAGER:
~~J. J. NEWBURY, M.B.E.~~
F.A.J. WOODWORTH

DIRECTORS:
~~W. M. DRAVERS, M. INST. T. (Chairman)~~
~~Col. Sir GODFREY LLEWELLYN, Bart., C.B., C.B.E., M.C., T.D., D.L., J.P.~~
~~Sir JOHN GUTCH, K.C.M.G., O.B.E.~~
~~T. V. WOODS, C.B.E.~~
~~F. K. POINTON, M. INST. T.~~

13th April 1970

Mr C. Scott,
Fort Erie,
32 Jubilee Road,
Bridgend,
Glam

Inspector F. CROSS
Traffic Office.

Dear Sir/~~Madam~~,

We thank you for your esteemed enquiry and have pleasure in submitting the following quotation for your consideration :

From ..... Bridgend
TO ..... Cheddar & Longleat House
via ..... Severn Bridge
.....
..... as per itinerary
on ..... day ..... July 1970
at the nett price of £ ..... 34 ..... per ..... 41 seater coach.
40 per 51 Seater Coach

This quotation is subject to the coach/es being available at the time confirmation of your acceptance is received.

We shall be grateful for an early reply, and would assure you of our best service at all times.

Yours faithfully,
p.p N. & C. Luxury Coaches, Ltd.

F Cross

For. TRAFFIC SUPERINTENDENT.

Cost would be 17/6 per Head. This would allow 2 free seats per 41 Seater Coach and up to [illegible] seats on a 51 Seater Coach

FC

secret was this: once those kids were aboard, I grabbed their pocket money as a deposit for the next trip!

Looking back, these hires were incredibly frequent and so were never big money spinners, but I was painfully aware that the writing was on the wall for the legendary N&C company. They were extremely happy days, albeit a bit of a worry in case no-one turned up, but I never paid more than £50 for a coach and driver for the day. If I occasionally had to top up the takings from my newly found salary, so what? It was a small price to pay for all these wonderful, unforgettable memories. But how I wish I'd had a better camera and could have afforded more film! Many of the photos that I did think to take have not stood the test of time.

The precious few I took were square format snapshots gained with a Kodak Instamatic.

Alan Old, my travelling buddy, had a Halina and took colour slides, but they were slow rated Agfa transparencies, and when we reunited many years later I was horrified to find they had been thrown in an old shoe box, and were scratched and faded. Even when scanned and enhanced they are still of questionable quality, as are those that originated from a number of other friends whose photo skills were worse than mine!

Some 50 years on, they bear no comparison to the hi-res digital files of today, often taken by phone, but for historic reasons they remain priceless statements of a bygone period in time.

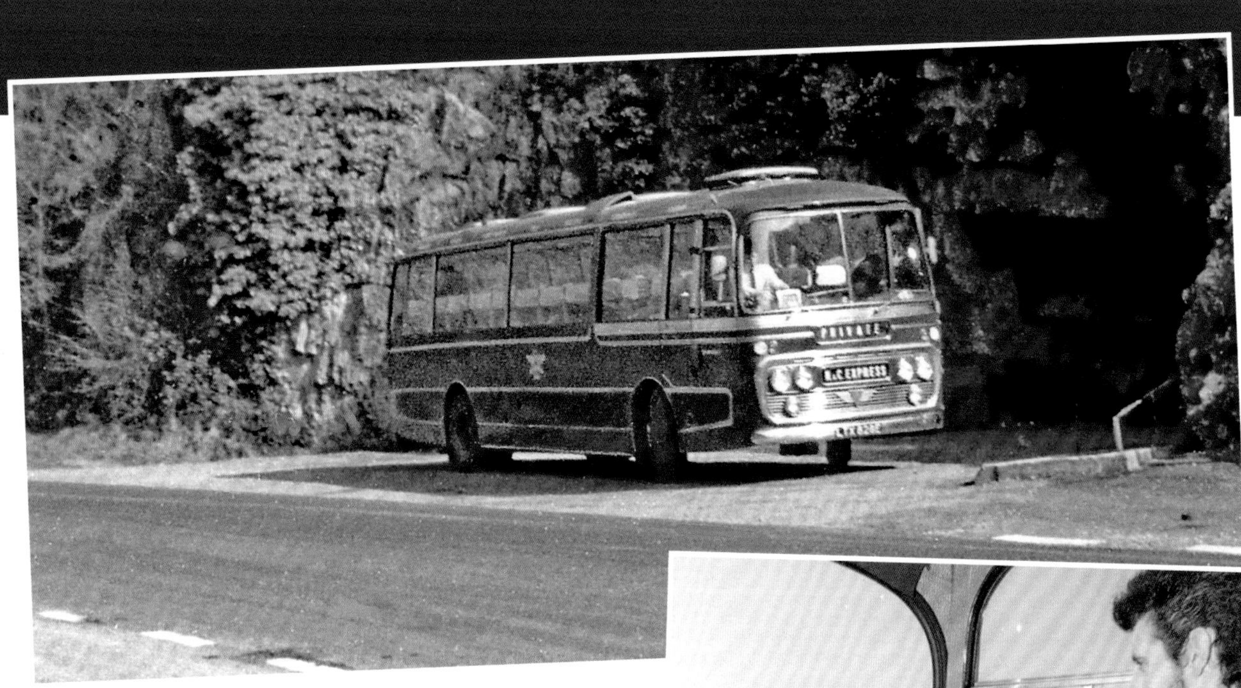

Tour No. 1 | 22 February 1969

Bath and Swindon
Driver: Selwyn Bowen
Coach: HTG600D Cost: £25

Regrettably, there is precious little to serve as a memento of my first trip. I was about to leave school and only just made it to my own meeting to announce the excursion, following a surprise call to an interview at Glamorgan County Council in Cardiff. Once again N&C saved the day! The party consisted mainly of members of Bridgend Boys' Grammar School's Model Railway Club, of which I was Chairman. Our destination was the GWR Museum, at that time housed in a former chapel at Swindon's Railway Village.

At the start of all my trips I cajoled one of my parents into chauffeuring me, together with specially invited guests, to Briton Ferry to squeeze every possible mile of N&C-derived pleasure that the day ahead would bring. On this auspicious occasion, for some unknown reason, I left my camera at home.

We first called at Bath, then went on to Swindon for the museum. We returned to pick up those who chose to spend the day at Bath, and just as we left, the front nearside tyre popped. It was changed at Bristol Omnibus Company's Brislington depot, but the following week Selwyn reported that the fitters there had replaced our radial tyre with a cross-ply. We thought it strange when 600 decided to roam across both lanes of the M4 as we rounded the bend on the descent at St Julians, Newport. The needle was a quarter of an inch off the clock at the time, so we must have been exceeding 80mph!

Selwyn Bowen at the wheel of LTX828E and above, preparing to leave Cheddar.

My diary noted: "Selwyn persuaded us to return later, so we eventually got back just over an hour late. Marks cut himself and Hughes fell into the Roman Baths, but apart from that all was well."

Tales of touring times

Tour No. 2 | 22 March 1969

Cheddar and Weston-super-Mare
Driver: Selwyn Bowen
Coach: LTX 828E Cost: £31

On arrival at Cheddar I was with my mate Alan Old and we sat in the cafe talking — about girls, naturally, while the rest of the party visited the caves. When everyone returned we continued to Weston-super-Mare on the premise of visiting the Model Village.

I took my 'Another Coach by Plaxtons' poster from one of the new Elites, given to me by Gerald Truran, but sadly I left it behind, still in the rear screen as I left the coach at Bryntirion when we headed home and watched it disappear into the night.

West House dip, Bridgend, on my 'Mystery Trip' to Woburn Abbey.

Tour No.3 | 24 May 1969

Oxford and Woburn Abbey
Drivers: Selwyn Bowen/Vic Greenwood
Coach: UNY832G Cost: £50

This trip was the biggest hire I ever undertook. The mileage was so great that we needed two drivers. Today it's incredible to think that at £50 it was also the most expensive. I advertised it as a Mystery Tour, so nobody knew what they were letting themselves in for!

Our first pick-up was at West House Dip, Bridgend. The tour guide was Gary Craddock. Note my trusty transistor radio, on the driver's side of the dashboard, always a must on our trips! Next came Bridgend Bus Station, where we always took advantage of N&C's stand 18 to pick up!

The service coach pulled up alongside and its crew — driver Jim Boucher and conductor Alan Williams — were keen to come aboard as our coach was only a couple of months old. Our co-driver Vic Greenwood joined at Ely, and we were all madly in love with Marge, his stunning partner.

Jim Boucher in the driving seat of UNY832G, the latest coach.

Tour No.4 | 27 September 1969

Bristol
Driver: Selwyn Bowen
Coach: HTG600D Cost: £24

The first photo taken on this day was of Selwyn Bowen and Brian Metcalfe the depot

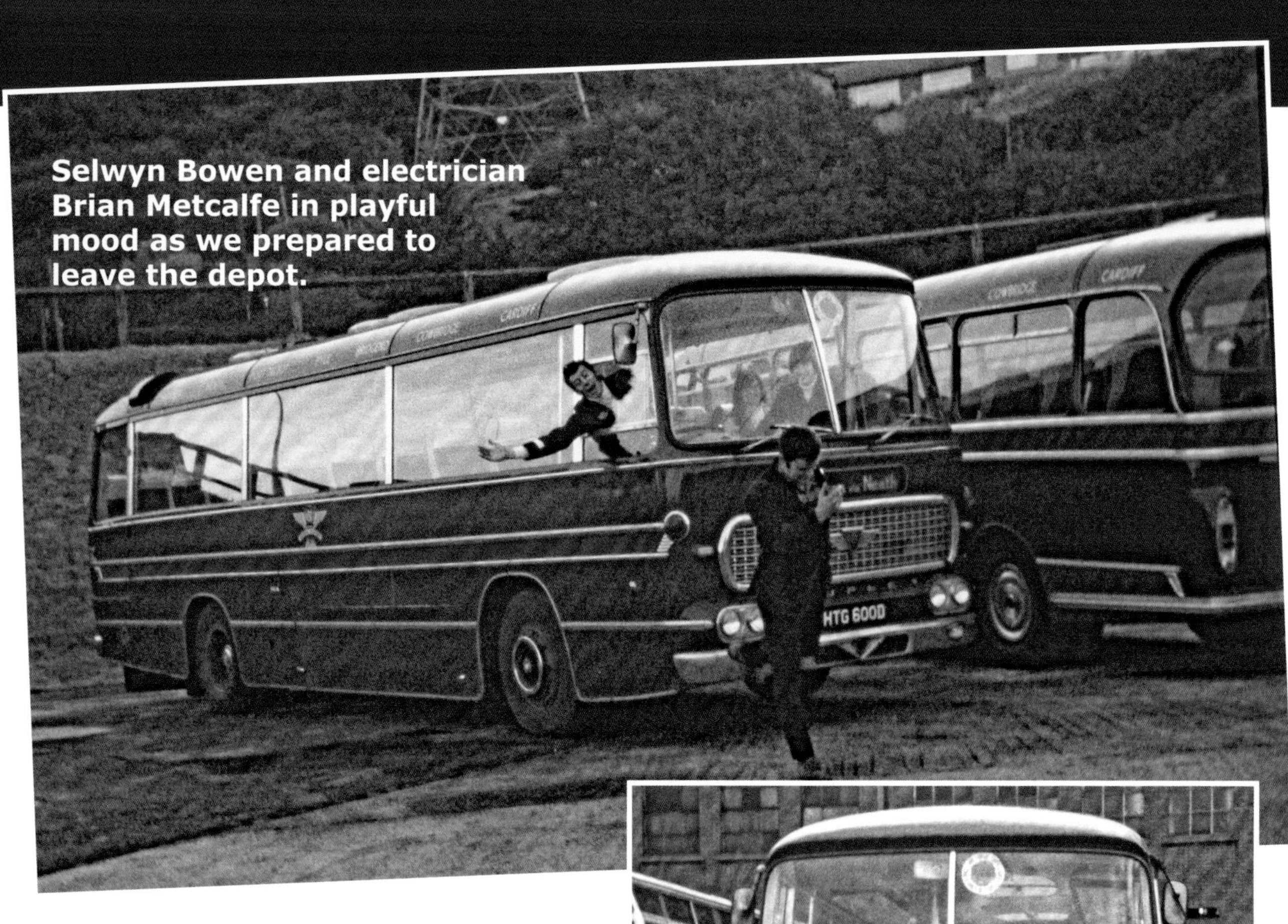

Selwyn Bowen and electrician Brian Metcalfe in playful mood as we prepared to leave the depot.

electrician, playfully posing for Alan Old's lens as we prepare to depart the garage. The Longleat sticker was from an earlier tour, and who were we to remove it? The second photo was taken on arrival at Bristol and shows Selwyn, his wife Marlene, and yours truly at the coach park in Anchor Road. I am enjoying a Manikin cigar – smoking a cigar was a far more acceptable thing to do in those days, and besides, it was Selwyn Bowen's trademark — and anything Selwyn did, we hero-worshipped!

Selwyn, his wife Marlene and myself at Anchor Road, Bristol.

Tour No.5 | 17 January 1970

Bristol
Driver: Selwyn Bowen
Coach: UNY 831G Cost: £24

This was the most poorly patronised of all my trips, and (maybe for that reason) very little record of it remains. The photograph is at Aust Services, which we called the 'Motorport' in those days and always played host to us if we were crossing the Bridge.

It seems I have found the switches for all but one of the front lights, and proudly displayed in the windscreen is my N&C winged motif that came from one of the Guy Arabs, LCY783, courtesy of Gerald Truran.

I'm not sure where our meagre crowd went, but our select little gang climbed the Cabot tower and attempted to keep warm in cafes. Selwyn again brought his wife Marlene and

Tales of touring times

The N&C winged badge in the windscreen was from Guy Arab LCY783 which by this time was the mascot on our trips.

niece Julie, who was timid on the forward journey, but was the life and soul on our return journey home.

We usually brought with us some blue crepe paper which we taped over the interior lights to give a nightclub effect coming back.

With less than 20 passengers, it was a trip best forgotten. But what was the best thing to do when a trip is a failure? Organise another one, straight away of course!

Tour No.6 | 7 March 1970

Bourton on the Water
Driver: Selwyn Bowen
Coach: PTX 830F Cost: £30

Before setting off we went to Selwyn Bowen's home in Skewen, where we called to collect a silver N&C cap badge which I wore on my lapel and treasured enormously. Gary Craddock and Phil Williams, my assistant tour managers congratulated themselves on choosing the finest way to spend their day. On arrival at a snowy Bourton-on-the-Water, Selwyn Bowen courageously protected N&C property from a deluge of snowballs from some unruly passengers! Our vehicle was covered in a layer of road salt and at this time of year was the sole occupant of the coach park at this beautiful Cotswold village.

My sixth outing was probably my best and took PTX830F to Bourton-on-the-Water.

Tales of touring times

Trusty PTX830F at Bourton-on-the-Water looking a little worse for wear after ploughing through roads covered in snow and slush that day.

The trip turned out to be my favourite of all those I organised. We picked up as usual at Bridgend Bus Station, then boldly drove into Cardiff's Central bus station. By this time, I had been working in Cardiff for a year and some of my colleagues from the office wanted to come along. Everything went well and they had a great day. We had a pleasant drive through Chepstow and Lydney, then had a head-on encounter with the local hunt at Andoversford. The coach was surrounded by dozens of excited hounds for several minutes.

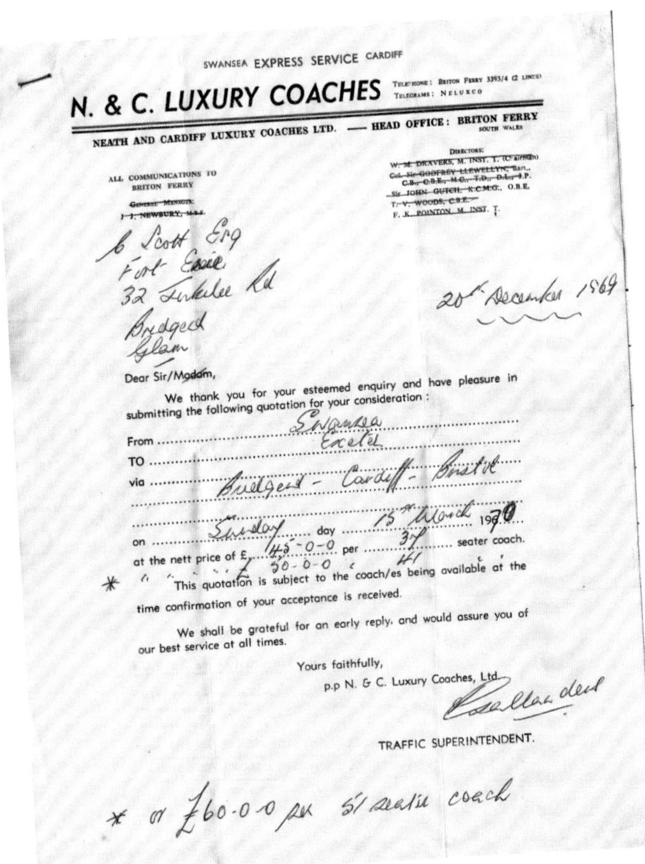

SWANSEA EXPRESS SERVICE CARDIFF

N. & C. LUXURY COACHES

TELEPHONE: BRITON FERRY 3393/4 (2 LINES)
TELEGRAMS: NELUXCO

NEATH AND CARDIFF LUXURY COACHES LTD. — HEAD OFFICE: BRITON FERRY SOUTH WALES

ALL COMMUNICATIONS TO BRITON FERRY

General Manager:
J. J. NEWBURY, M.B.E.

Directors:
W. M. DRAVERS, M. INST. T. (Chairman)
Col. Sir GODFREY LLEWELLYN, Bart., C.B., C.B.E., M.C., T.D., D.L., J.P.
Sir JOHN GUTCH, K.C.M.G., O.B.E.
T. V. WOODS, C.B.E.
F. K. POINTON, M. INST. T.

C Scott Esq
Fort Essie
32 Jubilee Rd
Bridgend
Glam

20th December 1969

Dear Sir/Madam,

We thank you for your esteemed enquiry and have pleasure in submitting the following quotation for your consideration :

From Swansea
TO Exeter
via Bridgend - Cardiff - Bristol

on Sunday day 15th March 1970

at the nett price of £ 45-0-0 per 37 seater coach.

* " " " £ 50-0-0 " 41 " "

This quotation is subject to the coach/es being available at the time confirmation of your acceptance is received.

We shall be grateful for an early reply, and would assure you of our best service at all times.

Yours faithfully,
p.p N. & C. Luxury Coaches, Ltd.
Gallanders
TRAFFIC SUPERINTENDENT.

* or £60-0-0 per 51 seater coach

The quotation for a proposed trip to Exeter for 15 March 1970. Instead we decided to visit Bourton-on-the-Water on the previous Saturday.

It was a great trip with everyone happy throughout. Selwyn spent the whole of the return journey singing, and we had a brief stop for chips at Gloucester. Returning to Bridgend around 11pm we were halted at the Embassy Bridge as a mass brawl rolled into town from the Palais de Danse, gathering momentum like a rugby scrum through Dunraven Place and up Market Street, where we stopped in the middle of the road and didn't let anyone off until the crowd had dispersed onto their various last buses and everything had quietened down.

Tour No.7 | 26 July 1970

Cheddar and Longleat
Driver: Selwyn Bowen
Coach: CTX 986C Cost: £40

We were allocated 986, the oldest coach we were ever given, and not normally used for private hire. We thought we were hard done by at the time, but looking back now, Mr Gallanders, the Traffic Superintendent, was no doubt playing safe as those monkeys

Regular driver Selwyn Bowen at Cheddar on 26 July 1970. We always altered the destination blind to Bridgend Only on our trips, as we felt our home town needed all the publicity it could get in those days!

climbed everywhere, poking their arms through the skylights, and could easily have wrecked the coach. The animals at Longleat were no better! I felt a pang of pride when 986 turned up twice for my journey to work the following week with its 'We've seen the lions of Longleat' sticker still prominently displayed in the windscreen!

Selwyn Bowen is seen above looking moody on the step of 986 at Cheddar in this, the only photograph of any relevance taken on the day. I'm not really sure why we chose to return to Cheddar, other than maybe to see the pretty girl who served coffee in the café.

This trip took place on a Sunday, a first for us as all the others were on a Saturday. This happened to be our only really wet day, which was a shame as 986's steamed-up windows prevented full enjoyment of the scenic drive through the animal compounds.

Two young ladies accompanied us on this trip, Michelle and Jayne, and the former took a shine to Selwyn and sat on the steps coming back, until she was knocked senseless by the heavy pivoting bar which served as the driver's door handle, and swung open unexpectedly. I ended up walking both girls home that night – well you have to be careful after a knock on the head!

SWANSEA EXPRESS SERVICE CARDIFF

N. & C. LUXURY COACHES

NEATH & CARDIFF
LUXURY COACHES LTD.
BRITON FERRY, NEATH, GLAM.
Telephone : BRITON FERRY 3393/4 (2 lines)

DIRECTORS :
B. GRIFFITHS (CHAIRMAN)
G. CARRUTHERS
SIR JOHN GUTCH
J. T. E. ROBINSON
F. PATERSON

RJG/NS.

Mr. C. Scott,
"Fort Erie",
32, Jubilee Road,
BRIDGEND.

5th, February, 1970.

Dear Sir,

We thank you for your esteemed enquiry of the 30th January and are pleased to quote you a price of £30. 0. 0. for a 41 seater coach and £38. 0. 0d. for a 51 seater coach for your tour to Bourton-On-The-Water. on Saturday 7th March. If our quotation is acceptable, we shall be pleased to make a firm booking and arrange for Mr. S. Bowen to be your driver.

Yours faithfully,
p.p. N.&.C. LUXURY COACHES LTD.,

R. J. GALLANDERS.
DISTRICT TRAFFIC SUPERINTENDENT.

A letter from Traffic Superintendent Ron Gallanders in connection with my third private hire booking.

Tour No.8 | 20 March 1971

Wye Valley and Cheltenham
Driver: Alan Williams
Coach: UNY 832G Cost: £39.15s

By this time, the N&C fleet and staff had transferred from Briton Ferry to the South Wales Transport depot at Clarence Terrace in Swansea. Many took this opportunity to seek work elsewhere, and Selwyn was one of them. SWT wasted no time in painting 832 into their coach livery, and she looked nice on the day of our eighth trip. With Selwyn gone, I requested the newly-qualified driver Alan 'Concorde' Williams, whose friendship had started when he was a conductor on my commuter runs. He was very pleased to be given such a prestige job!

> **The fastest I drove was 93mph and that was on the last service back to Neath, with nothing on the road.**
> ***Jim Boucher***

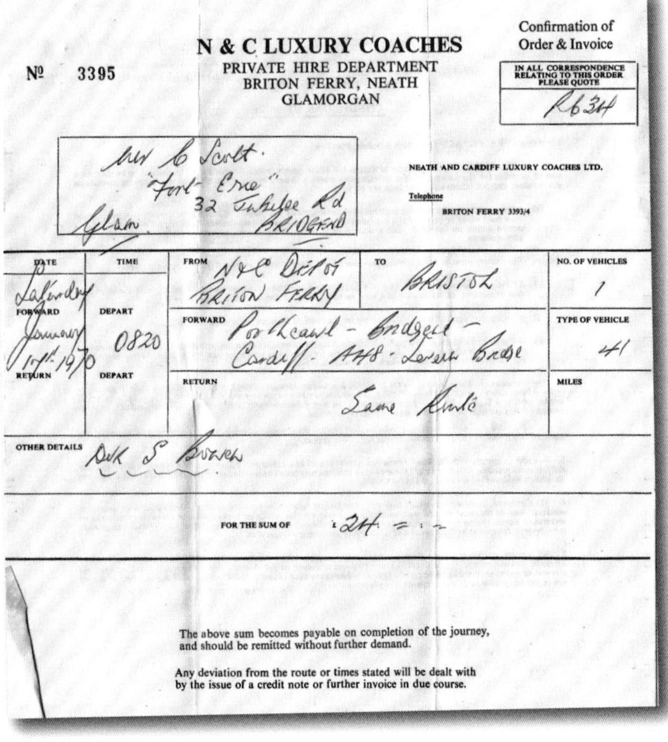

N & C LUXURY COACHES
PRIVATE HIRE DEPARTMENT
BRITON FERRY, NEATH
GLAMORGAN

Confirmation of Order & Invoice

Nº 3395

IN ALL CORRESPONDENCE RELATING TO THIS ORDER PLEASE QUOTE: R634

Mr C Scott. "Fort Erie" 32 Jubilee Rd BRIDGEND Glam

NEATH AND CARDIFF LUXURY COACHES LTD.
Telephone BRITON FERRY 3393/4

DATE	TIME	FROM	TO	NO. OF VEHICLES
Saturday		N&C Depot Briton Ferry	Bristol	1
FORWARD January 10th 1970	DEPART 0820	FORWARD Porthcawl - Bridgend - Cardiff - A48 - Severn Bridge		TYPE OF VEHICLE 41
RETURN	DEPART	RETURN Same Route		MILES

OTHER DETAILS: Dick S Bowen

FOR THE SUM OF £24 = : -

The above sum becomes payable on completion of the journey, and should be remitted without further demand.

Any deviation from the route or times stated will be dealt with by the issue of a credit note or further invoice in due course.

I cherish a picture I have that shows 832 (as SWT 173) leaving the abandoned Briton Ferry depot, where we pulled into the yard, and I like to think we were the last coach ever to leave this special place.

Alan Old, Phil Williams and Peter Cunningham had come down with me to Swansea to begin the day. The Black & White company's coach station at Cheltenham was in decline by this time, as the Severn Bridge and the M5 motorway had reduced the need for this once important interchange and hub for the Associated Motorways network.

Whilst my seventh trip was the last of the true N&C hires, No. 8 qualified in a way. But then things really changed. I ran a few more trips in the early 1970s, with the coaches and drivers coming from Morris Bros (Swansea), where Selwyn then worked. There were two trips to London, one to Symonds Yat & Cheltenham, and yet another to Bristol.

My requests to have Selwyn as driver were not always successful; Mr Henson at Morris Bros would instead send him off elsewhere at short notice, and I would get an apologetic phone call the night before, not from Henson but from Selwyn, who had just been informed of his change of duty. This resulted in the trips becoming less fun and eventually the coach hires ceased.

I was a driver myself by then, and so I hit on the idea of hiring 12-seater Transits or Bedford minibuses for self-drive trips.

The destination of these mini-adventures included Oxford, Worcester and the Wye Valley. It was the closest to becoming a coach driver that I was ever to get. Pleasant as they were, these trips never matched the thrill and spectacle of the N&C hires that sadly were now consigned to history.

The confirmation note for one of our Bristol trips.

Chapter 12

Days in a diary

There have been many great diarists throughout history and their jottings have played a big part in colouring our modern day views of events during times ranging from the mundane and everyday to the spectacular.

Keeping a diary is something that I chose to do during my formative years when my passion ranged from most forms of transport to discovering the various other pleasures associated with youth.

Little did I realise as I documented my adventures and exploits with the Brown Bombers that many years later it would prove most helpful in taking me on a nostalgic excursion down memory lane.

They say that if you can remember the Sixties, you weren't really there, but writing it down at the time has certainly helped clarify matters some 50 years later! Reading my notes revealed many interesting and amusing tales, particularly in the years up to and including the change of decade.

In the early days my diary-keeping was sporadic, to say the least, and dealt mainly with life at school in Bridgend. But 1969 was a milestone year in many different ways. I was 17 in January. By March, I was in full time employment with Glamorgan County Council in Cardiff and thoroughly enjoying the daily commute by my beloved N&C luxury coaches, as well as the social contact that came with it.

Those were memorable days in so many ways. The excellent service the N&C provided had yet to turn sour under the clutches of the National Bus Company. The writing may have been on the wall, but in the eyes of us passengers, things carried on just as they'd always done. We just felt a few hints from time to time that there were changes on the horizon. Scrutiny of extracts from my diary that follow will offer clues that there was much to take in, particularly during 1969. Changes didn't really hit us until 1970, and when they came, they were for the worse. It was a true transport tragedy for us all.

1967 - Memories are made of this - 1970

Tuesday 8 August 1967

Thrilled to see one of N&C's splendid Plaxton Panoramas, rare on daily service. LTX828E appeared in the evening.

Saturday 9 December 1967

A blizzard during the night resulted in chaos at bus station with LTX829E, 231BWN and TWN557 there, going nowhere at 10am. Ridiculous bringing a Plaxton out in such conditions! Cleared up pm so went to Cardiff and back on 231BWN. Good driver, good journey. 3281WB smashed and abandoned in the snow at St Nicholas."

Thursday 21 December 1967

WWN190 repainted. It seems the fawn and red N&C livery has fallen from favour.

Saturday 6 January 1968

Trips on the N&C becoming a common pastime now. An afternoon trip to Cardiff in RCY 804. Had that good N&C driver (Selwyn Bowen) and the English 'Alfred Marks' type conductor (John Friend). Very good journey up and fast journey back in 191. They all seem to go down the inner by-pass now.

Wednesday 17 January 1968

Selwyn Bowen had become a figure of hero worship. Peter Jones, a younger lad living nearby happened to be the grandson of Senior Inspector Mick Williams, and shared our admiration for this Jason King look-alike. My best friend Gary and I soon befriended Peter. It quickly reaped benefits with much-needed inside info on the N&C. Selwyn now familiar to me and Gary.

Friday 26 January 1968

Evening observations: HTG602D repainted into brown. 557 broken down at Bridgend, left 25 minutes late.

Saturday 27 January 1968

Made N&C game in afternoon. We had a three-hour non-stop game from 7pm to 10pm. Great fun! (I had devised a board game based on the N&C. Players spun a disc to select driver, conductor, turn of duty and coach, then raced up and down a diagrammatic route map to the throw of the dice. The coaches were made of balsa and there were hazards en-route, just like the real thing: bottlenecks, delays and accidents; then inspectors and speed cops to look out for. It occupied us for hours and went through several revisions.)

Saturday 3 February 1968

Home rugby international at Cardiff. Great day for N&C with almost every coach including HTG601D on the road. It was the last in the fawn and red livery and normally kept back for private hire. Mainly running in threes to Cardiff and twos to Swansea.

Monday 12 February 1968

Peter Jones, Mick Williams' grandson, continued to enthral us with his inside information. Peter told us that N&C's new coach is PTX830F which had arrived on the 1st of the month.

Monday 19 February 1968

Saw Selwyn in 567ECY. Driving very slowly. Most unusual.

Wednesday 21 February 1968

An N&C day out: Bridgend-Cardiff-Bridgend-Swansea-Bridgend, recording all movements. First went down bus station to catch coach to Cardiff. Decided to make a day of it and it went as follows:

11:00 Bridgend – Cardiff 11:45 232BWN with Chris Shylon/Twiggy;

13:30 Cardiff – Bridgend 14:15: CTX986C with Doug Thomas/Herbie Gibbon;

14:45 Bridgend – Briton Ferry 15:20: HTG602D with Tom Jones/Bill Collier - 602 had a problem so we went into depot. Selwyn Bowen just coming out in a 'Box'.

Driver John Hughes, conductor Herbie Gibbon and the author, who during the summer of 1969 walked over to Cardiff Central bus station most days in his lunch hour, making many good N&C friends over a coffee in Asteys.

15:20 Briton Ferry – Swansea 16:00: RCY804 with Mel Powell/Bill Collier;

17:00 Swansea – Bridgend 18:00: WWN190 with Reg Hoare/Jack Handford.

Thursday 7 March 1968

The fawn and red livery still hasn't gone. HTG601D is the sole survivor and something of a recluse, seen today in Ewenny Road.

Friday 15 March 1968 and

Saw my hero Selwyn Bowen in NCY885 with his girlfriend.

Saturday 16 March 1968

Selwyn in NCY again on same service as yesterday and again with girlfriend in front seat, except as I discovered later that it was not his girlfriend, but his wife!

Saturday 23 March 1968

Another N&C day out: Bridgend – Cardiff – Bridgend – Swansea – Bridgend. Late start due to poor weather.

13:10 Bridgend – Cardiff 13:50: LTX829E with Bryn Maggs/Ronnie Ware. 14:30 Cardiff – Bridgend 15:15: HTG602D with Doug Thomas/Basil Jones.

15:45 Bridgend – Swansea 16:00: 568ECY with Dai Goodland/Gwilym — pulled into depot for crew change: PTX830F was there inside.

18:00 Swansea – Bridgend 19:00: 567ECY with Vic Greenwood/unknown conductor.

Saturday 30 March 1968

Saw Selwyn Bowen in NCY887 on 20:00 Bridgend to Cardiff.

Friday 5 April 1968

Two coaches vying for stand 18 resulted in a highly amusing exchange of banter. Went down town in evening and saw Selwyn and Basil in WWN189, and Reg pull up alongside.

Saturday 6 April 1968

Two trips to Cardiff to buy model railway items from Bud Morgan. Caught 10:00 Bridgend – Cardiff 10:45: WWN190 with Tom Jones/Harry Jones.

13:30 Cardiff – Bridgend 14:15: CTX986C with unknown driver/Basil Jones.

16:00 Bridgend – Cardiff 16:45: 568ECY with Mel Hughes/Ronnie Ware.

17:30 Cardiff – Bridgend 18:15: with Reg Hoare/John Friend.

Monday 15 April 1968

Easter Bank Holiday. It was always rewarding to stroll down to Waterton on a bank holidays to see the dozens of Rhondda buses returning from Porthcawl and Aberavon, and many of the municipalities hired in, plus of course the N&C.
Went down by-pass in evening. Saw HTG601D, LTX828E (on tour), and Selwyn Bowen on service in WWN191.

Tuesday 16 April 1968

Saw Doug and John Friend in 3283WB stuck in Wyndham Street for some reason. Saw Doug again later in CTX986C – with AEC badge now on radiator grille.

Friday 19 April 1968

Another full N&C day. Off I went as follows:

12:45 Bridgend – Swansea 14:00 via Neath: NCY887 with Tom Jones/Twiggy to depot, then Ivor Hughes/Harry Jones.

15:00 Swansea – Cardiff 16:45 via BFB: TWN557 with unknown crew to depot, relieved by John Hughes/Herbie Gibbon.

17:25 Cardiff – Swansea non-stop 18:40: 232BWN with Len Bradey. Pre-booked by Alwyn.

19:00 Swansea – Bridgend 20:00: NCY887 with Doug Thomas/Harry Jones, also Len Brady passenger. Passed Selwyn in 558 four times in all. 231 being overhauled. Flyer was quite good, but should have been a better coach: 829 was on service.

Saturday 4 May 1968

Missed getting a ride with Selwyn Bowen time and time again. Went down town and caught coaches as follows:

11:30 Bridgend – Cardiff 1215: RCY803 with Tom Jones/Ray Dukes.

12:30 Cardiff – Swansea 14:15: CTX986C with Tom Jones/Ray Dukes.

15:15 Swansea – Cardiff 17:15: TWN558 with Dickie Bach/Basil Jones to depot, relieved by Doug Thomas/Herbie Gibbon.

18:00 Cardiff – Bridgend 18:40: 3284WB with Ivor Thomas/ Ronnie Ware.

Selwyn Bowen went up same time as the 11:30 in 986 but did not pull into the stand so I didn't know until it was too late. I got straight on to 986 at Cardiff but Selwyn just had to get on to 803 instead! When they got to Swansea he came back on 602 via Neath so I missed him again!

Saturday 11 May 1968

Another Saturday in heaven: Went to Cardiff in afternoon. HTG602D with Reg Hoare and Harry Jones. 568ECY with Tom Jones/Chris Bond. Saw Peter and Gary on return in 804. He said 231 and 232 are being reseated and that one of the WBs had a smash.

Friday 24 May 1968

A rare mechanical fault led to a delay. Saw 568ECY in repair bay with faulty windscreen wiper. Left at 4:55, 25 minutes late.

Wednesday 5 June 1968

O-Level exams were fast approaching; I'd written a bold reminder that serious revision from today was needed. Went down town and caught 10:30 Bridgend – Cardiff 11:15:

TWN558 with Vic Greenwood/Ronnie Ware. Came back on 12:00 Cardiff – Bridgend 12:45: WWN190 with Danny/Gwilym.

Friday 7 June 1968

Mick Williams was at the bus station and went off in TWN557. Little did we realise the significance of this sighting.

Saturday 8 June 1968

Friday was a tragic night for the N&C, as TWN557 came to grief by skidding on a wet surface at the junction of Splott Road and Habershon Street in Cardiff, and ploughing into a shop window, causing the shop façade to collapse on to the coach.

Got the Echo after reading the placards and discovered to my shock that TWN557 with Philip Evans was involved at Cardiff – we were only remarking last night on the poor tyre wear. Went to Swansea as a result.

Bridgend – Swansea: 231BWN with Jim Boucher/Jack Handford: good journey.

Swansea – Bridgend: NCY886 with unknown crew: awful, but 557 had not arrived at the depot. We pulled right down too so that the conductor could get tickets. Some new types (green card) found on 231. Presumably emergency tickets.

Thursday 13 June 1968

The demise of TWN557 still very much the main focus: Tonto told Gary and Peter that 557 will have a new body.

Senior driver 'Jock' Cross takes charge of a tour in new Duple Commander MkII HTG601D, 1966.
Geoff Lumb

Sunday 15 June 1968

Plenty of activity on the Bridgend by-pass. Went down by-pass in evening with Gary. Some 38 Rhondda/ PUDC buses. HTG600/1D on tours. 601 still good in buff livery.

Thursday 27 June 1968

An afternoon trip to Cardiff with Selwyn: Went down town in morning. Saw Selwyn Bowen on 10:15 to Swansea (568) so decided to meet him when he returned on the 1pm. It was 567, however. 13:00 Bridgend – Cardiff 13:45: 567ECY with Selwyn Bowen.

Saturday 20 July 1968

After my 'O' Levels I lay low on account of my embarrassing acne. My travels recommenced during the summer holidays and – I regret this now – I always preferred the new coaches to the old.

Went to Cardiff with Dave Hart. Got down bus station by 9.30am. It had to be NCY886! Bloody coach. I feel like writing a letter of complaint to N&C! After all, NCYs are 1956.

Wednesday 24 July 1968

Trip to Cardiff with various observations: 11:00 Bridgend – Cardiff 11:45: RRC237 with Jim the Fish and Alwyn.

13:00 Cardiff – Bridgend 14:15: 568ECY with Dickie Bach and John Friend.

237, 600 and 602 on service today. The WBs seem to be having a rest lately, not so the NCYs and TWNs.

Saturday 31 August 1968

Saw Selwyn with Eddie Jones in 3279. Ed put on a good show for about 10 minutes.

The faster drivers such as Selwyn could often have 10 minutes to spare at Bridgend. They arrived several minutes early, and could easily make up a few more if they chatted beyond booked departure time.

Saturday 7 September 1968

We carried out an N&C Survey, noting all departures from Bridgend over the entire weekend. Made survey all morning and continued in the afternoon.

Sunday 8 September 1968

Made another survey. Thirteen each way departures on Sunday, compared with 33 (or 39?) on Saturday! Top half of Market Street was closed. Wyndham Street was later made one way from York Road up."

Friday 27 September 1968

Saw 828, 600 and 602. Saw Selwyn Bowen earlier in 803 on Cowbridge Road and later in 887 which had relieved 828.

Sat 28/Sun 29 September 1968

Night of the 'Yog Jog' charity walk from Cardiff to Porthcawl. I took the short cut home from Waterton. What would Health & Safety say to all that today?

Got a lot more sponsors from neighbours in evening. Got to bus station – soaked already. Diabolical weather. Met Jim and Richard and caught 985 with John Friend. Poured with rain towards midnight and we were really drenched by the time we set off. It was great going as fast as possible overtaking everybody in sight at first, but the pace slowed down after Ely Works. It was very hard going but an experience to say the least, despite some cramp. Got to Waterton at 6.15am.

Monday 7 October 1968

A trip to the National Museum for art appreciation, and we took advantage of the shortage of seats in Tom the art master's car. Made plans for afternoon in Cardiff so we left at 11.30am. We had planned to catch the 16:00 back and when we saw 601 going down at 12.15 I worked out it would depart Cardiff at 16:00 so all the better.

12:30 Bridgend – Cardiff 13:15: RCY804 with Eddie Owens and Harry Jones; heard quite a lot of gossip about depot, Eddie Jones, etc. Enjoyed sketching at museum.

16:00 Cardiff – Bridgend 16:45: HTG601D with Doug Thomas and unknown conductor.

Thurs 10/Sat 12 October 1968

3283WB has been seen by Gary with Morris of Pencoed. NCY886 must have gone, according to Peter. Talked to him for most of afternoon at the N&C stand. Quite a lot learned about WBs, 557, etc. 3280 has gone also. Has 3279? Saw Gary after who said he had seen 3280 in Pencoed.

Monday 28 October 1968

Rained torrentially so didn't go down Briton Ferry until afternoon. It's the wettest summer and autumn I have ever known. Journey down in 567ECY. Saw Selwyn Bowen, Eddie Jones, etc at depot. Also, D N Flower was talking to Mr Truran the tall engineer for some time. Quite a lot of interesting news: UNY831/2G coming next year. No second-hand vehicles yet. 885/7 and 3281/2/4 staying. 191, 231 and 568 being overhauled. Got fleet list and took quite a few photos. Came back on CTX986C from depot yard.

Wednesday 30 October 1968

Serious hold ups affected all services. N&Cs not running to any schedule due to roadworks or something at Pyle. Some Cardiffs were diverted via Kenfig Hill and running about 30 minutes late. Coming back from Cardiff, most were late also.
Saw Selwyn rushing like hell to catch up on his 15 mins break. Also, Leyshon rushing to

Swansea. Rather chaotic at bus station all day really – wonder what can be wrong.

Sunday 3 November 1968

One of the most eventful, never-to-be-forgotten journeys to Swansea, caused by the continuing roadworks at Pyle.

Tuesday 5 November 1968

Daimler demonstrator KKV800G was being trialled by N&C until 24 November, when it went to Western Welsh for use on route 302. It became a familiar sight on the A48 for the next month.Gary said that his father saw the demonstrator at 17:00 so I went to see it return at 18:45 and again at 21:30. Very nice. Twiggy and Graham Matthews driving it. PTX830F went up at 16:00 with Tom Jones and Basil Jones actually on service. Didnot come back.

Saturday 9 November 1968

Decided to go somewhere, in afternoon. Went down bus station. Ended up going down to Swansea.

Immediately saw KKV800G with NCY885 going to Cardiff at 12:00 so worked out time of return and went home to have lunch. Went back and waited for demonstrator as planned. Selwyn Bowen came in meantime in 567 (to Cardiff).

13:45 Bridgend – Swansea (via Neath) 15:00: KKV800G with John Hughes and John Friend, with another bloke as 'pilot' from Coventry, undoubtedly. He got off at depot. Found it rather stuffy inside 800 but ride was smooth despite some jumpy gear changes.

Returned quite late: 16:15 Swansea – Bridgend (via Neath) 19:30: 231BWN with Tom Jones and old John Knox. Very good journey back. 828 and 829 on service also.

Saturday 7 December 1968

3282WB seen overhauled – was also seen in yesterday morning's murky light but could not tell then. Saw Eddie Jones at bus station and was joking with him for a while.

Saturday 14 December 1968

Went over bus station. Saw 189, 3284, 238. 3284 had apparently failed as they were messing with it and eventually it went with the N&C lorry which suddenly appeared from behind the scenes. They've done a bit of work on 567 (roof and some of front and rear). 828 on service all lit up.

Friday 20 December 1968

Came home after final assembly in afternoon. Went to Cardiff in late afternoon.Bridgend – Cardiff: CTX985C Cardiff – Bridgend: HTG602D with Man from Uncle, Vic Greenwood. Fantastic journey back through torrential rain."

Monday 23 December 1968

N&Cs running at no regular pattern today – probably because of heavy traffic.

Monday 30 December 1968

14:15 Bridgend – Swansea via Neath: CTX986C. 237, 238, 600 and 601 were there on hire to Thomas Bros. Depot very empty

The diaries which helped the author tell the story of N&C Luxury Coaches.

with only NCY, RCY and a Harrington there on way down, but nothing at all on the way back.

16:00 Swansea – Bridgend via Briton Ferry Bridge: CTX986C with same crew again.

Saturday 4 January 1969

Quite a busy day for N&C: three went up at 13:30pm (829, 556 and 558).

Sunday 5 January 1969

First trip of the year. Had dinner late but arrived at bus station at 14:15pm. Man from Uncle turned up with RCY805 on 14:30pm. Quite a good journey. Returned on HTG602D with Tom Jones.

Wednesday 8 January 1969

Rumours down the grape vine. Could it be that N&C are extending their service to Llanelli? Come to think of it, the Man from Uncle did say something about it.

Monday 13 January 1969

The 1967 Panorama 1s still making an impact. LTX829E on service. Great illumination at rear.

Sunday 19 January 1969

An unforgettable day out for all the wrong reasons. We came across a fatal crash.

Monday 20 January 1969

My first thoughts on hiring an N&C coach for a day for the model railway club. Saw Gary after school. Told him all the news. Trip was to have been supported by school but it was soon decided it was far too ambitious in every respect and so the idea was dropped.

Monday 27 January 1969

Hiring an N&C coach, with Selwyn to drive it, was still the number one priority in my life. Had brilliant idea hiring coach for trip to Weston-super-Mare (or Swindon) for visits to model railway or museum. Me, Jim Boyles, Geoff Stokes and Ieuan agreed to be responsible jointly which we will be great as we can all take charge and sit at the front of the coach.

Tuesday 28 January 1969

After school I phoned Weston, to learn that the model railway won't be open. I therefore think it best to go to Swindon instead.

Thursday 30 January 1969

Walked down town after school, seeing Selwyn in a freshly repainted RRC237. Really good going for them to do that.

Saturday 1 February 1969

I had an interview with Glamorgan Council but was more concerned about my plans to hire a coach from N&C.

Had letter for interview at Cardiff's planning office 9.30am Monday morning, but no letter from N&C. Rather nervous about former, will I get back to school in time to duplicate leaflets for the trip.

Met Phillip and caught the 10:15 coach (232BWN with Mel Joseph and Ronnie Ware) to depot. Unfortunately, there is a delay due to a teething problem with the doors so the new ones won't be coming for a fortnight at least. Very disappointed. Still, Truran and Gallanders kindly informed us that we would

Ready to roll at Briton Ferry, 1968.

be able to have Selwyn and get on at the depot. 830 and 601 are in Scotland now. 829 in London. 828 was at the depot waiting for Selwyn in the morning when we were there. Chatted to Gerry Truran for a while.

Monday 3 February 1969

Job interview in Cardiff and the school meeting to announce my Swindon trip. Caught 08:00 non-stop coach to Cardiff. CTX985C with Eddie Owens and Fred Little. Arrived council offices at 09:20 and went straight into the interview to emerge at long last at 12:15.

They were very pleased with me, but in more than one way I shan't be at all disappointed if I don't get the job.

Came back at 12:30. RRC238 with same crew. Went straight up to school for meeting then home for lunch. N&C letter had come!"

Saturday 8 February 1969

Snowed more at lunchtime so went back down town in afternoon and caught 14:30 Bridgend to Cardiff: WWN189 to Cardiff with Man from Uncle and Philip Evans. Back at 16:00: TWN556 with Mel Joseph.

Wednesday 12 February 1969

My future had been decided. Received reply from council offices in morning: I've got the job. Appointed Plotter/Draughtsman. So, it's up to me to decide when to start."

Monday 17 February 1969

Decided to have not one, but two, dry runs prior to starting work on 3 March. Unfortunately, was a bit of a rush in morning, as didn't wake up until 07:30. However, got down bus station by 08:00. (LTX828E on Flyer but no hope of boarding.)

Did not catch coach until 08:30 Bridgend - Cardiff: RCY805 with Reg Hoare and Harry Jones. Returned on 11:00 Cardiff – Bridgend: CTX986C with Ivor Hughes. Selwyn Bowen came in on 828 at 16:30 so, regardless of time, I got on it!

16:30 Bridgend – Cardiff: LTX828E with Selwyn Bowen.Returned on next coach: 17:30 Cardiff – Bridgend Only: RCY804.

Monday 3 March 1969

The first working day of my life. I was part of the in-crowd, the select elite who could claim

to be N&C regulars. But not exactly off to a good start. 07:30 coach, 567ECY. That terrible ex-Black & White driver. Arrived 08:25 having travelled in 5th and 6th all the way at 20mph – or so it seemed!

Tuesday 4 March 1969

Lift to bus station. There at 07.20. One person in queue before me. No standing on coach today as yesterday. Same terrible crew though and he does definitely use 6th gear without cause. Only six minutes late though, so got there just after 08:30 (986). Permission given to leave 10 minutes early on condition that I make it up, so I caught the 5pm coach (191). I realised that in saving the half hour, it will result in me no longer catching the same coach in both directions, except for Mondays which is much better than all week otherwise.

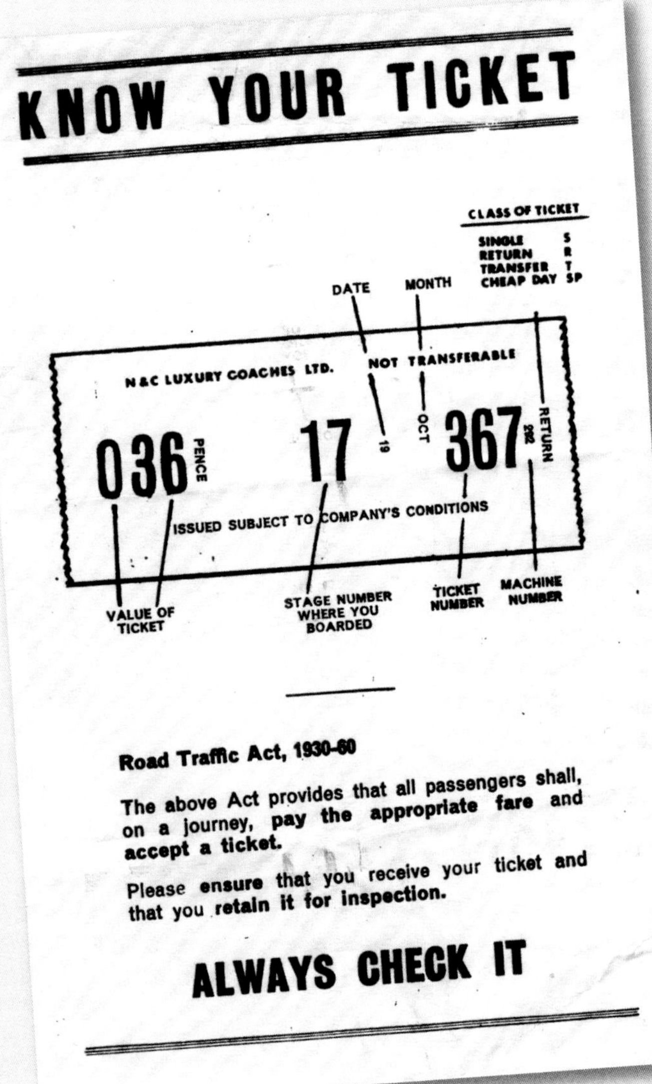

Saturday 8 March 1969

Selwyn swept into the bus station in 887. He got out to have a word. He said he'd framed the cutting from the Gazette story reporting our Swindon trip. He also said UNY831/2G have come and are 'no good', having some 'trouble' in having to use clutch to shut door. He reckons they'll be putting the destination transfers on 831/2 along the bottom of the windows.

Thursday 13 March 1969

Saw 600 and 601 on relief turnover at Cardiff lunchtime. 567 seemed a bit pepped-up but we were in 1st up Cowbridge Hill, as I heard later.

Saturday 15 March 1969

A trip to the depot to see the new Elites. Caught 11:15 Bridgend – Briton Ferry 11:55: 232BWN with Ivor Hughes and Herbie Gibbon. Arrived at depot to see the Elites in the garage.

Paid the coach fare for Weston trip to duty inspector in the presence of Reg Hoare and Selwyn Bowen who was just off in RRC237 to Tredegar. He said we definitely won't have an Elite, as did another inspector, but after an examination I think, except for the looks, 829 will be better for the journey.

Saw Truran and he did not know of the hire but seems to think 829 will be available. He says it is a better coach than 828. He said that Selwyn had two endorsements and that he smashed up 3281WB and NCY887 three weeks ago on the Bwlch (3281 quite badly into the back of a lorry), and tore the side off HTG602D 18 months ago at Morriston. Also saw Peter Jones so we had more freedom then and have now been inside every coach (including 830). Saw some remains of TWN557. Gerry Truran took us round in 831 so we could photograph it.

Thursday 20 March 1969

A brace of mechanical hiccoughs. Saw Selwyn Bowen at lunchtime at Asteys with Cyril Shackson, Dai Goodland, Alwyn and others. It seems Gerry Truran wants to give us 828 on Saturday now. Selwyn changed 189 due to something wrong with the speedo and a maximum speed of 55 mph. Returning home, 602 went well until Cowbridge when smoke started pouring from rear offside wheel. So, we were late getting into Bridgend and Selwyn had to take the coach over the pits at the bus station. Still some smoke coming from wheel when he drove down York Road at 18:55.

Saturday 22 March 1969

My second N&C private hire. Went to Cheddar and Weston-super-Mare, with Selwyn Bowen in LTX828E.

Monday 24 March 1969

LTX828E seemed forever to be allotted to Turn 1 on a Monday. Very surprised at today's coach being 828 yet again. The stickers were on it in morning but were removed by evening. Thinking to have trip to Woburn Abbey but it's a long way.

Friday 28 March 1969

Had Jock Cross on way up (232). Jack Handford said 'hello' at Bridgend - it's great to be a regular. Ivor Hughes on way back in a terrible 567. 831 was on Flyer. Got paid before lunch. Went to CWS Bank to cash cheque: came home with £26-8s-10d from a taxable £29-12s-6d.

Monday 31 March 1969

Yet another Monday 'doubler' with 828. Had the new little chap (Ken Cochran) with John Friend in morning and John Hughes with Gareth Evans (new conductor) in afternoon. Saw Selwyn in evening and he likes the idea of a Mystery Trip to Woburn Abbey.

Tuesday 1 April 1969

Same crew in morning as yesterday (829); Eddie Owens and Eddie Jones on way back (3282). Saved a lot of time in going through St Fagans as there were serious jams at Ely. 885 went out about 10 mins before us and did not get to Bridgend until 15 mins after us. Alan Williams came in so we asked him if Selwyn was about. He said he'd been given the sack for smashing up 803 at Laleston.

Tuesday 22 April 1969

The quote for our mystery trip to Woburn came in at £50, and needs two drivers. Didn't hesitate to accept, regardless of lack of passengers. John Allen was there and he said he saw the accident at Laleston and the coach had hit both vehicles.

Wednesday 23 April 1969

Rumours of Selwyn's dismissal were proved false. Phoned Mr Gallanders. Great! He sounded much friendlier over the phone and everything's all right for 24 May, with Selwyn. (And an Elite, if possible).

Saturday 26 April 1969

Saw Selwyn Bowen at 11:15 with Alan Williams. Told him about date for Woburn and he admitted smashing up 803, but it wasn't his fault. Returned to town in afternoon and caught 15:30 to Cardiff as it was Selwyn in 568ECY with John Friend. Quite a good journey (35mins approx). Returned with him at 5pm with Jack Handford. 558 cut out at St Hilary but we weren't late. Tudor may be our second driver; Reg Hoare has apparently had a stroke so he's out.

Monday 28 April 1969

Had Tudor Reynolds and Fred Little in morning (568), and Ivor Hughes and Derrick Parry in evening (568). Return trip really good, racing 231 which was on non-stop!.

Wednesday 30 April 1969

Had that slow Graham (Isaac) bloke with Alan Williams on way back (568). Alan said I could ask for Vic Greenwood so I did.

Went down to see Selwyn at 8.30pm. He said not to have anything to do with Alan Williams as he reported him for some joke.

Monday 5 May 1969

The massive delays at Ely during the bridge replacement were becoming unbearable.

Had Bill Drury and Herbie Gibbons in morning (567) and Chris Shylon on Flyer in evening (568). Getting fed up of Ely Bridge.

COACHES

The last of the Guy Arabs (KCY488-490 and LCY781/2) were withdrawn on New Year's Day, 1967. Their replacements, six Burlingham-bodied AEC Reliances (3279WB - 3284WB), had arrived from Sheffield United Tours the previous November. The first to enter service, 3282, can just be seen outside the paint shop, while others including 3280, await attention. The two Weymann Fanfares that came from Trent Motor Traction at the same time (RRC237/8) were in better condition and put to work in Trent livery, as soon as makeshift fleet names had been applied. One of the pair can be seen in the middle distance awaiting its next duty. INSET: One of the last AEC Regal IIIs in service takes a well-earned rest at the garage in the summer of 1964. *Richard Evans*

Friday 9 May 1969

Vic Greenwood was on 828 in evening for the Western Welsh LUH-F coach came along and brushed it so I'm hoping there's not much damage. (Accident report was filled in.) Came back with Bill Phillips and Archie (602). It seems like Dickie Bach is a good driver to have on the return journey — he avoids the jams as much as possible.

Wednesday 14 May 1969

Dai Goodland on the Bridgend Only tonight (232); quite good racing Twiggy in 231 as far as Cowbridge turn off.

Tuesday 27 May 1969

Working for the council meant that as well as Bank Holidays, an additional day's holiday was given on the Tuesday. Time, therefore, for something a little different, accompanying Selwyn Bowen on a very strange working duty: "Down bus station by 9am. Selwyn came in with Eddie Jones in 568. Had quite a good run up to Cardiff where we had until 12:30 to mess about. Got 'Buses' mag then returned to Asteys with Selwyn. Then we moved to 602 where all his serious proposals for an independent firm were discussed, very seriously. Went all the way to Swansea then in 885.

Had a trot around Swansea then returned to Selwyn in the cafe. He departed at 15:00 so I caught the 15:15 (Bill Drury, Mel Hughes) and met him at the depot, this time in 829 with Cyril Shackson. Got off at Mid Vale and went home for tea. Joined him yet again at 9pm but this run wasn't worth it. Selwyn liked the idea of Gwyn Reed retiring and selling his business.

Wednesday 28 May 1969

Had Mel Joseph with Fred Little on way up (231). Saw Alan Williams (out at 13:30) and we had quite a good talk. He will be leaving and joining Swansea Constabulary, or so he says. Back with Selwyn (231), but a very slow journey, probably because he ran over a Dalmatian dog on the way up and was upset. We stopped at Cowbridge police station for him to report it.

Friday 30 May 1969

602 both ways today. Back with Selwyn via St Fagan's, Peterston-super-Ely, etc! It took no longer, but going via Peterston wasn't planned - we were lost! Incident with Cortina estate car at Sycamore Cross, whose driver had a fright when he saw 602 bearing down at him as Selwyn had begun to cross the central reservation in anticipation of the gap. The chap swerved, stopped and waved his arms about. Dai Goodland beat us, of course, in 568. He went on to Western Avenue and we would have followed but assumed he'd gone straight on at the lights.

Monday 2 June 1969

A battle of the slow coaches coming home. Had Ivor Thomas, with Selwyn's brother-in-law, Dai Hughes, as expected in morning (985), and Ken Arthur and Eddie Jones coming back (985), as Danny Vaughan was on Flyer in 828. We were ahead of him at Ely and he passed us at the top of Cowbridge by-pass. We got to Bridgend together.

Monday 3 June 1969

Saw Herbie Gibbons in bus station in afternoon, without uniform. He recognised me and informed me that Selwyn is up the mountain this week. (An early form of rail replacement service, due to the state of the Blaengwynfi tunnel.)

Wednesday 18 June 1969

Had John Hughes with Alan on Turn 1 as expected (231). Learned quite a few things from him at 13:00, mainly the names of such people as Peter Parker (new boy), Dai Hughes (Selwyn's brother-in-Law), Jimmy Vaughan ('The Fish'), Jimmy Walters, and Len Brady.

Thursday 19 June 1969

Alan again, this time with Mel Joseph. Alan distributed the new timetables this morning and it will now require a lot of learning and experience before this is mastered. This service will leave at 07:40 in future.

Friday 20 June 1969

Had Alan with John Hughes (985). By 13:00 he had swapped with the new boy Peter Parker. Alan said he was working on to duplicate the 6pm with Selwyn, so I waited. Went down bus station to see, very surprisingly, Selwyn, who had brought up a coach for John Hughes following the injector failure of RCY803 went up to Laleston with Selwyn taking 803 back - really enjoyed the standing at the front. Walked back to see Vic, with Madge, at 20:45pm.

Monday 23 June 1969

Had Tom Howells and Basil Jones (567), but doubt they'll be on tomorrow as they aren't very friendly [with each other] ... Had Jim the Fish on return (232). Kind of Gareth to keep the front seat.Alan said Selwyn has had another bump: a puncture caused him to slide into some flagstones. Gareth, surprisingly, also said this later. Jock Cross came on coach and talked about a job to Birmingham yesterday, and that he enjoyed being with Selwyn.

Thursday 3 July 1969

Went up to see Turn 1 return: Dickie Bach and Alan on it. Saw him when he returned at 12:40 and I said I might travel up for the ride tomorrow.

Friday 4 July 1969

Went up to Cardiff and back with Alan and Dickie Bach (567). It does not seem as if the new service is working properly. Selwyn came in speeding like hell into Stand 13, then Shylon came around again and Peter Parker came in but had to pull up out on the road. Selwyn's invited me up the mountain Monday or Tuesday.

Tuesday 8 July 1969

Saw Tudor, with Jack Handford, after meeting Alan in morning, and we were told Selwyn wasn't on the mountain contract. So, we did not go up. Stayed with Tudor in 556 and he eventually pulled around and went out at 12:00. Also saw Eddie Jones with a friendly John Hughes. Went to Swansea in afternoon to meet Sel at 16:02 at the Ferry. Went down with Tom Jones and John Knox on 190 and came back with them via Neath to the depot. Tom was chatting on way back. Sel got on at Neath and we were joined by Alan at Briton Ferry. Went right up to Cardiff and came back, with Selwyn all the time.

Wednesday 16 July 1969

Saw Selwyn on the 7.45am turn back, with Alan. Particularly good because that girl I fancy was looking on when Alan came up, and when I boarded 567. Danny Vaughan came in on 829 and then Jim Boucher on 231, as Ken Cochran had failed to turn up. We crawled all the way — terrible journey — and the 8am flyer had passed us at the top of Tumble! Got in at 08:45 and was greeted by time clerk Mike Hulbert. Still, it wasn't my fault... Came back on the flyer with Hedleigh Pope and Dai Goodland.

Friday 18 July 1969

Saw Selwyn at Cardiff lunchtime and had a good chat, including details of his court case next Thursday. Arrived bus station just before 5pm. Peter Parker came up when I called him but could not get on his bus, 558, because it was full. So, waited for Bridgend flyer (602, Hedleigh Pope) although if I had known I would have got on 832 'cos that's what was on the next service... Saw Alan in evening... apparently 568 is the first of seven coaches to have a white triangle for a

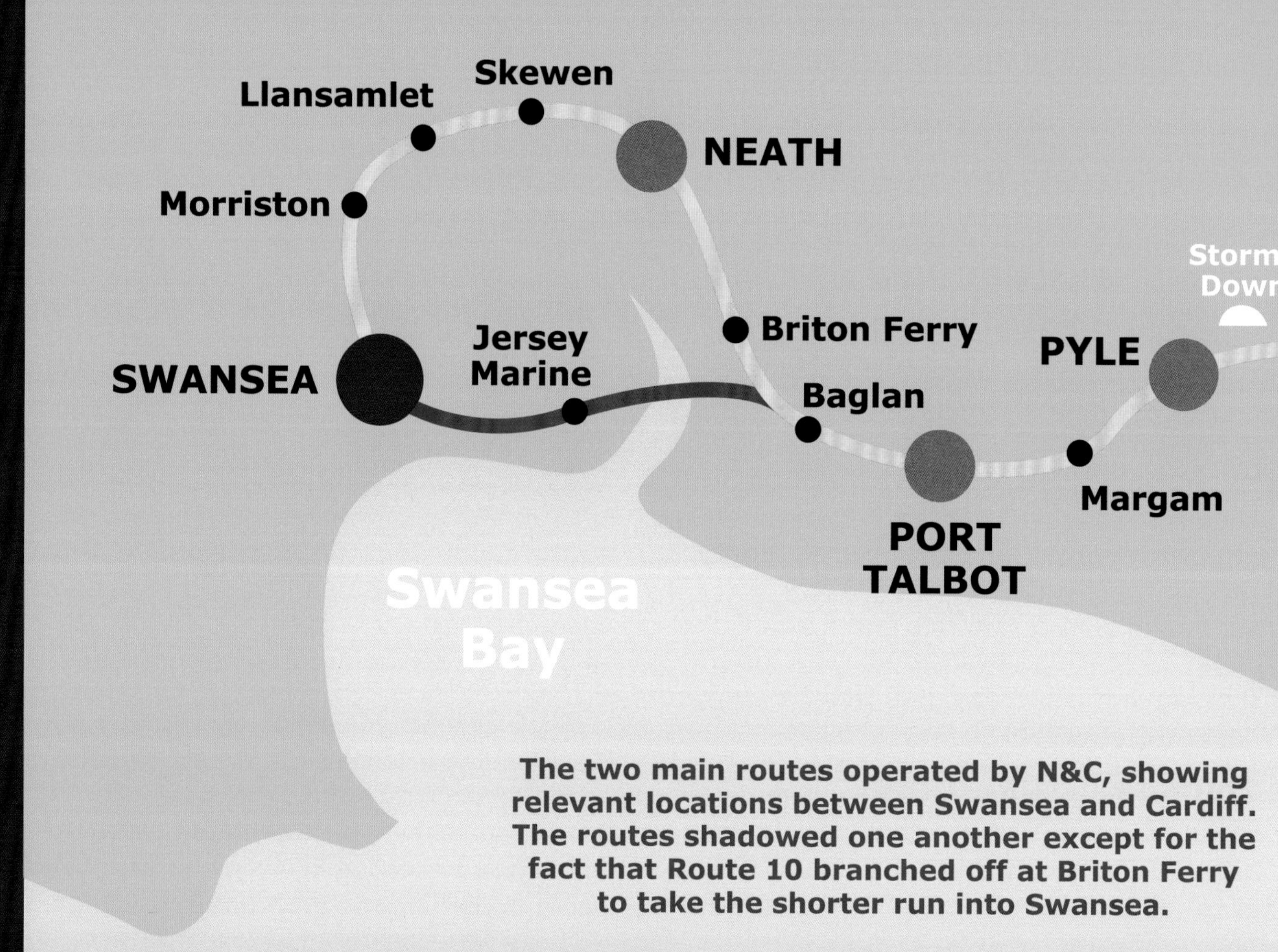

The two main routes operated by N&C, showing relevant locations between Swansea and Cardiff. The routes shadowed one another except for the fact that Route 10 branched off at Briton Ferry to take the shorter run into Swansea.

Cardiff allocation. 828/9 and 600 are also supposed to be going there.

Monday 21 July 1969

Man on the Moon – not a nickname for a driver, but an historic day in space exploration. Also in this month, Prince Charles was invested as Prince of Wales, and in a far more ominous sense, 'Something in the Air' by Thunderclap Newman was top of the pops.

Upwards with Selwyn and Jim Bond as expected (232). Peter Parker on the 07:45 Bridgend-Swansea. Got to Cardiff early and was in work just after 08:30.

Saw John Hughes in bus station before Selwyn came in at 1.20pm. Also saw Vic. Saw him again after rushing for the 17:30. He was talking to Jock Cross, with Dai Goodland, then we set off for a really fast trip to Bridgend (568).

Wednesday 23 July 1969

Peter Parker was on the turn back again and was apparently racing Selwyn on way in.

Thursday 24 July 1969

Had Ken Arthur and Bill Collier (231). Got in at 08:30 Selwyn was right: he's speeded up. Saw Gareth just before Selwyn came in at

SERVICE CARDIFF

Key

Route 7 via Neath

Route 10 via Briton Ferry Bridge

Laleston

BRIDGEND

Crack Hill

Primrose Hill

Tumble Hill

Ely

CARDIFF

COWBRIDGE

Culverhouse Cross

Bristol Channel

BRIDGEND COWBRIDGE CARDIFF

17:30 and said 'he'd got away with it', so all is well. He was cleared of both charges.

Tuesday 29 July 1969

Went up on Flyer with Arthur Bowen (602). Got in dead on time, just after Ken Arthur again. Came back with Selwyn and Harry Jones, as predicted (190).

Wednesday 30 July 1969

For the first time in my travels to work I had a 41-seater coach. Got into Cardiff just after Ken Arthur at 08:25! (189). Had a good ride despite five-gear coach which Selwyn reckoned was going flat out. Madge was on in both directions for a change. On arriving at the bus station at 17:15 I was greeted by most of the Cardiff crew and Selwyn, and N&C are on strike! All the Cardiff's had stopped by that time, after a WW crew were put on, and Gareth was there, who should have gone out at 15:05. Consequently, the Flyer didn't run and all services were then running down, and the 18:05 (Tom Howells, Eddie Jones) was returning to Briton Ferry after Swansea. The 18:00 out of Bridgend (Graham Matthews) returned light after reaching Cardiff. Don't know what Ken Arthur/Peter Bowen (18:25 out) did. All services had stopped

For the author the first day of his working career in local government meant joining Turn 1, the 7.30am from Bridgend to Cardiff, aboard 567ECY with driver Ken Arthur and conductor Chris Bond.

by 20:00 at Briton Ferry. As far as is known now, no services will be running tomorrow.

Thursday 31 July 1969

Got down bus station by 07:35. Fairly surprised to see everything back to normal, but before Turn 1 arrived I was called by my occasional travelling companion Eddie Davies in his car, who had been trying to attract my attention.

We arrived in Cardiff 8.10am so I was the first in work today. Saw Selwyn and Alan just before they left at 12.25pm. Selwyn had been on the Flyer and beat Ken Arthur in, and will be on it again tomorrow. They agreed to go back at last night's meeting under the promise that negotiations will start today. If nothing has been reached by Sunday, they will be out Monday and it looks as if they'll stay out.

Wednesday 6 August 1969

Learned a lot about the dispute. It seems it is justified and everyone's sympathetic. Things are coming to the boil. Western Welsh are putting pressure on N&C to join their union, and are blackmailing them by refusing to let them use Penarth Road depot. Apparently Gray and Flower are in battle.

Saturday 9 August 1969

The dispute was lingering now. There was a really angry incident this morning. Vic stormed off the coach at Bridgend's stand 13 after Gwyn Hare held him back. Vic really tore into Gwyn and they did not look at each other when Vic came back.

Thursday 14 August 1969

Had Chris Shylon on the Flyer (985) and we nearly smashed into a mini van at the junction by Victoria Park, Cardiff.

Wednesday 20 August 1969

Returned on Flyer with Vic on a good performing 829.

Friday 22 August 1969

A near miss on the Golden Mile. Vic on the Flyer again, with Roger Williams (829). Quite an exciting ride, especially when we had to swerve off the Golden Mile to avoid three oncoming cars.

Monday 25 August 1969

The men were still far from happy. Had Jim Boucher and Cyril Shackson today (567) and it was the worst ride ever! The WW 301 passed us on top of Cowbridge, and the Flyer a bit further on. Jim said he'd make sure they'd be in front of him tomorrow as well. We got in at 08:37. Will definitely report him if he's late tomorrow.

Tuesday 26 August 1969

What was going on? Waited for the Flyer, but Jim Boucher played a sly one and got in before us today. What came over him?

Friday 5 September 1969

Surprised to see 832 roar into stand 13 with Tom Jones and Eddie Jones. Again, I had the front seat saved for me. Lovely journey, but was slightly late getting to work.

Wednesday 22 October 1969

Was pleased to have a chat with John Hughes in Cardiff lunchtime. He makes very good company.

Friday 14 November 1969

Fridays at this time meant I didn't commute to Cardiff but instead attended Bridgend College along with many of my colleagues who travelled down from Cardiff. At first there was only three of us in Tech. We learnt that this was because the 8:05 from Cardiff had a smash at Penlline Dip. John-Paul had injured his hand and went down the hospital.

Saturday 15 November 1969

Alan said it was Jim the Fish and Raymond involved in yesterday's crash, in 191. Saw 602 in evening, repainted and looking very good except for the back bumper.

Monday 5h January 1970

Conductor Eddie Jones was one of my friends and would always sit next to me and talk shop, often in an amusing, camp, manner, which I enjoyed. But sometimes he could be serious and there were many issues he would raise with management. Eddie was saying he is on the committee and wants to dissolve Turn 21 into the rest and asked me if I could find a way to do it.

Wednesday 14 January 1970

Went up with Bill Drury and Cyril Shackson (602). Some choice phrases as always. It was like being in a foreign country.

Thursday 23 April 1970

The revised and dovetailed 301/7/10 timetable had always been hated by the N&C staff. They resisted the requirement to observe the extra stops and, for instance, at Crack Hill, some would deliberately be out in the centre lane to avoid picking-up.

There was a real witch of a woman who used to stand there flailing her arms about like Worzel Gummidge, and we never stopped! For many of us 'proper' commuters, it was an added touch of excitement to see these upstarts who were alien to the N&C jump out of the bus shelter and wave their arms about, by which time we had no way of pulling up and so swiftly passed them by! Up Dickie Bach/Ronnie Ware [for the fourth day running] (986). Left that duffer at Three Ashes behind. He's been asking for it.

Wednesday 10 June 1970

After 40 glorious years, we were clearly entering a time of confrontation between the road staff and the SWT management, and this was mainly a grievance over long-standing private hire arrangements and the substitution of Western Welsh men on N&C work. Private hire work was on hold, and this led to postponement of my next private party. Learned about 16:30 that N&C are once again on strike.

Wednesday 17 June 1970

Phoned Jock Cross and had a very pleasant chat with him. We have postponed the trip and they will let us know when they are back running private hire. The price for Tenby would have been £23.

Wednesday 9 September 1970

The N&C service was deteriorating, slowly but surely. Up Tom Howells/Fred Little (985) – he cannot maintain time. Back Ron Kent/Ronnie Ware (232) due to Daniel Vaughan being on Flyer. Had enough of him last week when he observed all stops and went through Cowbridge on the Flyer. I shall certainly never travel with him again.

Monday 14 September 1970

Up Dickie Bach/Ronnie Ware (231). There is now a ban on standing passengers. Left work slightly early expecting overtime ban thus no Flyer, but in fact was shocked to see a queue about a mile long! Evidently more than the dupes had been cut, so returned on train.

Wednesday 30 September 1970

In the fortnight since the overtime ban had been in effect, I had travelled by train on several occasions and of course at extra expense. Now it seemed I was to be hit from both sides. Fare increases next week. A return will be 9s/6d and a weekly £2-7s-6d! Incredible. Conductors have said they will refuse to charge them, so again there'll be chaos. Another strike in Cardiff tomorrow.

Monday 12 October 1970

The glory days were well and truly over, and I had witnessed at first hand every mortal wounding: Up Ken Arthur and Jack Handford (568). Not a very good ride and one semi-regular passenger played hell on arrival. The new fares were being charged, surprisingly. Returned on 301 duplicate. Have decided definitely to get monthly ticket on train from November.

The Plaxton Panorama Elite body was years ahead of its time. UNY832G with driver Tom Jones and conductor Eddie Jones, paused in Landore, Swansea in the summer of 1969. *Phil Trotter*

Chapter 13

Journey's end

The N&C coach company emerged out of one man's dream of providing fast comfortable and stylish coach travel between two prosperous commercial hubs. When its first vehicle took to the road it was heading on a route that would see it face many challenges.

That it overcame most of these and in doing so gained an enviable reputation for its provision of luxury travel between Swansea and Cardiff is a tribute to the sheer skill, management and determination of that same man, Colonel Godfrey Llewellyn, together with the staff in whom he placed his trust.

To achieve that reputation took much time and effort — something that in itself was no express journey — so it wasn't a surprise that its swift demise and dismembering was regarded by those who worked for, travelled on, or simply admired the company for what it was, as a tragedy and total travesty.

The end of the N&C came as a result of bus industry nationalisation in 1971. The proud operator was defenceless against its absorption into the Swansea-based South Wales Transport and Cardiff-based Western Welsh companies. Both had long envied N&C and by degrees couldn't wait to play their vicious individual roles in ripping the Brown Bombers' fleet and its service to shreds.

While the company's demise was painful for anyone who understood what it was all about, the witness for whom it must surely have cut deeper and hurt most was that same visionary who had built up the company and its proud reputation.

That was of course the Colonel, by now Sir, Godfrey Llewellyn. It was, after all, his 'baby'. The dream he had fought to create had come true, but had now been destroyed. When asked for his thoughts in 1971 he didn't hold back.

"In quite a short time the company, as such, was destroyed and was delivered into the

The two coaches acquired from Trent Motor Traction were put straight into service in the winter of 1966/67 as the paint shop was fully occupied with the former Sheffield United Burlinghams. Here RRC238 has arrived at Cardiff bus station at a busy time and is probably on its way to the perimeter road to await its next duty.
Mike Street

hands of the South Wales Transport and Western Welsh companies," he said.

"It was killed, as some claimed, by Nationalisation and mourned by all. In the 38 years of the company's existence under private ownership, we were a very happy company with a wonderful and loyal staff.

"The loss of the N&C's identity is a tragedy, but perhaps satisfying to those who for years had appeared to be possessed of jealousy of our success and cast envious eyes upon us."

Although all three companies were in the BET camp, they individually clung to their empires at all cost, until eventually the opportunity arose to destroy N&C in the interests of the National Bus Company's rationalised reforms. Up until then, both South Wales Transport and Western Welsh had felt restrained from having a go at N&C out of respect for its reputation under the highly-regarded J J Newbury. But as soon as the order came down from on high to destroy it, they acted swiftly. Its indecent hasty slaughter was a painful loss to the travelling public of South Wales.

The destruction came in two defined and catastrophic stages. Firstly, in July 1969, N&C's express service was dovetailed into Western Welsh's Limited Stop 301 service, forming a 20-minute headway between Briton Ferry and Cardiff. This forced N&C to observe additional stops at the cost of its end-to-end timings.

The result was visible. It was not unusual for the Western Welsh service, which often reverted to saloon or double-deck operation, to be overtaken by the following N&C

service, so it came as no surprise that passengers preferred to avoid the 301 for the two-manned comfort and speed that the N&C was still managing to provide.

The new joint service was badly researched and a major hitherto unforeseen problem arose that was difficult to resolve. Observation of the extra intermediate stops was difficult for the long-serving N&C drivers, many of whom would still be out in the centre lane when approaching these stops. Was this deliberate, was there an element of protest in this, in the interest of keeping their own N&C patrons happy? This is something that will never be known, but there were many frantically waving arms from would-be passengers with the habit of appearing from nowhere, jumping out from the hidden depths of the shelters only to be left standing as the coaches sped past, unable to cut in, and many too were the smiles from the comfortably ensconced, dyed-in-the-wool N&C regulars within.

The second, fatal wounding came in January 1971 when the fleet was physically split between South Wales Transport and Western Welsh. The coaches were delivered straight into the greedy hands of the vulture-like opposition, with no regard whatsoever for the needs of N&C's loyal customers — who it must be said wouldn't remain loyal for very much longer. After all, there was no company left to remain loyal to. It was not only indecent and uncalled for, but a terrible mistake, as Western Welsh's general manager, Ivor Gray, later admitted, off the record.

There didn't seem to be a sufficient awareness of brand loyalty in those days. There can be no doubt now that killing off N&C was an extremely ill-conceived decision, made by people who clearly possessed little knowledge of the industry they had been employed to manage.

As time passed and the end neared, the service that had spawned the N&C's long-held pride began to visibly deteriorate as the staff became more and more disgruntled.

Following the closure of Briton Ferry garage a number of them claimed they had been 'hoisted by their own petard' due to the lack of adequate transport available to get them to and from work following the merging of the N&C Company with South Wales Transport.

Things became progressively messy. At an industrial tribunal held at Neath during April 1971, six conductors, a fitter/cleaner and a coach builder were asked to explain why they had refused to take employment under the parent company, SWT, following the closure of Briton Ferry depot.

Idris Thomas, district organiser of the Transport and General Workers' Union, told the tribunal that in the beginning it was

> **"The N&C was a great way to travel, you thought you were proper posh on them!"**
> ***Helen Chislett***

understood that the merged companies would all retain their separate identities, with the N&C company operating the very fast schedules between Swansea and Cardiff. It was thought at first, said Mr Thomas, that the depot at Briton Ferry might be absorbed into one of the five different garages, but that did not come about and last January the firm switched its operations to Swansea. Each employee was given notice and offered work on the same terms under the SWT company, and it was agreed that transportation would be arranged for N&C workers to and from Swansea.

William Jones, a conductor for eight years, said that at no time had the company given any firm assurances about transport. This resulted in him having to find his own way home from Briton Ferry after 10.30pm. Mr Macnamara, the assistant general manager of the parent company, pointed out

that 17 drivers and 10 conductors had transferred to Swansea and were quite satisfied, to which Mr Jones replied that the majority of these men lived in Swansea, and that he himself was now unemployed.

Evan Havard, depot superintendent at Swansea, said that a convoy system had been worked out to suit the needs of the former N&C staff. This covered Morriston, Danygraig and Briton Ferry.

"I have bent over backwards to try to satisfy these people," said Mr Havard.

Mr Powell, the Chairman of the Tribunal, said they accepted Mr Havard's assurance, but Mr Jones lived at Taibach, Port Talbot and found the distance too great between there and Swansea, on early and late shifts. The convoy system suggested would take Mr Jones far off his homeward route. For these reasons, the tribunal had decided that the company's offer was not a suitable one, and the tribunal awarded him his claim of 12 weeks pay for his eight years' service.

Conductor Haydn Morris of Aberdulais, who said he was similarly placed owing to the

inadequate transport facilities, was awarded 21 weeks' pay for his 14 years of service.

Coachbuilder Malcolm Davies of Cimla, Neath, said he would lose money because he would not be allowed to take driving and private hire work at the Ravenhill garage. He had been receiving about £35 weekly. Mr Macnamara submitted that Mr Davies's refusal was not a reasonable one, but the tribunal thought otherwise and awarded him 14 weeks' pay.

Conductor John Day from Briton Ferry, who had been with the N&C coaches for 25 years, told the tribunal that his special domestic difficulties, due to his wife's blindness, had been met by the N&C company who allowed him to take permanent afternoon shifts since his wife's illness. Mr Macnamara said they were opposing this case only on technical grounds. Nevertheless, Mr Day was awarded 30 weeks' pay.

A staff gathering to mark the retirement, in December 1970 of chief inspector Mick Williams. Only Mick himself is missing although it is said by some that he was in disguise!

Grief at death of a legend

In the summer of 1970 the 'In Memorium' page of the Western Mail newspaper carried a piece entitled 'The Death of the Neath and Cardiff Luxury Coaches Service.' This told of its passing away suddenly on Sunday 29 June, 1970. 'Killed by Nationalisation, sadly missed and mourned by all.' The sentiments expressed in this cryptic message were reiterated in a mourning card pinned to the notice board at Briton Ferry Depot. The card lamented:

'In days of olde, when knights were bold,
And hearts were fancy free,
Date 1930, thereabouts
Was formed the N&C.
A scintillating service, this,
By everyone adored.
Alas! The jewel now is dimmed,
By NBC 'tis floored!
But we shall not forget, you know,
That gallant band of men.
Goodbye, Good luck to all the staff,
RIP and AMEN!'

On the face of the card was inscribed the words 'In Loving Memory from those who care.'

The foremost emotion from both staff and passengers was one of grief. The service had built up a fine reputation of courteous staff, proudly serving their public by adherence to the timetable, which is more than could be said about the bigger bus companies that eagerly planned its merger and loss of identity. The travelling public joined the staff in mourning the loss of their service, which they knew was as an outstanding example of how a bus company should be operated. They pleaded with National Bus Company management to take immediate steps to reverse the trend of lowering standards and revert to those set by the N&C.

Conductor Ronnie Ware, an employee of 21 years standing and living in Caewathan, Skewen, said that travelling would have meant a certain amount of hitch-hiking, and this was difficult during the winter months. He was awarded 26 and a half weeks' pay.

Conductor Bill Collier of Crythan Road, Neath, with 16 years' service, was awarded 21 weeks' pay. Eddie Thomas of Neath, who had been ill for three years, was awarded 28 and a half weeks pay. Graham Isaac, employed as a fitter/driver with 30 years' service and living in Longford, was awarded 21 and a half weeks pay.

There were to be further applications from an inspector, two drivers, and a cleaner, which were heard during the following week.

"Joe Louis, one time heavyweight boxing champion of the world, used to be known as the 'Brown Bomber'. So, it needs to be pointed out that a new booklet called 'Forty Years of Brown Bombers' has nothing to do with coloured boxers." Thus began a review of Gerald Truran's new book 'Forty Years of Brown Bombers' published in the Neath Guardian on 14 May, 1971. "Boxers, no! Buses, yes! For 'Forty Years of Brown Bombers' is all about the Neath and Cardiff Luxury Coaches Limited, and its author, Mr G H Truran, has given an explanation for their coaches being called Brown Bombers. One reason is the speed at which they used to travel, and the other is their colour – chocolate brown.

An unusually mixed line-up of coaches at Briton Ferry in 1967. Generally, vehicles were parked by type as an aid to drivers and conductors. *Gerald Truran/The Omnibus Society*

"Mr Truran wrote his booklet to mark last year's 40th anniversary of the company, and in the foreword, the firm's managing director, Sir Godfrey Llewellyn, says they had a 'most romantic career.' The book has pages devoted to details of every vehicle ever owned by the firm – registration number, make, model, name of the bodymaker, seating capacity and when first registered.

"Then comes notes on bodies, engines, etc. fitted to certain vehicles and of when and where vehicles were disposed of by the company when they no longer had use for them.

"Mr Truran even adds details of Longford coach bodies supplied to other coach operators. The booklet has ample illustrations, but here again they are for the bus lover rather than the bus passenger. For every photograph is of a coach."

This was a mixed review from a journalist who probably didn't know the N&C company, nor indeed its reputation. It was indeed a book for enthusiasts, as was the revised second edition in 1998. But there is indeed always more to the life of a bus company than simply the vehicles it operates, a story I have attempted to relate with the help of many people throughout this book.

My personal association with N&C came during the final days of one of the most highly respected companies in the UK. Every journey was a thrill for me, whether it was my daily commute, my extra-curricular runs or my private hires.

Even in my school holidays, it was an all-consuming desire on my part to jump aboard the first coach to sweep into Stand 18 at Bridgend bus station and ride up and down the A48 all day long. The adventures I had, the thrills and laughs, were countless. They were remarkable times, but just in case I was ever to forgot them, I wrote about them in my diaries which I began in 1968, aged 16, many of which I was persuaded to include in this book. On reflection they offer a unique glimpse of days in the life of N&C.

The statistics for the year ending 31 December 1969, show that 1,125,626 passengers were carried aboard the 26 N&C coaches. Together they operated 1,274,271 miles. On the payroll were 23 drivers, 21

The end of the road . . .

THE SOUTH WALES TRANSPORT COMPANY LIMITED
UNITED WELSH SERVICES, LIMITED
THOMAS BROTHERS (PORT TALBOT) LIMITED
NEATH AND CARDIFF LUXURY COACHES, LIMITED

NOTICE TO ALL STAFF

From 1st January, 1971, N. & C. Luxury Coaches, Thomas Bros. and United Welsh will cease to trade as individual companies and their assets will be transferred to the formal ownership of The South Wales Transport Company Limited. This will have the following effects:-

1. Employment

All staff will be employed by The South Wales Transport Company Limited and appropriate notices regarding the transfer of Contracts of Employment will be given.

2. Agreements

Formal agreements with unions will be honoured and unless specifically agreed to the contrary will continue unaltered. In cases where movement of staff is necessary, transfer to the appropriate agreement will be negotiated.

3. Seniority

Existing seniority as a one unit basis (within categories) will be observed.

4. Trading Name

(a) Stage Carriage Services

All stage carriage services will be operated under the name, "SOUTH WALES" and applications are now being lodged with the Traffic Commissioners for the transfer of all stage carriage licences to S.W.T.

(b) Coaching Activities

It is intended that the coaching activities of the four companies will be operated under a common trading name.

F. A. J. Woodworth
DIRECTOR AND GENERAL MANAGER

19th November, 1970

FAJW/MEW

THE SOUTH WALES TRANSPORT CO. LTD.

6TH JANUARY, 1971.

Dear Sir/Madam

The Neath and Cardiff Luxury Coaches Ltd., ceased to exist as a Company on the 31st December, 1970 and has now been incorporated into the Swansea Group of Companys under The South Wales Transport Co. Ltd. The Briton Ferry depot is closing on the 9th January, 1971 and, after this date, all business will be transacted at The South Wales Transport Co. Ltd, Coach Station, Singleton Street, Swansea (Telephone:Swansea 55116.)

Our reason for bringing the above information to your notice is that, during past years, you have been a regular hirer of N.&.C coaches. Your business has been greatly esteemed and we have always aimed at giving the best service possible. This standard we aim to maintain from our new address and can assure you that we look forward to your continued hiring of coaches although they will all now be under the name of South Wales Transport. Any request you may have for a particular driver will, whenever possible, be honoured. If you would direct your enquiries to the Coach Station at Swansea, either in writing or by telephone, we can assure you that they will receive our immediate and courteous attention.

Please accept our apologies for this being a duplicated rather than an individual letter but we are sure you will appreciate that we have many esteemed hirers to contact.

Yours sincerely,

R. J. GALLANDERS,
(DISTRICT TRAFFIC SUPERINTENDENT).

A letter advising of N&C's final closure, dated 6 January 1971. Significantly it bears no letterhead, as if wanting to escape blame. Ron Gallanders was clearly embarassed by it all, as explained in the final paragraph.

conductors, 4 inspectors, 10 mechanical support, 2 clericals, 9 cleaners and 3 others – 72 in total. The total revenue was £182,288 and expenditure was £167,878. The pre-tax profit was £14,410 – not a huge amount, but only around £6k less than SWT, which had 312 vehicles.

It is hard to accept now that back in the 1960s, if you wanted to travel between Cardiff and Swansea, you didn't have to consult a timetable because you knew that there was a regular pattern of services from early morning, right through the day until late in the evening. And they were truly services you could set your watch by. You didn't have to worry that you would become stranded in the early evening, or at best be faced with a long wait, and you also knew that during the day, the driver didn't have to disappear off on some school run just when you needed to get somewhere. The duty rosters allowed crews to get their meals without creating a gap in the service. These staff duties ensured spare crews were available in case the booked ones could not get in, and at busy times these spare crew would be out on the road, operating reliefs as required, or the rostered crew offered a relief journey after their main turn had been completed. The overtime could mount up without even turning a wheel!

The reason N&C made such a success of their timetable, come what may, in all weathers, despite hold-ups or other unforeseen incidents, is that adequate recovery time was built into the schedules at the end of each journey. There were a few exceptions, but this recovery time meant that the next journey could still leave on time and the crew would still get a comfort or meal break after their next trip. The sample of duty schedules

The range of N&C uniforms — TOP: the double breasted standard brown jacket; CENTRE: the lighter summer jacket; BOTTOM: the later SWT-inspired nylon dustcoat.

The final two N&C vehicles, enhanced Plaxton Derwent bus bodies arrived in August 1970. At this late stage, the company's management was based at Swansea and so SWT's fleet purchase policy applied, as did their registration numbers. Cardiff-bound UCY979J waits at Pyle, on what had sadly become the 'N&C Service' but no longer Express.
John Weager

earlier in this book illustrate this perfectly, and its perusal will serve as a lesson to modern day operators who allow neither recovery nor turn-around time over many journeys, as they squeeze every ounce of productivity from their stressed-out staff and overworked vehicles.

Many times, in conversations at preserved bus rallies, or aboard the tribute vehicle that I part-owned, or even while simply chatting with fellow enthusiasts, the question often arises as to what would have happened had the N&C survived. What coaches would they be operating now? Would they have grabbed the opportunities offered with the completion of the motorway network? Would there still be two-manning? Would they have specified high-floor coaches with on-board facilities? There can be no sure answer. Gerald Truran speculated many years after the firm's demise and believed they would have remained loyal to AEC for as long as they could, then gone with Volvo. Duple Dominants or Plaxton Supremes? Uncertain. Paramounts? Definitely. Two-manning would have been phased out with conductors being provided only at bus stations, then inevitably static ticket machines would have come into play also.

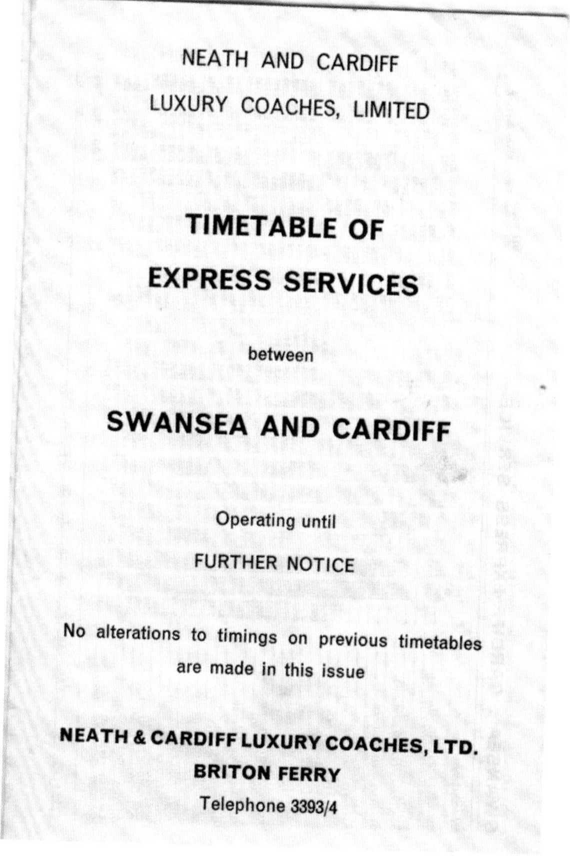

NEATH AND CARDIFF
LUXURY COACHES, LIMITED

TIMETABLE OF
EXPRESS SERVICES

between

SWANSEA AND CARDIFF

Operating until
FURTHER NOTICE

No alterations to timings on previous timetables are made in this issue

NEATH & CARDIFF LUXURY COACHES, LTD.
BRITON FERRY
Telephone 3393/4

The cover of the last traditional N&C only timetable, issued in 1968. After that the timetable was combined with that of Western Welsh.

SWANSEA EXPRESS SERVICE CARDIFF

N. & C. LUXURY COACHES

NEATH & CARDIFF
LUXURY COACHES LTD.
BRITON FERRY, NEATH, GLAM.
Telephone : Briton Ferry 3393/4 (2 lines)

Directors :
B. GRIFFITHS (Chairman)
G. CARRUTHERS
Sir JOHN GUTCH
J. T. E. ROBINSON
F. PATERSON

The letterhead in use by the company during its short lived existence at Briton Ferry depot.

With the deregulation of coach and bus services in the 1980s, services may have been extended to Bristol. Also, a London motorway service would have been likely, for which on-board toilets would have been specified, then removed for normal service after five years. It's all speculation, but there is little doubt the N&C would have continued to prosper and even lead the way.

The N&C was special and it felt special – a cut above the rest. When you stepped aboard you knew you were in for something extraordinary, and it never disappointed. When it was taken from us, it was regretted almost immediately that the goodwill attached to the N&C name and livery had not been kept.

With the benefit of hindsight, it should never have been wound up in the first place.

Those amazing times when I was accepted into the fabulous N&C family were without doubt among the happiest days of my life. I hope the tales and memories so freely shared within this book will keep the legend alive forever.

Born out of one piece of much needed legislation, there is perhaps an irony in the fact that the sad and sudden demise of the N&C Luxury Coach Company had been brought about by another, although the latter without any doubt lends itself to far more criticism than the former. Some may of course mount a counter argument.

On the balance sheet it may well be that the figures were more impressive once amalgamation had been achieved under the bus deregulation moves,but there is no hiding placed for the sentiment that it had done nothing for the improvement of service for he or she who paid the bill — the loyal passenger.

In the years that have passed since the demise of the N&C, coaches themselves have evolved in ways that would never have been possible when N&C ruled the road.
That said it is a company that will never be forgotten.

Caroline, or 'Carrie', widow of Captain J J Newbury, at 103 years of age, came to see the N&C Tribute Vehicle operated by the Brown Bombers Club in 2016. Sadly, she passed away some months later.

Chapter 14

Fleet facts

Many passenger transport companies which began around the same time as the N&C Luxury Coach Company Ltd experimented with a variety of vehicle makes and models in an attempt to evaluate their suitability.

For N&C things were slightly different however. In its embryonic years the company leaned on the C K Andrews firm which had provided its earliest vehicles.

This company not only supplied the Morris chassis, but built the bodies too. The result was a number of 20-seat Morris Viceroys with one 33 seater thrown in for good measure. These vehicles each helped establish the N&C's presence.

By the middle of the 1930s the company was experimenting with Dennis, Gloster, Albion and Maudslay vehicles. A number were still bodied by C K Andrews, but just before the outbreak of the Second World War, two emerged from N&C itself. Shortly after hostilities ended, N&C set up its own body building company, Longford Coachworks, which operated until 1952.

A glance at the fleet list that follows shows that almost every available make of vehicle was given the opportunity to shine as it was put through its paces.

The first of many AECs arrived in 1939 and gradually found favour, although not without a few Daimlers and Tilling Stevens vehicles added for good measure. In the mid-1950s, under BET control, the fleet was radically updated with 12 Guy Arab LUFs, believed to be unique to N&C. The choice of Park Royal coachwork for these led to that company rebodying the six best AEC Regals, extending their lives by a further eight years.

In 1956, N&C began a love affair that was to last until its demise, one with the AEC Reliance underfloor chassis. When the Guys were withdrawn in 1966, only AECs remained. This marked the realisation of a standardisation exercise by the forward thinking company engineer Gerald Truran.

Arrival	Reg. No.	Chassis / type	Body / Type	Withdrawn	Extra info
3/30	WN2835	Morris Viceroy	CK Andrews C20	?	
3/30	WN2836	Morris Viceroy	CK Andrews C20	?	Last reg. 1937
5/30	WN2977	Morris Viceroy	CK Andrews C20	?	
6/30	WN3133	Morris Viceroy	CK Andrews C20	?	
6/30	WN3134	Morris Viceroy	CK Andrews C20	?	
/30	WN3357	Morris Viceroy	CK Andrews C20	?	
12/30	WN3494	Morris Dictator	CK Andrews C33	c1941	
11/31	WN3118	Morris Viceroy	CK Andrews C20	?	
11/31	WN4205	Morris Viceroy	CK Andrews C20	7/47	Dorman engine fitted, 1934
4/32	WN4596	Morris Dictator	CK Andrews C32	7/42	
11/32	WN5087	Dennis Lancet I	CK Andrews C32	11/42	Gardner 5LW engine fitted
3/33	WN5391	Dennis Lancet I	Dennis C35	8/42	
4/33	WN5508	Dennis Lancet I	CK Andrews C35	7/42	
8/33	WN5884	Dennis Lancet I	CK Andrews C32	7/41	
12/33	WN6211	Dennis Lancet I	CK Andrews C32	12/42	
3/34	WN6536	Gloster Gardner 6LW	Gloster; Longford C32F	10/53	Rebodied 3/46
6/34	WN7126	Gloster Gardner 6LW	Gloster C32F	10/53	Ex-WWOC body fitted, 1946
4/35	WN8112	Albion SPW67	CK Andrews C32R	3/51	Gardner 5LW engine fitted
/36	WN9705	Dennis Lancet II	Dennis C32	1940	Requisitioned by Army
4/36	WN9973	Maudslay Magna SF40	Willowbrook C37F	1944	New to Jones, Danygraig, 5/36
5/37	AWN805	Dennis Lancet II	Dennis C32F	7/40	Requisitioned by Army
23/7/37	CTG293	Maudslay Magna	N&C; Longford C35F	1954	Gardner 5LW; Rebodied 12/48
4/38	WN4597	Dennis Lancet I	CK Andrews C32C	7/42	New to Bromham, 5/32
4/38	WN9380	Dennis Lancet II	Dennis C32F	1940	New to Bromham, 3/36; to Army
31/5/38	DNY713	Maudslay Magna SF40	N&C; Longford C37F	1953	Gardner 5LW; Rebodied 1/49
1/4/39	ENY64	Maudslay Magna SF40	Duple; Longford C32C	1953	Gardner 5LW; Rebodied 1/47
1/4/39	ENY65	AEC Regal Mk I	Strachan; Longford FC35F	1955	Rebodied 7/50
1/4/39	ENY66	Maudslay Magna SF40	Duple; Longford C33C	1955	Gardner 5LW; Rebodied 3/48
1/4/39	ENY67	Maudslay Magna SF40	Duple; Longford C33C	1954	Gardner 5LW; Rebodied 7/50

Arrival	Reg. No.	Chassis / type	Body / Type	Withdrawn	Extra info
1/4/39	ENY68	Maudslay Magna SF40	Duple; Longford C33C	1955	Gardner 5LW; Rebodied 3/48
3/44	FNY556	AEC Regal Mk I	Burlingham; Longford B36F	1956	Rebodied 9/49
9/9/46	FTX28	AEC Regal Mk I	Duple C33F	1956	
16/10/46	HB6138	AEC Regal 0662	LPTB C34F	1953	Ex-Army; new to Green Line
23/12/46	FTX27	AEC Regal Mk I	Duple C33F	1956	
/46		Crossley	? ?	?	Double-decker; not operated
/46		Crossley	? ?	?	Double-decker; not operated
/47		Daimler CF6	? C32	1947	Ex-War Dept; not operated
1/3/47	EM3855	AEC Regal 0662	LPTB C34F	1953	Ex-Army; new to Green Line
6/47	HB6406	Dennis Lancet III	DJ Davies C33F	1/48	
6/47	HB6423	Dennis Lancet III	DJ Davies C33F	1/48	
/47		Albion	Jeffreys ?	1947	New to N&C, sold unregistered
23/12/47	EWN556	AEC Regal Mk III	Duple C33F	1955	Rebodied – see later entry
1/1/48	HNY22	AEC Regal Mk III	Longford C33F	1955	Rebodied – see later entry
1/3/48	HNY913	AEC Regal Mk III	Longford C33F	1955	Rebodied – see later entry
1/7/48	HTG442	AEC Regal Mk III	Longford C33F	1955	Rebodied – see later entry
1/9/48	HTG951	AEC Regal Mk III	Longford C35F	1955	Rebodied – see later entry
21/10/48	HTX407	AEC Regal Mk III	Longford C35F	1955	Rebodied – see later entry
2/12/48	HTX545	Tilling Stevens K6MA7	Longford C33F	5/60	Gardner 6LW engine fitted
8/10/49	JTG887	Maudslay Marathon III	Longford C33F	13/5/58	
1/1/50	JTX58	Daimler CVD6DD	Longford C33F	12/1/62	
1/1/50	JTX121	Daimler CVD6DD	Longford C33F	9/58	
19/1/50	JTX339	Daimler CVD6DD	Longford C33F	9/58	
5/4/50	JTX960	Tilling Stevens K5MA7	Longford C33F	31/8/59	Gardner 5LW engine fitted
23/5/50	JTX633	Tilling Stevens K5MA7	Longford C33F	31/8/59	Gardner 5LW engine fitted
23/5/50	KNY197	Daimler CVD6DD	Longford C33F	1959	
23/5/50	KNY198	Tilling Stevens K5MA7	Longford C33F	31/8/59	Gardner 5LW engine fitted
2/5/51	KTX549	AEC Regal Mk IV	Longford	C39C	11/62

Arrival	Reg. No.	Chassis / type	Body / Type	Withdrawn	Extra info
1/1/52	LTG226	AEC Regal Mk IV	Longford C39C	11/62	
1/5/52	LTX111	AEC Regal Mk IV	Longford C39C	11/62	
3/6/54	KCY488	Guy Arab LUF	Park Royal C41C	1/1/67	
3/6/54	KCY489	Guy Arab LUF	Park Royal C41C	1/1/67	
3/6/54	KCY490	Guy Arab LUF	Park Royal C41C	1/1/67	
4/6/54	KCY492	Guy Arab LUF	Park Royal C41C	1/11/65	
1/7/54	KCY491	Guy Arab LUF	Park Royal C41C	1/11/65	
1/7/54	KCY493	Guy Arab LUF	Park Royal C41C	1/11/65	
4/4/55	LCY778	Guy Arab LUF	Park Royal C41C	1/12/66	
6/4/55	LCY779	Guy Arab LUF	Park Royal C41C	14/12/66	
6/4/55	LCY781	Guy Arab LUF	Park Royal C41C	1/1/67	
15/4/55	LCY782	Guy Arab LUF	Park Royal C41C	1/1/67	
19/4/55	LCY783	Guy Arab LUF	Park Royal C41C	1/11/66	
4/5/55	LCY780	Guy Arab LUF	Park Royal C41C	1/12/66	
20/5/55	HNY913	AEC Regal Mk III	Park Royal C37F	9/64	
20/5/55	HTG951	AEC Regal Mk III	Park Royal C37F	9/64	
25/5/55	HNY22	AEC Regal Mk III	Park Royal C37F	9/64	
22/3/56	HTX407	AEC Regal Mk III	Park Royal C37F	9/64	
27/3/56	HTG442	AEC Regal Mk III	Park Royal C37F	9/64	
29/3/56	EWN556	AEC Regal Mk III	Park Royal C37F	9/64	
19/5/56	NCY885	AEC Reliance MU3RV	Burlingham Seagull C41C	1/1/70	
19/5/56	NCY886	AEC Reliance MU3RV	Burlingham Seagull C41C	22/10/68	
1/6/56	NCY887	AEC Reliance MU3RV	Burlingham Seagull C41C	9/69	
1/6/58	RCY803	AEC Reliance MU3RV	Weymann Fanfare C41F	5/71	SWT 101 from 11/70
1/6/58	RCY804	AEC Reliance MU3RV	Weymann Fanfare C41F	5/71	SWT 102 from 11/70
1/6/58	RCY805	AEC Reliance MU3RV	Weymann Fanfare C41F	5/71	SWT 103 from 11/70
1/10/59	TWN556	AEC Reliance 2MU3RV	Park Royal C41F	5/71	SWT 104 from 11/70
1/10/59	TWN557	AEC Reliance 2MU3RV	Park Royal C41F	7/6/68	Chassis to Brewer, Caerau
1/10/59	TWN558	AEC Reliance 2MU3RV	Park Royal C41F	5/71	SWT 105 from 11/70
22/7/60	WWN189	AEC Reliance 2MU3RV	Harrington Cavalier C41F	1/72	SWT 111 from 11/70
29/7/60	WWN190	AEC Reliance 2MU3RV	Harrington Cavalier C41F	9/71	SWT 112, 11/70; WW 101, 12/70
29/7/60	WWN191	AEC Reliance 2MU3RV	Harrington Cavalier C41F	9/71	SWT 113, 11/70; WW 102, 12/70
6/4/62	231BWN	AEC Reliance 4MU3RA	Harrington Cavalier C51F	8/76	SWT 151 from 11/70

Arrival	Reg. No.	Chassis / type	Body / Type	Withdrawn	Extra info
6/4/62	232BWN	AEC Reliance 4MU3RA	Harrington Cavalier C51F	12/76	SWT 152 from 11/70
18/3/63	567ECY	AEC Reliance 4MU3RA	Harrington Cavalier C51F	9/76	SWT 153 from 11/70
18/3/63	568ECY	AEC Reliance 4MU3RA	Harrington Cavalier C51F	8/76	SWT 154 from 11/70
14/4/65	CTX986C	AEC Reliance 4MU3RA	Duple Commander C51F	8/76	SWT 159, 11/70; WW 104, 12/70
16/4/65	CTX985C	AEC Reliance 4MU3RA	Duple Commander C51F	1974	SWT 158, 11/70; WW 103, 12/70
11/4/66	HTG600D	AEC Reliance 2MU3RA	Duple Commander II C41F	12/76	SWT 127 from 11/70
11/4/66	HTG601D	AEC Reliance 2MU3RA	Duple Commander II C41F	12/76	SWT 128 from 11/70
11/4/66	HTG602D	AEC Reliance 4MU3RA	Duple Commander II C51F	7/76	SWT 160 from 11/70
24/3/58	3280WB	AEC Reliance MU3RV	Burlingham Seagull C41C	1/10/68	Ex-Sheffield United Tours, 11/66
2/5/58	3279WB	AEC Reliance MU3RV	Burlingham Seagull C41C	1/10/68	Ex-Sheffield United Tours, 11/66
2/5/58	3281WB	AEC Reliance MU3RV	Burlingham Seagull C41C	13/5/70	Ex-Sheffield United Tours, 11/66
2/5/58	3282WB	AEC Reliance MU3RV	Burlingham Seagull C41C	1/1/70	Ex-Sheffield United Tours, 11/66
2/5/58	3283WB	AEC Reliance MU3RV	Burlingham Seagull C41C	1/10/68	Ex-Sheffield United Tours, 11/66
2/5/58	3284WB	AEC Reliance MU3RV	Burlingham Seagull C41C	11/69	Ex-Sheffield United Tours, 11/66
2/5/60	RRC237	AEC Reliance 4MU3RA	Weymann Fanfare C37F	7/71	Ex-Trent, 11/66; SWT 106, 11/70
2/5/60	RRC238	AEC Reliance 4MU3RA	Weymann Fanfare C37F	7/71	Ex-Trent, 11/66; SWT 107, 11/70
1/2/67	LTX828E	AEC Reliance 6MU4R	Plaxton Panorama I C51F	10/76	SWT 163 from 11/70
1/2/67	LTX829E	AEC Reliance 6MU4R	Plaxton Panorama I C51F	10/76	SWT 164 from 11/70
11/67	TWK502	AEC Reliance MU3RV		11/67	1957 chassis ex-Morris, Pencoed
1/2/68	PTX830F	AEC Reliance 6MU4R	Plaxton Panorama I C51F	3/79	WW 105 from 12/70
1/3/69	UNY831G	AEC Reliance 6MU4R	Plaxton Pan.Elite C51F	10/78	WW 106 from 12/70
1/3/69	UNY832G	AEC Reliance 6MU4R	Plaxton Pan.Elite C51F	12/80	SWT 173 from 11/70
1/8/70	UCY979J	AEC Reliance 6MU2R	Plaxton Derwent DP51F	2/82	SWT 460 from 12/70
1/8/70	UCY980J	AEC Reliance 6MU2R	Plaxton Derwent DP51F	6/82	SWT 461 from 12/70

Preserving the memory

It is still possible to see, and ride on, two surviving N&C coaches that have been preserved by enthusiasts. Above is WWN191, one of the 1960 trio of Harrington Cavalier bodied AEC Reliances, while below is PTX830F, a 1968 Plaxton Panorama 1.

Words of thanks

Telling the story of a coach company which vanished from our roads half a century ago might normally be a daunting task. However in the case of the legendary N&C this was not the case.

The N&C's pioneering express service made such an impact on passenger transport in South Wales that it has never been forgotten. The lasting memories of employees, passengers and even casual observers have played a huge part in the building of this book, the foundations for which were laid by my own enthusiasm for ensuring that the memory of the N&C lives on into the future as a tribute to all who ran the company from beginning to end.

It has been a help that my publisher and friend David Roberts of Bryngold Books has long shared my love for the N&C, and for his guidance and support through the preparation of this book, I will always be grateful.

I am grateful to many others for their contributions to **Life on the Luxury** and for vividly describing the unique character of the N&C company and its people through treasured memories and valued artefacts. Regrettably, some of those mentioned below are no longer with us. Hopefully, their memory too, will live on through this book.

I am particularly indebted to Trevor Burley, Michael John and Phil Williams for their many contributions. Without them this book would be a mere shadow of what it is. The contributions of those listed below has also helped create a fitting tribute to the legend that is the N&C.

For their remininscences I thank:
Mansel Abraham, Eddie Bailey, Glyn Bowen, Fay Chick, Norman Chinnock, John Cole, Clive Coulson, Tudor Davies, Enid Dewitt, Darrel Edwards, Linda Feltham, Barbara Genery, Sylvia Hawkins, John Hughes, Mary jones, Joan Lloyd, Janet Magness, John McDonald, Brian Metcalfe, Peter Parker, Hedley Picton, Dennis Preston, Bill Price, Lyndon Rees, Debra Richardson, Alan Roberts,

Tributes to a legend

In 2014, a Duple Dominant bodied AEC Reliance 760 of 1979 vintage, was bought by a group of enthusiasts, including the author, and converted into a tribute coach to the N&C company. Used as a mobile exhibition and hospitality vehicle it contained display panels, memorabilia and a scale model of Briton Ferry garage, seen right.
A shortage of volunteers resulted in the coach, being sold in 2019 and the displays put into storage, pending future display at Swansea Bus Museum & Transport Heritage Centre.

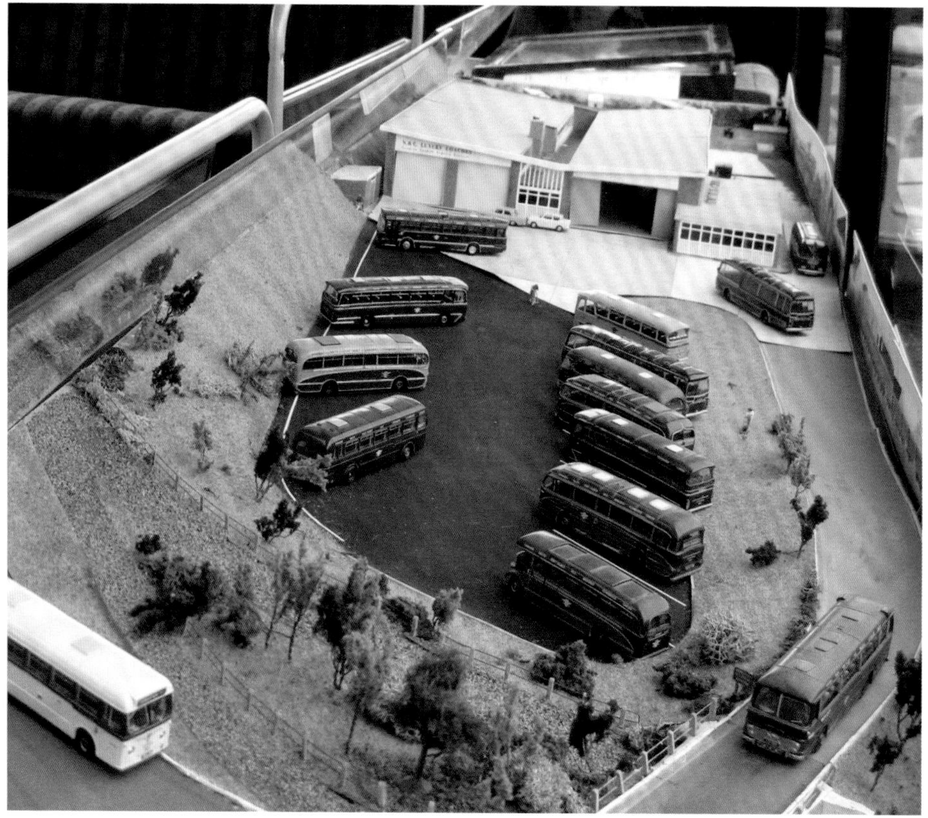

Richard Sanders, Colin Simper, Charles Smith, Robert Thomas, Gerald and Margaret Truran, Byron Westlake, Roy Wilcox, Colin Williams, and Mick Williams.

For use of their photographs and artefacts: Pauline and Jason Aitken, Glyn Bowen, Selwyn Bowen, Alan B Cross, Clive Coulson, Philip Curnow, Gerald Dodd, Richard Evans, Stephen Howarth, John Hughes, David Jones, Michael John, Kathryn Jones, Lucy Llewellyn, Geoff Lumb, Brian Maguire, Penny Matthews, Geoffrey Morant (courtesy of Michael and Richard Morant), Richard Morgan, Caroline Newbury, Steve Powell, Michael Rooum, Alan Snatt, Chris Stanley, Strachan & Brown/The PSV Circle Collection, Mike Street, Robert Thomas, Phil Trotter, Gerald, Margaret and Helen Truran, Anthony Warrener and John Weager.

I acknowledge the assistance of The Bus Archive, The National Newspaper Archive, The Omnibus Society Photographic Archive, Port Talbot Historical Society and The Transport Library for the many ways in which these organisations have supported me in my quest to salute and commemorate the legend that was the N&C.

To anyone whose image has been used, but for which I have been unable to identify ownership, I hope you will be understanding and pleased to have played a part in this book.

And finally I must offer my thanks to Professor Stuart Cole CBE for agreeing to write the foreword to Life on the Luxury.

Colin Scott, 2021.

Bibliography

Forty Years of Brown Bombers

Gerald Truran

First edition 1971; Revised second edition 1998

British Bus Fleets 18 – South Wales

Ian Allan

First edition 1963; Revised second edition 1966

History of British Bus Fleets – South Wales

David Holding and Tony Moyes

Ian Allan 1986

Red, Cream and a Touch of Gray

Colin Scott

Bryngold Books; First edition 2012; Revised second edition 2019

Return Ticket

Jonathan Isaacs

Bryngold Books 2014

On 31 December 1970, the last day of operations from Briton Ferry garage, RRC238 sweeps around the yard for a crew change en-route to Swansea. South Wales Transport fleet numbers have already been applied and soon the mighty crests will be replaced by SWT's fleet names. The vehicle behind is UCY980J, the final N&C coach. *Robert Thomas*